Breaking the Silence: Recognizing the Social and Cultural Resources Students Bring to the Classroom

Catherine Compton-Lilly, Editor

International Reading Association
800 BARKSDALE ROAD, PO BOX 8139
NEWARK, DE 19714-8139, USA
www.reading.org

The International Reading Association attempts, through its publications, to provide a forum for a wide spectrum of opinions on reading. This policy permits divergent viewpoints without implying the endorsement of the Association.

Executive Editor, Books   Corinne M. Mooney
Developmental Editor   Charlene M. Nichols
Developmental Editor   Tori Mello Bachman
Developmental Editor   Stacey L. Reid
Editorial Production Manager   Shannon T. Fortner
Design and Composition Manager   Anette Schuetz

Project Editors   Stacey L. Reid and Christina Lambert

Cover   Design, SR Nova; Photographs (from top), © iStockphoto.com/Robert Hunt, © iStockphoto.com/Aldo Murillo, © iStockphoto.com/Thomas Perkins

Illustrations on pp. 99, 100, and 104 by Sarah Jackson.

Library of Congress Cataloging-in-Publication Data

Breaking the silence : recognizing the social and cultural resources students bring to the classroom / Catherine Compton-Lilly, editor.
    p. cm.
  ISBN 978-0-87207-466-8
  1. Multicultural education—United States. 2. Critical pedagogy—United States.
I. Compton-Lilly, Catherine.
  LC1099.3.B735 2008
  370.11'5   dc22
                                                                                        2008032317

This book is dedicated to teachers around the world who are working hard to break the silence despite mandates and policies that fail to recognize the remarkable strengths that children and families bring to our classrooms.

CONTENTS

ABOUT THE EDITOR   VII

CONTRIBUTORS   IX

PREFACE   XI
Catherine Compton-Lilly

INTRODUCTION   1
Sociocultural Considerations for Students and Classrooms: The Case of Alicia Rodriguez
Catherine Compton-Lilly

PART I
Considerations for Sociocultural Teaching

CHAPTER 1   13
New Literacy Studies: Literacy Learning Through a Sociocultural Lens
Joanne Larson

CHAPTER 2   24
"Decontextualized Language" and the Problem of School Failure
James Paul Gee

CHAPTER 3   34
"O Say, Do You See?": Using Critical Race Theory to Inform English Language Arts Instruction
Arlette Ingram Willis and Kimberly N. Parker

CHAPTER 4   49
"First, Do No Harm": A Cautionary Consideration of Classroom Research From a Sociocultural Perspective
Deborah Appleman

CHAPTER 5   60
Cultural–Historical Approaches to Literacy Teaching and Learning
Mariana Pacheco and Kris Gutiérrez

PART II

Working With Diverse Students and Families

CHAPTER 6   81
Unpacking the Science Fair: Sociocultural Approaches to Teaching English-Language Learners
Margaret Hawkins and Kathleen Nicoletti

CHAPTER 7   92
Posing, Enacting, and Solving Local Problems in a Second-Grade Classroom: Critical Literacy and Multimodality in Action
Melissa Mosley and Rebecca Rogers

CHAPTER 8   109
This Is How We Do It: Helping Teachers Understand Culturally Relevant Pedagogy in Diverse Classrooms
Adrienne D. Dixson and Kenneth J. Fasching-Varner

CHAPTER 9   125
Diverse Families, Welcoming Schools: Creating Partnerships That Support Learning
JoBeth Allen

CHAPTER 10   141
Basketball, Rap, and SmackDown: Popular Culture and Literacy Learning
Catherine Compton-Lilly

CONCLUSION   151
Catherine Compton-Lilly

INDEX   154

ABOUT THE EDITOR

Catherine Compton-Lilly is an Assistant Professor of Literacy at the University of Wisconsin–Madison. She was formerly a reading teacher and Reading Recovery teacher in Rochester, New York, USA, and she taught in New York state public schools for 18 years. Catherine received her EdD in Curriculum and Human Development from the University of Rochester in 1999.

Catherine spent most of her teaching years working in a vibrant community that brought passion and hope to the school doors. Despite difficult circumstances in relation to employment, housing, and health care, families in this community were committed to their children. These experiences taught Catherine important lessons about resiliency and the potential of children.

Catherine is the author of *Reading Families: The Literate Lives of Urban Children*; *Confronting Racism, Poverty, and Power: Classroom Strategies to Change the World*; and *Re-reading Families: The Literate Lives of Urban Children, Four Years Later*. She is the author of several articles and book reviews and is the editor-in-chief of *Networks*, a teacher research online journal. Her current research interests focus on a 10-year longitudinal research project involving eight of her former first-grade students. Catherine is particularly interested in the role that time plays in the educational trajectories and in the lives of students and their families.

Author Information for Correspondence

Please feel free to contact the editor with comments and questions about this book. Catherine's e-mail address is comptonlilly@wisc.edu.

CONTRIBUTORS

JoBeth Allen
Professor of Language and Literacy
Education
University of Georgia
Athens, Georgia, USA

Deborah Appleman
Professor
Carleton College
Northfield, Minnesota, USA

Catherine Compton-Lilly
Assistant Professor of Literacy
University of Wisconsin–Madison
Madison, Wisconsin, USA

Adrienne D. Dixson
Assistant Professor
The Ohio State University
Columbus, Ohio, USA

Kenneth J. Fasching-Varner
Instructor
Department of Education–Literacy
St. John Fisher College
Rochester, New York, USA

James Paul Gee
Fulton Presidential Chair of Literacy
Studies
Curriculum and Instruction
Arizona State University
Tempe, Arizona, USA

Kris Gutiérrez
Professor
University of California, Los Angeles
Los Angeles, California, USA

Margaret Hawkins
Associate Professor
University of Wisconsin–Madison
Madison, Wisconsin, USA

Joanne Larson
Michael W. Scandling Professor
of Education
Chair, Teaching and Curriculum
Department
University of Rochester
Rochester, New York, USA

Melissa Mosley
Assistant Professor
The University of Texas at Austin
Austin, Texas, USA

Kathleen Nicoletti
Doctoral Student
University of Wisconsin–Madison
Madison, Wisconsin, USA

Mariana Pacheco
Assistant Professor
University of Wisconsin–Madison
Madison, Wisconsin, USA

Kimberly N. Parker
PhD Candidate
University of Illinois–Urbana Champaign
Champaign, Illinois, USA

Rebecca Rogers
Associate Professor
University of Missouri–St. Louis
St. Louis, Missouri, USA

Arlette Ingram Willis
Professor
University of Illinois–Urbana Champaign
Champaign, Illinois, USA

PREFACE

Catherine Compton-Lilly

Enter a school staffroom almost anywhere in the United States and you will hear teachers talk about their professional lives. We discuss the lack of quality resources and irrelevance of federal and state mandates. We lament the narrowing of curricula that has accompanied the implementation of high-stakes tests and the pressure we face to ensure that students pass these tests. In addition, we express our concerns related to the growing diversity of our students: language differences, cultural diversity, and the economic difficulties faced by some of our students' families. We complain about student behaviors that disrupt our instructional agendas, and sometimes in our frustration we point our fingers at families, blaming them for the challenges we face. Despite our concerns, silence surrounds the complexities that accompany our work; we are told to teach children more information, ensure that they meet standards, and prepare them to pass tests. Too often we fail to ask tough questions, engage in difficult conversations, and examine our own assumptions. In this book, we attempt to break that silence by providing educators with compelling examples of rich instructional practices and provocative discussions of difficult issues.

Official responses to teachers' challenges generally do not address our everyday concerns. Since the publication of *A Nation at Risk* (National Commission on Excellence in Education, 1983), business and political leaders have played an increasingly powerful role in designing educational policy and practice (Hursh, 2004). In recent years, standards-based reforms and standardized testing initiatives have proliferated. Although to some these practices promise to improve student achievement, these initiatives have generally failed to acknowledge and address the growing diversity of students. For instance, in the year 2000, the National Reading Panel Report (NRP) identified alphabetics, fluency, comprehension, teacher education, and computer technology as the critical topics to be examined (National Institute of Child Health and Human Development, 2000). No Child Left Behind (NCLB) legislation in the United States in 2002 focused on phonemic awareness, phonics, fluency, vocabulary, and comprehension. Although each of these topics has a place in literacy education, focusing only on the surface skills of reading does the following:

- Isolates teaching and learning from social and cultural contexts
- Negates the relevance of social and cultural diversity
- Simplifies teaching and learning to transference of skills and knowledge
- Ignores the fact that teaching and learning are human activities that involve individuals with unique interests, goals, and experiences

All of us are deeply concerned about the literacy development of our students, and we understand the place of reading skills; however, students' difficulties with literacy are not separate from the worlds in which their families live and the historical failing of schools to educate some groups of students. Issues of policy, economics, identity, access, race, class, and social relationships are closely intertwined with our teaching and with the literacy development of our students. While official discussions focus on the skills and strategies of reading, issues of access and equity are ignored, or even worse, they are assumed to be irrelevant.

In this book, we explore sociocultural theories that recognize the complexity of learning and literacy. Sociocultural theories about learning and literacy recognize that learning does not occur separately from other aspects of children's lives. The following tenets characterize sociocultural understandings about learning and literacy:

- **Learning always occurs within a particular context.** It involves particular people and particular expectations; learning can occur in both formal and informal contexts (Hull & Schultz, 2002; Street, 1995).

- **Learning is a social process.** It occurs though interaction with others rather than as an individual accomplishment occurring within an individual's mind (Barton & Hamilton, 1998; Street, 1995).

- **Learning is grounded in the histories of people.** Historical precedents have preceded us and our ideas; we learn with other people's words, and these words have historically served other people's interests (Bakhtin, 1994).

- **Literacy is not just about reading and writing.** Literacy learning involves learning multiple types of literacy practices that are useful in multiple contexts (Barton, Hamilton, & Ivanič, 2000).

- **Literacy learning and literacy practices are not separate from people's identities.** Literacy is among the tools that we use to enact particular identities (Ferdman, 1990; Gee, 2000).

- **Literacy learning and literacy practices are ideological.** Becoming literate involves particular ways of understanding the world and the role of written text within the world (Street, 1984, 1995). Children not only learn how to read, but they also learn the messages that are conveyed through texts. They learn about gender, race, class, and the ways the texts operate in the world.

- **Literacy learning and literacy practices are situated within contexts that involve power.** Some literacies are valued while others are devalued. Some literacy practices provide access to power while other literacy practices are marginalized.

Our goal is to introduce educators to a growing body of work that examines the ways literacy is contextualized within larger social contexts and to present various instructional practices that extend beyond the recommendations of the NRP and NCLB legislation. This book offers solutions and possibilities that recognize the strengths that students bring to classrooms and presents the inspirational experiences of thoughtful teachers. In this book, you enter classrooms in which literacy is treated as more than just a set of skills, language is recognized as a complex contextualized system, teacher research is treated as a tool to inform instruction, race and language differences are contemplated and are critical to the decisions made by teachers, relationships with families are nurtured and developed, and students' media experiences are treated as resources to support literacy learning.

How to Use This Book

This book is presented in two parts. Part I, "Considerations for Sociocultural Teaching," introduces the foundational ideas that provide us with a basis for creating classrooms that reflect and honor the social and cultural worlds of students. The chapters in Part I explore issues of meaningful learning, language, race, learning from our students, and cultural-historical approaches. Although these are only some of the considerations that teachers who strive to honor the social and cultural worlds of the students must consider, they provide a rich starting point for rethinking educational practice and breaking the silences that too often constrain teaching and learning.

In Chapter 1, "New Literacy Studies: Literacy Learning Through a Sociocultural Lens," Joanne Larson introduces us to theory related to new literacy studies and takes us into two remarkable classrooms in which teachers are exploring the potential of literacy instruction to provide students with experiences that have very real effects in students' lives. Her goal is to help each of us rethink what literacy is and how it is used. The chapter shows us that literacy is not just a set of skills that we teach children; it is a set of social practices that children use in school, at home, and in their communities. This chapter helps us to consider what we can do to revise existing classroom literacy practices so that they are meaningful and relevant to students and to reflect upon what we can do to engage children in meaningful and personally relevant instructional activities.

In Chapter 2, "'Decontextualized Language' and the Problem of School Failure," James Paul Gee explores the role that language plays in literacy and questions assumptions that surround the assumed relationship between language and school success. Language is often blamed for the academic difficulties faced by diverse students and children living in poverty; however, Gee takes us on an engaging journey through various linguistic constructs that complicate this explanation by demonstrating that *all* language requires contextual understandings. This chapter challenges us to contextualize learning for students within meaningful activities, experiences, and inquiries, and it invites us to rethink many of our assumptions about language and the types of language practices that schools tend to privilege.

In Chapter 3, "'O Say, Do You See?': Using Critical Race Theory to Inform English Language Arts Instruction," Arlette Ingram Willis and Kimberly N. Parker offer critical race theory as a means of hearing counternarratives that challenge entrenched ways of thinking. They invite teachers to participate in a series of reflections involving autobiography and memoir and to examine multicultural and multiethnic literature as means to explore these counternarratives and ultimately our own belief systems. This chapter asks us to consider how race can affect teaching and how we can begin to examine our own racialized position and seek ways to come to terms with the racialized histories that we bring to our classrooms.

Through these experiences we can each begin to rethink the ways we understand race in our own lives and in our classrooms.

In Chapter 4, "'First, Do No Harm': A Cautionary Consideration of Classroom Research From a Sociocultural Perspective," Deborah Appleman invites us to apply sociocultural constructs as we examine our own instructional practices and the ethical issues that accompany that exploration. Teacher research recognizes that learning always occurs in social contexts that involve people with unique histories and experiences. Knowing students and recognizing the resources they bring is critical, but it requires a deep ethical commitment to students and a respect for the information they share with us. The chapter illustrates how can we learn about the experiences and cultures of our students and begin to recognize and build upon the rich resources that they bring to our classrooms, while at the same time it asks us to consider the dangers of entering students' worlds through teacher research and shows us how we can become ethical and honorable stewards of the information they share with us.

In Chapter 5, "Cultural-Historical Approaches to Literacy Teaching and Learning," Mariana Pacheco and Kris Gutiérrez explain that humans interact with their worlds through mediational means that involve cultural artifacts, tools, signs, and symbols, including language. They explore how the everyday cultural practices of students can be honored and used to inform discussions about teaching, learning, and curricula. Pacheco and Gutiérrez challenge us to recognize the potential of creating spaces that welcome multiple ways of being and knowing. Specifically, the authors explore classroom discourse patterns and how these interactional patterns can either honor or silence the knowledge and resources that students bring to classrooms.

Part II, "Working With Diverse Students and Families," takes us into particular classrooms and presents various pedagogical practices and insights that we can apply to our own classrooms. Specifically, insights related to teaching second-language learners, discourse analysis, culturally relevant teaching, working with families, and popular culture are presented. Each of these chapters addresses some of the silences that often accompany traditional educational practices.

In Chapter 6, "Unpacking the Science Fair: Sociocultural Approaches to Teaching English-Language Learners," Margaret Hawkins and Kathleen Nicoletti welcome us into the classroom of an experienced, dedicated, and well-meaning, prototypical fourth-grade teacher who invites his students to participate in a common, perhaps quintessential school experience: the science fair. However, while recognizing the great potential this activity may hold for student learning, Hawkins and Nicoletti problematize the assignment by thinking carefully about what this experience entails for English-language learners (ELL). They examine the science fair assignment as presented by this teacher with attention to language, opportunities for social interaction, the resources that ELL students bring to classrooms, and issues related to familial expectations. The chapter ends with an insightful alternative presentation of the science fair experience that takes into consideration the strengths of and challenges faced by ELL students.

In Chapter 7, "Posing, Enacting, and Solving Local Problems in a Second-Grade Classroom: Critical Literacy and Multimodality in Action," Melissa Mosley and Rebecca Rogers argue that there is a pervasive silence in literacy research on matters of race. They describe a research project in which a professor and a teacher researcher introduce texts about race in U.S. history within the literacy block in a second-grade classroom. Mosley and Rogers documented their experiences with video and audio recordings and took observational and reflective notes that provided them with information that allowed them to create and refine spaces for exploring race with students. Using a form of mediated discourse analysis, the authors demonstrate how to make sense of the racialized enactments that students created through analysis of the props, costumes, and actions. A thoughtful and promising approach to video analysis is presented that can easily be adapted to a range of educational settings. Ultimately the authors argue that "reading race" needs to be guided just as other literate processes are guided in the classroom.

In Chapter 8, "This Is How We Do It: Helping Teachers Understand Culturally Relevant Pedagogy in Diverse Classrooms," Adrienne D. Dixson and Kenneth J. Fasching-Varner invite us to tour two classrooms in which the possibilities and potential of culturally relevant teaching are not realized. Although the teachers' good intentions are noted, these scenarios invite us to rethink various common but rarely interrogated classroom practices that work against the creation of classrooms designed to serve diverse students. A third classroom is then presented. This classroom brings salient issues related to race and gender to the forefront. Rather than relegating the issues of agency and identity to the margins of classroom life, Dixson and Fasching-Varner report on how the classroom teacher incorporated issues of gender, race, power, and access into history lessons, directly addressing issues related to racial oppression. Insights and possibilities to support us in moving toward more culturally relevant classroom spaces are shared.

In Chapter 9, "Diverse Families, Welcoming Schools: Creating Partnerships That Support Learning," JoBeth Allen presents a disturbing depiction of families to challenge each of us to think about the assumptions and beliefs that we hold about families. Allen describes the practices of experienced teachers who have been successful in bringing home and school literacy knowledge together. She draws upon her vast experiences with teachers and families to detail how we can develop rich partnerships with families that support teaching and learning processes while challenging dangerous assumptions. Suggestions are made for how we can create extended literacy communities that demonstrate respect for families while developing rich learning experiences in classrooms.

In Chapter 10, "Basketball, Rap, and *SmackDown*: Popular Culture and Literacy Learning," I present the case of Kenny, a 6-year-old student, who was initially reluctant to engage with reading and writing. I describe how connections to media and cultural resources helped Kenny to become a successful reader and writer. The chapter shows us that cultural and media knowledge are not just about preferences and favorite television shows—the characters and scenarios that engage students are often intimately connected with their identities and the kinds of people they view themselves to be. Literacy is one of the many tools we use to play out our identities. We discover how accessing students' interests and cultural knowledge can be a means for inviting students to use literacy in personal and purposeful ways and to begin to see themselves as people who possess meaningful and purposeful reasons for learning to read and write.

In the book's Conclusion, I briefly return to Alicia's story and reflect on how she might have benefitted from school experiences that drew more upon her home experiences and beliefs, demonstrated respect for her as a learner, and involved rich and meaningful personal relationships. I examine four issues that were raised in the book (language, self-reflection, observation, and instructional practices) and invite us to choose a starting place for our own explorations and as we begin to incorporate some of the lessons from this book to create classrooms that break silences and present possibilities.

Acknowledgments

Writing is always a social practice, and many people have been involved in the conception and the writing of this book. I have been fortunate to work with a remarkable group of authors. Each of them has been a joy to work with and has expanded my thinking in many ways.

I am very grateful to Alicia, Kenny, and their families for allowing me to tell their stories. I am constantly in awe of the strength and the commitment that families bring to our schools and greatly appreciate the generous help families have given me over the years as I attempt to understand the complex work of teachers. Teacher research grants from the International Reading Association, National Council of Teachers of English, and a grant from the Spencer Foundation have been critical in enabling me to do this work.

I would like to thank all of my colleagues who have supported me as I worked on this project: James Gee, Maggie Hawkins, Dawnene Hassett, Paula Wolfe, and Mary Louise Gomez. In particular, I am grateful to John Capuano, Christopher Crowley, Jennifer Grandone, Mary Guay, Yun-Ju Huang, Anne Karch, and Tanya Morin for providing me with feedback on sections of this text.

Finally, I continually thank my family, Todd and Carly, for helping me to follow my dreams and joining me on the journey.

REFERENCES

Bakhtin, M.M. (1994). From M.M. Bakhtin, the dialogic imagination. In P. Morris (Ed.), *The Bakhtin reader: Selected writings of Bakhtin, Medvedev, Voloshinov* (pp. 74–87) London: Edward Arnold.

Barton, D., & Hamilton, M. (1998). *Local literacies: Reading and writing in one community*. London: Routledge.

Barton, D., Hamilton, M., & Ivanič, R. (2000). *Situated literacies: Reading and writing in context*. London: Routledge.

Ferdman, B. (1990). Literacy and cultural identity. *Harvard Educational Review, 60*(2), 181–204.

Gee, J.P. (2000). Identity as an analytic lens for research in education. *Review of Research in Education, 25*(1), 99–125.

Hull, G., & Schultz, K. (2002). *School's out! Bridging out-of-school literacies with classroom practice*. New York: Teachers College Press.

Hursh, D. (2004). Undermining democratic education in the USA: The consequences of global capitalism and neo-liberal policies for education policies at the local, state and federal levels. *Policy Futures in Education, 2*(3 & 4), 607–620.

National Commission on Excellence in Education. (1983). *A nation at risk: A report to the nation and the secretary of education*. Washington, DC: U.S. Department of Education.

National Institute of Child Health and Human Development. (2000). *Report of the National*

Reading Panel. Teaching children to read: An evidence-based assessment of the scientific research literature on reading and its implications for reading instruction (NIH Publication No. 00-4769). Washington, DC: U.S. Government Printing Office.

Street, B. (1984). *Literacy in theory and practice.* Cambridge, England: Cambridge University Press.

Street, B. (1995). *Social literacies: Critical approaches to literacy in development, ethnography, and education.* London: Longman.

Sociocultural Considerations for Students and Classrooms: The Case of Alicia Rodriguez

Catherine Compton-Lilly

Many years ago, Alicia (pseudonym)—now a high school senior—was a student in my first-grade class. Since then, I have returned to visit her and her family every three or four years. When I visited her at school last year, I found her sitting in the long term detention room because of a history of fighting, gang connections, and general disaffection from school. Although her cumulative school records are most certainly filled with assessments of her reading ability, reports on her behavior, old report cards, and state test scores, these records do not come close to telling her whole story.

In this chapter, stories about Alicia and her family are presented. These stories are part of a 10-year longitudinal case study that I feel demonstrates the importance of sociocultural understandings about literacy and learning. First, I describe incidents from Alicia's story to present and define *historical precedents*, *literacy practices*, and *ideological awareness* as aspects of sociocultural theory. Then, I share more of Alicia's story to demonstrate how literacy learning and sociocultural considerations are interwoven and inextricable from each other.

Examining Sociocultural Influences on Alicia's Literacy Learning

In the following section, excerpts from Alicia's story that extend from first grade through eighth grade are presented to illustrate the historical precedents, literacy practices, and ideological awareness that shaped Alicia's views on literacy and learning.

Historical Precedents That Informed Alicia's Literacy Learning Experiences

In first grade, Alicia was an energetic, African American child with a big smile. In my field notes, I described her as a bright child who enjoyed the social aspects of school. My research focused on the ways Alicia, her peers, and their parents viewed reading. Historical precedents related to learning to read involve ways of understanding reading that are grounded in people's collective experiences over time; historical precedents became evident when I asked Alicia, "What do children have to do to be able to read?" Alicia offered three interrelated answers: "Sound it out . . . sound out the letters . . . sound out the words." This response was not unique to Alicia. It was echoed by the other students whom I interviewed, and it was repeated by those students as they moved through the grade levels. In fifth grade, Alicia explained, "I practice sounding [out] the words and I read the books and I know how to read and I started learning how to read by myself." In eighth grade, she still reported "sounding out words."

"Sounding out" has a history that is reflected in the ways students, their parents, their siblings, their peers, and their teachers talk about reading. For example, Alicia's mother and older brothers used the term *sounding out*, and this usage of the term was related to their own experiences with learning to read. Thus, Alicia's use of the phrase reflected a long history of uses. Her mother described helping Alicia learn to read as follows:

> When she's reading along, she comes to me, and if she don't come to me she goes to her brothers, and we tell her the same thing: "Sound it out!" [Ms. Rodriguez laughs.] We help her sound it out . . . and then she be like, "OK, OK, OK, wait a minute, wait a minute." And then we keep going until she gets it, because we don't want to tell her the word because . . . she's not going to get it if you just tell her. Let her do it on her own.

In this quote, we witness Ms. Rodriguez and her sons offering sounding out as a decoding strategy that Ms. Rodriguez associates with independent word solving, perseverance, and accomplished reading.

Although sounding out is grounded in historicized notions of reading and is associated with independent reading, it also conveys a range of meanings. Through my research, I learned that sounding out refers to more than the letter-by-letter decoding of words. Some people in the study used sounding out to refer to word solving in general. One parent was observed telling her daughter to sound out a word, and then she immediately directed the child's attention to the accompanying picture, encouraging the child to think about the story. Other parents described sounding out as being able to identify known parts within words; one child offered the word *without* (with-out) as an example. All these meanings circulate via language potentially contributing to the meanings Alicia and her family members convey when they use the phrase *sounding out*.

The sociocultural approach to literacy and learning reminds us that all words bring a history of meanings that intersect with our lives in complex ways while revealing much about the social worlds we construct (Bakhtin, 1994). Sounding out has a powerful history grounded in our collective experience of learning to read. Words enter classrooms, bringing with them messages and meanings that we might not realize. Sounding out can be problematic if it silences alternative word-solving strategies and is the only available reading strategy available to students.

Other educational terms can also be problematic. Terms such as *at-risk, student-centered, hyperactive, whole language, scientifically based, developmentally appropriate, teacher-proof, minority*, and *special education* carry histories of meanings that reflect particular ways of understanding students and schooling and reveal our assumptions about particular groups of people; the histories these words bring can be dangerous and can infect our intended meanings and messages.

Alicia's Family's Literacy Practices

Literacy practices are regularly performed activities that involve the use of written texts (Street, 1984, 1995). During the interviews that took place across the grade levels, Alicia made reference to a range of literacy practices (see Table I.1). Alicia's mother described one of her own literacy practices of trading and sharing books with her friends. This literacy practice has been repeated on many occasions and is social in nature and grounded in personal relationships. It is a literacy practice that is often not associated with a mother of six children living in a poverty-stricken, inner-city community.

Having heard Alicia describe school literacy tasks as "boring" and hearing her mother describe Alicia's interests in the social aspects of school, I was surprised when in eighth grade she described the poetry she wrote. She agreed to share a poem with me (see Figure I.1). Alicia's poem reflects her fears and hopes. She presents her faith in love and fear of bullies. Alicia explained that she did not learn to write poetry in school and that she taught herself. Poetry writing is a literacy practice that Alicia values and enjoys. As these examples reveal, literacy practices can be surprising and unexpected. In some cases, literacy practices remain unrecognized even by people who participate in those practices. Reading recipes, newspapers, food labels, signs, advertisements, and bus schedules are all common

Table I.1. A Sampling of Alicia's Literacy Practices

Grade	School	Home
1	• Reading trade books with her friends • Participating in guided reading groups (defines reading groups as being about reading with friends) • Writing in her journal • Using friends' names as characters in her writing • Reading independently	• Getting help with reading from her brothers • Playing school • Reading books from a large box of trade books and textbooks
5	• Taking tests • Reading independently assigned chapter books • Defining vocabulary words	• Reading chapter books and series books (The Baby-Sitters Club and Goosebumps) that her friends also enjoy • Reading her brother's book about Dr. Martin Luther King Jr. • Reading "baby books" to her sister
8	• Reading classic literature (e.g., Poe) • Preparing for tests	• Reading chapter books and "love" novels she gets from her neighbor and mother • Reading books with Black characters • Writing poems • Reading teen magazines • Surfing the Internet • Using the computer at friends' homes to do puzzles and activities

Figure I.1. Alicia's Poem "Scared"

Don't be afraid of love.
Remember your faith of the person who live up above.
Don't be afraid.
Don't be afraid.
Be afraid of the bullies.
Their self does.
They're afraid of making changes.
Don't be afraid of yourself.
If you dare to stop the praise above,
there's nothing you are scared [of].

literacy practices that people do not always identify when asked about their reading and writing practices.

Ideological Awareness in Alicia's Family

An awareness of ideologies, the particular ways people understand the world, and specifically the role literacy plays in the world, affect the ways people view literacy and learning. During the first-grade interviews, Ms. Rodriguez told me a story to illustrate her views on African American speech patterns and how they might affect her children's futures. Ms Rodriguez explained that she tells her children, "You can walk around saying, 'Yo, what's up' and 'Chill,' but once you get out there into the business world—that 'yo, chill'—throw that out the window and you start talking like you got some sense." She explained that she periodically tests her children to see if they can code switch, as illustrated in the following description:

> I didn't think they could . . . you got to test them out every now and then. Now this one, when he goes to a job interview he can do it because he always proper. But them [her other two sons] I gave [them a test] to see whether they can do it. And I was like now go talk to so-and-so and so-and-so and he was like "What?" I says, "Now you got to *walk the talk*, like you got some sense." He goes up to him [the person Ms. Rodriguez had indicated], "Excuse me." You know. . . . And I'm sitting there looking at him like now this is the same kid that works his mouth all over town, I was like "uh-uh" [shaking her head as she speaks]. So I know that they can make that conflict and I'm glad about it because it's easier for them. It's not, it won't be hard as they grow up changing. When they get to work, then when they get home "OK, chill." All right, fine. I'm glad they can do it though.

Although some teachers may insist on students using standard forms of English, Ms. Rodriguez's story suggests that context is critical and that her goal is for her children to know when and how to use various language codes and systems. Ms. Rodriguez associates knowing how to speak in formal contexts as key to economic access and social success. She "tests" her sons on their ability to "talk like you got some sense" and celebrates their ability to do this. Ms. Rodriguez also demonstrates her understanding that particular ways of using language are associated with access and power. Her ideological beliefs about language include the understanding that some language variations are more highly valued than others in particular contexts. Ms. Rodriguez realizes the importance of her sons being able to access and use mainstream English patterns to gain access to opportunities and to participate in some social networks. She also recognizes that other forms of language work in other contexts. She displays her belief that getting a good job is contingent upon more than literacy achievement; it is related to the ways people present themselves and the language systems that they access. Ideological beliefs like this reveal people's understandings about the ways power operates through language and within social networks.

Entanglements: Literacy and Sociocultural Considerations

In this final section, I present more of Alicia's story to illustrate the many ways in which literacy and sociocultural considerations are interwoven and inextricable from each other. Although policymakers and curriculum developers often fall victim to the temptation to separate literacy from issues of class, identity, access, race, and social relationships, Alicia's story illustrates how these issues are inherently intertwined with literacy learning and literacy practices.

Social Relationships and Their Effect on Alicia's Literacy Practices

Throughout the time I have known Alicia, reading has always been a social activity caught up in her relationships with her friends, family, and teachers, as illustrated in many of the literacy practices listed in Table I.1. In first grade, she often wrote about friends and family members. During independent reading time, she was surrounded by a group of friends; when they finished one book, they would proceed together to the book corner to select their next title. Although I grouped students for reading instruction on the basis of their strengths and weaknesses as readers, Alicia surmised that I grouped students together so they "could be friends."

Alicia had a reputation in her family for being talkative. In first grade, Alicia qualified her talkativeness as relative to reading, saying, "I'm getting [to be] a better reader . . . I just talk a little and then read." Alicia had clear ideas about learning to read. She explained that her friend Jasmine is a good reader because she "don't play" and she "don't hit people." She described students who have trouble learning to read as "fooling around." I asked Alicia how being good in school affected learning to read:

Alicia: If you be good in school you might get something for free and the teacher might give you something. A treat or something.

CL: But does being good help you learn to read?

Alicia: Yes.

CL: How does that happen?

Alicia: Because if you don't read good you won't be like the people say, if you don't do what the teacher say you might go to the office.

CL: Well, how does, how does being good help you learn then?

Alicia: If you don't learn and read and learn and read 'cause if you don't read you won't go outside or you might be on punishment at home or [if] you won't read a book when it's time to read a book on the rug, you might stay at the table and put your head down.

Access, opportunity, and learning to read are described as contingent upon demonstrating good behavior. Alicia clearly identified a relationship between being good and learning to read but struggled to articulate the details of this relationship.

In fifth grade, Alicia still described reading with friends. She reports that her best friend Rizette is a good reader. She said, "I help her read some of the words. And she'll be like, 'What's this word?' And I'll be like, 'Sound it out,' or 'Try to look in the dictionary.'" Alicia says that school has changed since first grade because she is older now and she's "got more friends." Alicia's mother remained worried that Alicia talks too much in school: "It's just she just got to stop running her mouth." Alicia confirmed her mother's fears, "I read a lot and I talk a lot, and it gets me in trouble." Unlike her description in first grade—when she would "just talk a little and then read"—her talking is now a problem.

In fifth grade, Alicia reported that she reads a variety of books: "I read chapter books and I read baby books and sometimes I read to my sister. And I read big, big dictionaries." Her favorite books were from The Baby-Sitters' Club series. She had read eight books from the series. I asked if there were any Black characters in those books, and she reported that one of the characters was Black but that she forgot the character's name. She shook her head when I asked whether it was important that there were Black characters in the books she read. Alicia wrote about reading books from the Goosebumps series with a sense of bravado: "I always like to read the Goosebumps books because they are funny and sometimes they scary 'cause [but] I don't believe in the things they think they make kids scared."

In contrast to her own reading, Alicia generally described school and teachers negatively. She explained, "Some of my classes get on my nerves, like usual," and that her teacher "yells for no reason . . . because I tell people to shut up, because they be 'dissing' me." Although Alicia's words alone are not conclusive, on the basis of my eight years of teaching in this school I can attest that teaching at this school is difficult. Serving more than 1,000 children from a struggling and diverse community with a 97% poverty rate, while managing on very minimal classroom budgets and large class sizes, with little administrative support and extreme pressure to raise test scores, teachers at this school are prone to frustration. We often chose between spending our own money on books and supplies or going without. These are factors that affect Alicia's school experiences.

In eighth grade, Alicia was still reading The Baby-Sitters' Club books as well as teen magazines and "love books," which Alicia described as being "mostly about sex." At that time, Alicia reported that she enjoyed reading books with Black characters. However, Alicia said that she never reads with her friends, reporting, "We don't read nothing." Instead she said, "We have fun." She explained that reading is something she does when she is "bored."

Ms. Rodriguez continued to report that Alicia talks too much in class. At the beginning of eighth grade, Ms. Rodriguez reported that so far things were going well but that she was "getting ready for the middle of the year when she gets to know everybody and she starts talking a lot." She remarked, "Every year we go through that." Ms Rodriguez reported that Alicia loves her school, "It's just all her friends and everybody is there." She says that Alicia's friends are very nice, but they talk a lot. She explains that their conversations are not generally focused on school. Instead of talking about what they should be talking about, "it's 'Ooooh girl, you know what you got on.' 'I'm wearing that tomorrow.' 'I'm wearing this color and di-di-di-di-di.' You know. 'Oh he's cute.' You know, girl talk."

Ms. Rodriguez explained that Alicia was "more interested in how she looks" than reading or academics. At this point, the social dimensions of reading have become distractions for Alicia. No longer is reading a socially defined, shared activity; reading is juxtaposed with friends and fun.

The School Context and Its Impact on Alicia's Learning

By eighth grade, Alicia described her school and her teachers negatively, saying "when the kids fight in class, they [the teachers] don't try to break them up. They don't. They think that the kids will try to hurt them or something" (see Table I.2). She reported that "[teachers only help children] when they feel like it." School is "kinda fun [but] it's a lot of fighting going on . . . I got a lot of friends there so I'm not alone." It is her friends rather than her teachers that Alicia credits with keeping her safe from the fighting at school. Alicia describes her teachers as fearful of students; the current barrage of negative media depictions of African American youth who share similar social class, dress, and language styles with Alicia and her peers contribute to this unwarranted fear.

In contrast to her critique of her teachers, Alicia thought highly of the school's principal, saying, "I don't hear her say nothing bad about kids or they don't say nothing bad about her. . . . She be polite to everyone. She don't always got to be

Table I.2. A Comparison of Alicia's Attitudes Toward School Across Grade Levels

First grade	Fifth grade	Eighth grade
Likes her friends and teachers	"Some of my classes get on my nerves, like usual." "[The teacher] yells for no reason . . . because I tell people to shut up, because they be 'dissing' me." "[My teacher] don't do nothing. She don't help me." "The teacher just yells at you."	"When the kids fight in class, they [teachers] don't try to break them up. They don't. They think that the kids will try to hurt them or something." "[Teachers only help students] when they feel like it." "Let the kids be who they are instead of trying to change them." "I don't hear her [the school principal] say nothing bad about kids or they don't say nothing bad about her. . . . She be polite to everyone. She don't always got to be mean about everything, so [that's] probably why."

mean about everything." When asked, Alicia offered three poignant pieces of advice to her teachers:

1. Talk to kids more.

2. Be respectful to kids.

3. Let the kids be who they are instead of trying to change them.

Ms. Rodriguez confirmed Alicia's critique of her teachers:

> When we used to go to school it's like the teacher was there to teach and not just get their paycheck. And it seem like [now] they just get her paycheck. And that's wrong. 'Cause you got a lot of kids that need help, and they ain't helping them.

Alicia's literacy learning occurs within a context where race, class, and the identity positionings that Alicia is constructing all cohabitate and interact in complex ways. As Gee (2001) argues, "we do not have a reading crisis in our schools. Rather we have what I would call an affiliation crisis" (p. xviii). The problem is not merely about reading ability; Alicia's literate and learning identities are difficult to reconcile with her school and peer affiliations. If we explore Alicia's literacy and school experiences through the lens of sociocultural theory, we reveal the ways literacy and sociocultural considerations are intertwined and inextricable from each other. Issues of class, identity, access, race, and social relationships have affected and will continue to affect Alicia's trajectory as a reader and a learner. Instruction in alphabetics, fluency, vocabulary, and comprehension is not enough.

Sociocultural Considerations Matter to Alicia and Her Peers

This chapter's brief description of Alicia over time illustrates how her school literacy learning has occurred within particular school contexts involving particular people and expectations. Alicia's teachers and her mother, Ms. Rodriguez, bring expectations related to Alicia's behaviors and her interactions with other children; by eighth grade her relationships with her teachers seem to have deteriorated. Alicia complains that her teachers do not respect students and suggests that they fear their students. Both Alicia and her mother agree that teachers do not provide students with enough help to be successful in school.

Although Alicia treated reading as a social activity when she learned to read and continued to report helping her friends in grade 5, by eighth grade she reports that her friends never read together. Talking in class is presented as a problem. Although Alicia continues to read books and write poetry at home, she reports that she reads when she is bored and teaches herself to write poems.

Alicia's identity as a reader and a writer is developing in conjunction and sometimes in opposition to her more general identity positionings. Alicia is becoming a young woman who values her friends and her many social relationships. Although her public persona involves "hanging out" with her friends, talking about clothes, and having fun, her personal identity involves reading books and writing poetry. Alicia does not share her literacy activities with her friends.

Alicia's story reflects historical precedents that define learning in school as antithetical to talking in class or fooling around. Although Alicia's complaints about her teachers are echoed by her mother, her complaints may also reflect her developing identity as an adolescent girl who is supposed to be interested in her appearance and who values her friendships with peers. Adolescents have traditionally been depicted in opposition to teachers, reflecting historically constructed precedents that contribute to the distancing that is often reported between adolescents and their teachers.

Despite Alicia's negative reports about school, she describes a range of literacy practices at home including using the Internet, writing poetry, and reading "love stories" and teen magazines. She reports that she reads books that her mother brings home and shares them with her brothers. At the end of eighth grade, Alicia could easily decode text at a sixth-grade level; although her accuracy rates were close to 100%, she struggled significantly with answering questions about the nonfiction passages she read. According to these assessments, she is at least two years behind.

Literacy is enmeshed with various ways of understanding the world and the role of written text within the world. When Alicia was in first grade, she associated literacy learning with good behavior and not talking. The separation between learning and social activity is maintained over time as both Alicia and her mother describe social activity as an obstacle to learning; it also supports the idea that accomplished reading is independent reading. The ways Alicia and her mother portray teachers can also be viewed ideologically. Teachers are positioned by Alicia and her mother as "others"—people from the outside who are not committed to students. These views of schooling, learning, and literacy are immersed in issues related to power and access. Teachers are assumed to have the capacity to help students but choose not to exercise that power. Teachers are described as negligent and uncaring. Understandings about race are ideologically laden. When Alicia was in fifth grade, she reported that the race of the characters in the books she read did not matter to her; by eighth grade, it matters.

Although phonemic awareness, phonics, fluency, vocabulary, and comprehension have all played a role in learning to read for Alicia, her story reveals additional complexities that are addressed by various sociocultural understandings about literacy. These are often the same issues that consume our professional lives as teachers. Student diversity, language differences, and the economic difficulties faced by some of our students' families all contribute to the challenges we face as we bring our own experiences and understandings to classrooms of students who do not always share those experiences and ways of being.

Exploring Silences: Identifying Possibilities

The pages that follow break the silences that accompany official descriptions of literacy learning by exploring the connections that exist among teaching and learning and the sociocultural contexts in which schooling occurs, highlighting the relevance of social and cultural diversity, acknowledging the complexities of teaching and learning, and reminding us that teaching and learning are human activities that involve individuals who bring unique interests, goals, and experiences to schools and classrooms. Leaders in sociocultural research describe a set of the key understandings that hold promise. Together, these research exemplars provide not only a lens for focusing on dimensions of literacy learning that are often ignored in official discussions, but also reveal a range of classroom practices that promise to address the challenges that so many of us face as we enter our classrooms each day.

REFERENCES

Bakhtin, M.M. (1994). Selected writings. In P. Morris (Ed.), *The Bakhtin reader: Selected writings of Bakhtin, Medvedev, Voloshinov* (pp. 88–122). London: Edward Arnold.

Gee, J.P. (2001). Foreword. In C. Lewis (Ed.), *Literacy practices as social acts: Power, status, and cultural norms in the classroom* (pp. xv–xix). Mahwah, NJ: Erlbaum.

Street, B. (1984). *Literacy in theory and practice.* Cambridge, England: Cambridge University Press.

Street, B. (1995). *Social literacies: Critical approaches to literacy in development, ethnography, and education.* London: Longman.

PART I

Considerations for Sociocultural Teaching

CHAPTER 1

New Literacy Studies:
Literacy Learning Through a Sociocultural Lens

Joanne Larson

The students are running full force up the hill along a narrow path on a warm, sunny day. They had been here before, in all four seasons, and today they let it all loose. Some of the kids notice a snake and shout, "Ahhh! Look at the snake!" One student finds a small frog and stops short to observe it. The teacher, Lynn Gatto, stops with her, and all the kids gather around to look. They proceed to "their" trees to write down changes that have occurred since their last visit. Gatto spends time with each student, asking questions, pointing out her own observations, and guiding their journal entries. At the end of the daylong visit, they all gather in the park's community house to discuss their findings. This is an opportunity to think about the changes they observed and build scientific vocabulary as they name the "stuff" they found on the trees (e.g., buds, twigs, lichen). Each student's observational notes go into the ever-growing data for the information kiosk they are building for park visitors.

The rich learning described above illustrates how sociocultural theories of learning and a new literacy studies (NLS) perspective can inform curriculum and pedagogy. This chapter briefly defines NLS, describes its origins in sociocultural theory, and contextualizes its central concepts in descriptions of robust learning contexts. I use data from my research in urban schools to demonstrate how understandings gained through NLS can inform teaching and instruction, and I illustrate that in order for schools to remain relevant in students' lives, educators must rethink how literacy is defined and used. Drawing on the sociocultural approach, shifting our definition from one that is limited by reductionist notions of skills to one that is focused on the social practices in which literacy is used is crucial in a global knowledge and information economy. Without such foundational shifts in thinking, school-based literacies will not recognize the extraordinary changes going on in the world and the varieties of modes and practices needed for today's students. Furthermore, the existing marginalization of students in urban schools and poverty stricken countries around the globe will worsen.

Breaking the Silence: Recognizing the Social and Cultural Resources Students Bring to the Classroom, edited by Catherine Compton-Lilly. © 2009 by the International Reading Association.

What Is NLS?

In the late 1970s and early 1980s, several key literacy scholars argued that literacy learning is linked to social practices of literacies in use in communities (e.g., context-specific and purposeful uses of literacy), and that a sociocultural (or practice) perspective challenged traditional reading and writing pedagogies (Graff, 1979; Heath, 1983; Scribner & Cole, 1981; Street, 1984). Scribner and Cole's (1981) study of Vai literacy claims that people used multiple literacy practices as means to accomplish social and cultural ends in everyday life, and that literacy did not necessarily link to cognitive ability. Researchers therefore began to understand that literacy is not simply cognitive but is also a communicative tool used by different social and cultural groups with social rules about who can produce and use particular literacies for particular social purposes and particular audiences (Barton & Hamilton, 1998).

Heath (1983) establishes the concept of literacy events as occasions where written text and talk around that text construct interpretations, extensions, and meanings. Street (1995) expands on the concept of literacy event to argue that

> the concept of literacy practices is pitched at a higher level of abstraction and refers to both behaviour and the social and cultural conceptualizations that give meaning to the uses of reading and/or writing. Literacy practices incorporate not only 'literacy events', as empirical occasions to which literacy is integral, but also folk models of those events and the ideological preconceptions that underpin them. (p. 2)

Street (1995) builds on his cross-cultural ethnographic research to develop the concept of a continuum ranging from autonomous models of literacy to ideological models of literacy. On one end, autonomous models define literacy as a unified set of "neutral" skills that can be applied equally across all contexts (Street, 1995). From this perspective (the perspective most common in schools), there is no need to adjust instruction for different contexts of use or diverse learners. However, on the other end, ideological models define literacy as a social practice grounded in social, historical, cultural, and political contexts of use. In this view, the nature and meaning of literacy are constructed in the specific social practices of participants in particular cultural settings for particular purposes (Larson & Marsh, 2005). Thus, literacy is more than acquiring content, but in addition, locates reading and writing in the social and linguistic practices that give them meaning (Street, 1995). Historically, the concepts of context-specific uses of literacy, literacy events and practices, and autonomous and ideological models of literacy all helped to form what is now called NLS.

Most recently, researchers in this tradition have been asking what counts as "new" in NLS (Lankshear & Knobel, 2003, 2007). Research on the impact on literacy practices from technological innovations (computers, Internet, handheld games, cell phones, anime music videos, video games) have challenged us to think about dangers of colonizing out-of-school practices for school purposes and of pedagogizing youth literacies (Gee, 2004; Ito, 2007; Ito, Okabe, & Matsuda, 2006; Lankshear & Knobel, 2007; Street, 2005). Ito (2007) asks us to shift from thinking about what youth are doing with digital literacies as something they will grow out of (e.g., not thinking of youth as growing up to use technology like "we" do) but to understand their practices as what are shaping future worldviews and practices. What does all this mean for teachers? What are teachers to do with a more complex understanding of literacy, especially in the current political context of high-stakes accountability that is based on an autonomous definition? One way teachers can begin to rethink literacy instruction is to understand their own theories of literacy teaching and learning by asking themselves these questions: What are my literacy practices? How do I write? How and what do I read? What kinds of things do I write and read? When? For what purposes? How do my students use literacy in their communities? When? For what purposes? The answers to these questions require us to adopt a sociocultural approach to literacy, an approach that is embodied by NLS. Curriculum and instruction will then include a deep understanding of teachers' and students' local literacy practices and the connection of these practices to those needed in a global knowledge and information economy. Once teachers understand their own practices, they can take that knowledge to what they do in their classrooms, and together with their students, understand how these practices have changed and are changed by new technologies. Larson and Marsh (2005) propose a set of NLS principles that can be used as a tool to help rethink traditional classroom literacy practices (see Table 1.1).

Table 1.1. Principles of NLS

1. Literacy practices and events are always situated in social, cultural, historical, and political relationships and are embedded in structures of power (Barton, 1994; Barton & Hamilton, 1998; Cope & Kalantzis, 2000; Street, 1995, 1997, 1999).
2. Being literate involves being communicatively competent across multiple discourse communities (Barton, 1994; Gee, 2001). Literacy practices and events are embedded in Discourses (Gee, 2001; Gee, Hull, & Lankshear, 1996) and are integrated into people's everyday lived practices on multiple levels (Gee et al., 1996).
3. Social inequalities based on race, class, gender, ability, sexual orientation, and so forth structure access to participation in literacy events and practices (Barton & Hamilton, 1998).
4. Literacy practices involve the social regulation of text, that is who has access to them and who can produce them (Barton & Hamilton, 1998; Luke, 1994).
5. The impact of new information and communication technologies changes the nature of literacy and thus what needs to be learned (Kress, 2003; Lankshear & Knobel, 2003).
6. The changing nature of work also demands a new view of language that is multimodal (Kress, 2003) and more complex than traditional conceptions. The notion of multiliteracies emerges (Cope & Kalantzis, 2000). In other words, people use different kinds of literacy across domains of life (discourse communities).
7. Literacy practices are purposeful and embedded in broader social goals and cultural practices (Barton & Hamilton, 1998; Gee, 2001; Street, 1995).
8. Literacy practices change, and new ones are frequently acquired through processes of informal learning and sense making (Barton & Hamilton, 1998).

From Larson, J., & Marsh, J. (2005). *Making literacy real: Theories and practices in learning and teaching.* Thousand Oaks, CA: Sage. Reprinted with permission.

Tips and Possibilities for Including NLS in Classrooms

- Engage students in rich personally and socially meaningful experiences through authentically related fieldtrips, art projects, science investigations, and inquiry-based projects.

- Provide students with opportunities to use spoken language for multiple purposes and with various audiences. Have students interview each other, address different audiences, improvise and role play, participate in literature discussions, and perform poetry and music.

- Provide opportunities for students to create written documents that address authentic issues and target multiple audiences. Posters, song lyrics, spoken word poetry, podcasts, blogs, webpages, and newspaper editorials are just a few possibilities.

- With students, seek out books, magazine articles, online resources, poetry, and music lyrics that are compelling and interesting to students and will help accomplish classroom goals.

- Use literacy to accomplish the students' and the community's collective goals. What problems in your community need to be examined and addressed? How can students in your classroom learn about these issues and work for change in their community?

NLS in the Classroom

Building on these principles, we might think of school as one of the many kinds of practices people have in which literacy/literacies play a role. What are the pedagogical implications of these propositions? I suggest possible answers to this question through the classroom examples of Lynn Gatto and her fourth-grade students and Maryrita Maier and her first-grade students in the sections that follow. The practices used by these exemplary teachers offer possible models for others to use as guides in transforming their own practices. I am not suggesting a "replicable" model; rather, I present these examples as ideas upon which others can draw and then connect to their local contexts.

Ms. Gatto's Fourth-Grade Classroom

Gatto's classroom is full to the brim with curriculum materials she has collected in more than 35 years of teaching in this urban district. She has snakes, hamsters, turtles, fish, a tarantula, and all the associated food needed. Students take care of the animals and the entire classroom in a carefully orchestrated routine they developed with Gatto. She centers her pedagogy and instruction on principles of team, conversational classroom discourse, and curriculum as inquiry. Curriculum activities are centered on an extended thematic unit that lasts 3–4 months and that build on each other as the year progresses. Gatto selects the themes on the basis of U.S. standards in all content areas (e.g., International Reading Association/National Council of Teachers of English's *Standards for the English Language Arts*) and her determination about how to best meet the content requirements of her district while maintaining her commitment to construct authentic, theoretically sound literacy learning events that are grounded in her framework of literacy as critical social practice (Gatto, 2007). The use of thematic units, supported by extensive field trips and culminating projects, enables her students to understand how actions, knowledge, language, and materials in the world are interrelated (Larson, 2005).

The Urban Botanists Project conducted in a local park is one example of Gatto's extended, interdisciplinary curriculum units that facilitate students' learning multiple literacies in their contexts of use. This unit began with students reading biographies of three botanists: George Washington Carver, the famous Black botanist; Alice Eastwood, the first female botanist; and Carl Linneaus, the developer of the classification system for plants. The students selected a biography of their own choosing to read. Biography group members discussed the aspects of their books that were interesting and determined the elements of the biography genre in preparation for writing their own biographies. The research on what botanists do that students learned as part of the biography was used as one data source for the extensive research they conducted on trees in the park over the course of the year. Also, students conducted research for an information kiosk they planned to build and install in the park and for the teacher's manual and walking guide they produced. The idea for the teacher's manual came about as the students realized that although there were many schools near the park, they rarely used it. Students hoped the manual, kiosk, and walking guide would promote more use of the park. Gatto used students' insight to guide them in what she calls a critical literacy practice (e.g., literacy used for social action).

The project itself involved extended research in Rochester's Ellison Park every month over the course of the year to observe the trees and document how they changed over the course of the seasons. Each student adopted a tree to observe and document the changing tree characteristics as it interacted with its environment. Students recorded questions and predictions in their journal, described each park trip from their point of view, took notes using field guides for identification, logged measurements, illustrated with labels, and drew maps and pictures of the trees. Figure 1.1 shows the students as they share some observations of a tree.

The walking guide students produced included digital pictures of the trees and activities they conducted. During the production process, students divided the guide into parts and small groups worked on different parts, and then they came together to assemble it. Students placed the digital photographs and descriptions of the common plants found in the park in the information kiosk for visitors. The kiosk included a botany map of the park with their trees' location marked and information about the trees posted. The unit and associated activities is full of authentic literacy practices that build on school-based learning and multimodal literacies needed for participation and *use* in contemporary society.

Gatto's curriculum and pedagogy demonstrate the principles of NLS and sociocultural theories in a number of ways. For instance, Gatto embeds instructional practices in multimodal literacies used in local and global communities and on the children's out-of-school literacies. In addition, she learns about their out-of-school lives and literacy practices through her deep connection to students' families gained via home visits, frequent parent events in her classroom, and ongoing conversations with families. Further, her students understand the purposeful nature of literacy practices and their connection to wider sociocultural practices through rich activities that have real audiences and real purposes. The Ellison Park project, for example,

Figure 1.1. Urban Botanist Students Observing a Tree

has as its audience current and potential users of the park, including teachers and students in surrounding schools.

Ms. Maier's First-Grade Classroom

Another teacher with whom I have worked, Maryrita Maier, uses a social practice perspective of literacy in her instruction of school-based literacy practices. She begins from a fundamentally different starting point, the ideological model of literacy, as she constructs her curriculum and pedagogy. Her more than 6,000 children's books and explicitly articulated theories of literacy as a social practice and learning as changing participation in culturally valued activity (Rogoff, 2003) affords rich, engaging, and authentic practices for her beloved first graders.

Grounded in her belief in children as social learners, Maier designed a rich, engaging, and relevant literacy curriculum that reconciles the increasingly constraining external mandates that reduce literacy to the so-called "basics" with what she understands to be sound practice. Describing Maier's literacy curriculum in detail would take its own book, so for this chapter I focus on one key activity— modeled writing. Specifically I focus on how the modeled writing activity facilitates learning school-based literacy from an NLS perspective.

In Maier's classroom, writing occurred every day, without fail, for one and one half hours each day and included both modeled writing and student writing time.

Maier's practice of modeling writing illustrated her own processes as a writer for students, to take off the top of her head as Atwell (1998) calls it, and model for students what writers think about as they write. She demonstrated the processes by which writers choose a topic, think about the audience and purpose of their texts, and tell a good story. As she wrote in front of students, saying aloud all her thinking as she wrote, she addressed many of the so-called "basics" of school-based literacy, but in what she calls a "humane" way: orthographic competence, composition strategies, prediction, sentence and paragraph construction, punctuation, spelling, and audience awareness; all curriculum elements demanded in the district's literacy curriculum (Larson & Marsh, 2005).

Figure 1.2 shows Maier at the easel as she models writing for research on a nonfiction topic: Antarctica. This project culminated in the students planning an imaginary world tour for which they produced passports and information guides for the trip. For the research project, students identified things they might see in Antarctica while Maier wrote down all their ideas, even those that were incorrect (e.g., that they would find Eskimos). Maier sent them off to do research in her collection of hundreds of penguin books that included both fiction and nonfiction, leaving it up to students to learn what books would be good resources for learning. The students came back with all they learned, and they revised their list as they put together all the information needed for the voyage.

In sum, Maier carefully integrated the teaching of traditional writing conventions as she made her own authorship processes explicit for her students in an interactive context in which student knowledge and capabilities as writers and authors were

Figure 1.2. Teacher Modeling How to Research a Nonfiction Topic

taken seriously (Nystrand, 1997; Rose, 1995). Thus, she did not simply model writing as a discrete technique or set of skills but modeled authorship as a meaningful writing practice and did so in authentic contexts of use (Larson & Maier, 2000).

Maier's curriculum and pedagogy draws specifically on the principles of NLS that define literacy as complex social practice grounded in social, cultural, historical, and political relationships by authentically using children's culture as content for writing. By modeling her own writing practices in which she reveals her life outside of school, she facilitates children's use of family events and popular culture in their own writing. The literacy practices in her classroom help children bring their out-of-school practices to school and to learn the school practices in authentic ways; that is, they become communicatively competent across multiple discourse communities.

Conclusions

As NLS proposes, understanding the purposeful nature of literacy practices and their connection to broader social, historical, and political goals and cultural practices means that school texts need to have real audiences and real purposes. Schools need to move beyond a narrow focus on literacy exercises (Edelsky, 1991) to a broad focus on authentic practices connected to larger social and cultural practices, beginning with the practices of their students and local communities. Students need to be a part of constructing the purposes of the activities they are asked to do. For example, Gatto's students did not just practice reading skills on random texts or books that are considered appropriate for fourth-grade students; Gatto engaged students with real-life experiences and relevant readings, and the students used these experiences and reading to craft new texts that would benefit the larger community. Similarly, Maier's students also enjoyed meaningful experiences with text. Maier carefully modeled the writing process for her students and demonstrated the process of choosing a topic, considering audience, and telling a story. Maier demystified the writing process and then provided her students with daily opportunities to record their own stories. In both of these classrooms, children had opportunities to engage in rich and authentic literacy activities.

NLS emphasizes literacy as a more complex social practice than traditional pedagogy, curriculum, and assessments address. As Street (1997, 1999) has argued, curricula and assessment that reduce literacy to simple, mechanistic skills fails to recognize, or use meaningfully, the richly complex literacy practices of teachers and students in everyday life. In order for students to learn and contribute to the richness and complexity of literacy practices in contemporary society, we need literacy curricula and assessment that reflect that richness and complexity. NLS offers a lens within which to develop, implement, and research just such practices (Larson & Marsh, 2005).

Given that literacy practices change—sometimes rapidly—educators need flexibility and adaptability. Professional reading in the literacy field may be a valuable resource for teachers to be aware of new research or emerging practices that ought to be taken into account when developing curriculum and may help avoid reducing literacy practices to simplistic school lessons. NLS helps us see the process and consequences of this pedagogization (Street, 1995) and provides a valuable lens through which to understand the complex processes of teaching and learning literacy in new times.

The current focus on narrow definitions of literacy and literacy learning and on dichotomous debates that assume a universal definition of literacy has taken the form of a near-continuous argument over which instructional approach is best able to solve student reading and writing problems (Larson, 2001). From an NLS perspective, the story is not simply about method. The question should not be What is *the* best way to teach reading and writing?

All programs work to one degree or another for the purposes for which they were designed. Phonics-only programs shape different pathways and practices to literacy than do literature-based programs. For example, process-writing approaches tend to create different kinds of practices and texts than genre-based programs. Using NLS, educators can take into account larger social, historical, cultural, and political issues and realize that literacy methods, like definitions of literacy, are radically context specific. Teachers, administrators, and researchers must take into account the local context and practices within which they are located. In the United States that means looking at the following:

- Government cutbacks and institutional downsizing
- Shrinking resources and taxation bases
- Crowded classrooms with diminishing specialist assistance and support
- Uneven political support for education, students, and communities
- Teacher and schools trying to cope with rapid and unprecedented economic, social, and technological change
- Oppressive external surveillance and accountability demands

Our decisions about how to think about and how to teach literacy need to begin with a critical social analysis of the dynamic communities in which students live. Our students already live in a complex world: a globalized economy; new, hybrid forms of identity; and new technologies that are transforming traditional print and generating wholly new, unprecedented forms of expression. What we need to ask is grounded in an understanding of social, historical, cultural, and political contexts within which a given community exists: What are the practices needed to participate in communities facing new and old technologies, media, and modes of expressions, emergent hybrid cultures and institutions, and forms of cultural identities and life pathways for which we have few precedents?

Recommendations for Educators and Classroom Applications

We need to be engaged as critical participants in these new cultures and media with our students to understand their meanings in relation to social context. Specifically, teachers need to be conversant and competent with the some of the new technologies and practices that students use in their everyday lives. We need to view these technologies as valid and purposeful literacy practices and help students to understand how technological and media literacy can overlap and intersect with academic literacies. Both can be used to accomplish students' goals and to explore students' interests. Students are often engaged in complex and sophisticated literacy practices that baffle their teachers. Not only do children benefit from mastering school literacies but also our work as teachers can benefit from the lessons we learn from our students about their literacy practices.

NLS can help teachers and researchers move beyond dichotomous debates to understand how best to construct literacy learning in our classrooms. Literacy learning is no longer about identifying the best ways to teach reading but is about using literacy to address authentic interests and significant issues. Students can contest school policies, address environmental issues, target problems in their school community, address problems in their community, or help people who have particular needs. Literacy must be viewed as more than a skill that is learned in school; it is a means to address issues that are important to them.

Finally, NLS requires teachers to recognize their students as individuals who bring rich histories, interests, and passions to classrooms. Literacy teachers cannot rely on test scores and assessment profiles to obtain information about their students. We need to know our students as individuals and as members of communities and invite students to share their interests in class and talk to each other. Students can work together to identify issues that they believe are important. Teachers should provide opportunities for students to read and write about issues that interest, concern, or intrigue them. The information we learn about our students will provide us with clues on where to begin.

Each group of students is different and every teacher brings his or her own experiences to classrooms. NLS offers a rich set of possibilities for helping all children engage with literacy in rich, productive and personally meaningful ways.

REFERENCES

Atwell, N. (1998). *In the middle: New understandings about writing, reading, and learning* (2nd ed.). Portsmouth, NH: Heinemann.

Barton, D. (1994). *Literacy: An introduction to the ecology of written language.* Oxford, England: Blackwell.

Barton, D., & Hamilton, M. (1998). *Local literacies: Reading and writing in one community.* London: Routledge.

Cope, B., & Kalantzis, M. (Eds.). (2000). *Multiliteracies: Literacy learning and the design of social futures.* London: Routledge.

Edelsky, C. (1991). *With literacy and justice for all: Rethinking the social in language and education.* New York: Falmer.

Gatto, L. (2007). Success guaranteed literacy programs: I don't buy it! In J. Larson (Ed.), *Literacy as snake oil: Beyond the quick fix* (2nd ed., pp. 73–90). New York: Peter Lang.

Gee, J.P. (2001). Reading, languages abilities and semiotic resources: Beyond limited perspectives on reading. In J. Larson (Ed.), *Literacy as snake oil: Beyond the quick fix* (pp. 7–26). New York: Peter Lang.

Gee, J.P. (2004). *Situated language and learning: A critique of traditional schooling.* New York: Routledge.

Gee, J.P., Hull, G., & Lankshear, C. (1996). *The new work order: Behind the language of the new capitalism.* Boulder, CO: Westview.

Graff, H. (1979). *The literacy myth: Literacy and social structures in the nineteenth century (Studies in social discontinuity).* New York: Academic.

Heath, S.B. (1983). *Ways with words: Language, life, and work in communities and classrooms.* Cambridge, England: Cambridge University Press.

Ito, M. (2007, February). *Amateur, mashed up, and derivative: New media literacies and Otaku culture.* Keynote address at the annual mid-winter conference of the National Council of Teachers of English Assembly for Research, Nashville, TN.

Ito, M., Okabe, D., & Matsuda M. (Eds.). (2006). *Personal, portable, pedestrian: Mobile phones in Japanese life.* Cambridge, MA: MIT Press.

Kress, G.R. (2003). *Literacy in the new media age.* London: Routledge.

Lankshear, C., & Knobel, C. (2003). *New literacies: Changing knowledge and classroom learning.* Buckingham, England; Philadelphia: Open University Press.

Lankshear, C., & Knobel, C. (2007). *A new literacies sampler.* New York: Peter Lang.

Larson, J. (Ed.). (2001). *Literacy as snake oil: Beyond the quick fix.* New York: Peter Lang.

Larson, J. (2005). Breaching the classroom walls: Literacy learning across time and space in an elementary school in the United States. In B. Street (Ed.), *Literacies across educational contexts: Mediating learning and teaching* (pp. 84–101). Philadelphia: Caslon.

Larson, J., & Maier, M. (2000). Co-authoring classroom texts: Shifting participant roles in writing activity. *Research in the Teaching of English, 34*(4), 468–498.

Larson, J., & Marsh, J. (2005). *Making literacy real: Theories and practices in learning and teaching.* Thousand Oaks, CA: Sage.

Luke, A. (1994). *The social construction of literacy in the primary school.* Melbourne, Australia: Macmillan.

Nystrand, M. (1997). Dialogic instruction: When recitation becomes conversation. In M. Nystrand (Ed.), *Opening dialogue: Understanding the dynamics of language and learning in the English classroom* (pp. 1–29). New York: Teachers College Press.

Rogoff, B. (2003). *The cultural nature of human development.* New York: Oxford University Press.

Rose, M. (1995). *Possible lives.* Boston: Houghton Mifflin.

Scribner, S., & Cole, M. (1981). *The psychology of literacy.* Cambridge, MA: Harvard University Press.

Street, B. (1984). *Literacy in theory and practice.* New York: Cambridge University Press.

Street, B. (1995). *Social literacies: Critical approaches to literacy in development, ethnography, and education.* London: Longman.

Street, B. (1997). The implications of the "New Literacy Studies" for literacy education. *English in Education, 31*(3), 45–59. doi:10.1111/j.1754-8845.1997.tb00133.x

Street, B. (1998). New literacies in theory and practice: What are the implications for language in education? *Linguistics and Education, 10*(1), 1–24. doi:10.1016/S08985898(99)80103-X

Street, B. (Ed.). (2005). *Literacies across educational contexts: Mediating teaching and learning.* Philadelphia: Caslon.

SUGGESTIONS FOR FURTHER READING

Gutiérrez, K., & Larson, J. (2007). Discussing expanded spaces for learning. *Language Arts, 85*(1), 69–77.

Lankshear, C., & Knobel, M. (2006). *New literacies: Everyday practices and classroom learning.* Maidenhead, NY: Open University Press.

Larson, J. (Ed.). (2007). *Literacy as snake oil: Beyond the quick fix* (2nd ed.). New York: Peter Lang.

Pahl, K., & Rowsell, J. (2006). *Travel notes from the new literacy studies: Instances of practice.* Clevedon, England: Multilingual Matters.

Shannon, P. (2007). *Reading against democracy: The broken promises of reading instruction.* Portsmouth, NH: Heinemann.

CHAPTER 2

"Decontextualized Language" and the Problem of School Failure

James Paul Gee

W hy do students from some minority groups and students living in poverty often perform more poorly in school than White, middle class students in the United States? Researchers have offered a number of different answers to this question (Miller, 1995). One of the most popular answers has been based on the notion of "decontextualized language" (Brandt, 1990; Cummins, 1984; Goody & Watt, 1963; Havelock, 1986; Olson, 1977, 1996; Snow, 1991; Street, 1984). The point of this chapter is to argue that this widely influential answer is wrong and misleading (see Gee, 1996, 2005).

What Is Decontextualized Language?

Most of students acquire a native language at home among the members of their community. All of these students learn to use this language effectively in face-to-face communication with parents, peers, and others. Face-to-face communication is "contextualized language." What this means is that in face-to-face communication a good deal of meaning comes not directly from the words and sentences uttered but from the "context," that is, from facial expressions and gestures, intonation, pausing, a shared physical and social setting, and shared knowledge, background, and culture. The decontextualized language argument contends that poor and minority students often fail in school because "school-based language" is "decontextualized," and these students cannot handle this type of language.

In certain situations—writing and reading essays is often taken as a prime example—the shared context of face-to-face communication is missing. The words, phrases, and sentences of the text must carry nearly the whole burden of communication. If they are vague, shared context will not make up for that fact, as it does in face-to-face communication. Furthermore, it is part of the convention of these forms of language that the communicator (in this case, the writer) is not supposed to assume any great deal of shared knowledge, background, or culture with the reader, as the reader could be anyone. Such communication where the communicator puts as much meaning explicitly in the words, phrases, and

Breaking the Silence: Recognizing the Social and Cultural Resources Students Bring to the Classroom, edited by Catherine Compton-Lilly. © 2009 by the International Reading Association.

sentences of the language as possible and assumes as little as possible about the receiver of the language, is called decontextualized language.

The distinction between contextualized and decontextualized language is not the same as the distinction between speaking and listening and writing and reading. Some forms of speech (e.g., everyday informal conversation) are heavily contextualized, some are less so (e.g., college lectures). Some forms of writing are heavily contextualized (e.g., love letters) and some are not (e.g., essays).

All students get a lot of practice at home with contextualized language. However, some students experience many more models of, and get a lot more practice with, decontextualized language than do other students. This is because they are surrounded by adults and older peers who have good control over decontextualized forms of language and use such language in different social practices (with and in front of the students). Because so much of schooling is centered on decontextualized language, these students are heavily advantaged in school.

There is a good deal of research documenting practices in middle and upper middle class homes that stress early practice with decontextualized language for young students (e.g., Heath, 1983; Scollon & Scollon, 1981; Snow, 1986; Taylor, 1983). To take one example of many, parents from these homes often ask young students to give explicit reports on one or more of the day's activities at the dinner table (e.g., "What did you do at Aunt Mary's with Mommy today?"). Parents often scaffold these productions with requests for explicit labeling and clarifying information. And of course, such parents often supply their students—well before school starts—with lots of books, including information books and not just storybooks.

Thus, the decontextualized language explanation for school failure claims that students from some minority groups, poor students, and some English as a second language students get too little support (in terms of models and practice) from their homes and local communities in decontextualized language, early on and throughout their school years.

In addition, after the first grade, the most important correlate of school success is a student's ability to handle the ever-increasing complexity of school-based (so-called "academic") language, in terms of its vocabulary and its structure (Dickinson & Neuman, 2006; Sénéchal, Ouellette, & Rodney, 2006). This is the sort of language associated with school content like mathematics, science, literature, and social studies. Students who learn to decode well early on, but who do not get ready to use reading for learning content fuel the well-known (and now pervasive) phenomenon of the "fourth-grade slump," the situation in which students pass early reading tests but cannot read well for content learning in the later grades, when the complex language of school-based content really begins to kick in in earnest (American Educator, 2003; Chall, Jacobs, & Baldwin, 1990; Snow, Burns, & Griffin, 1998).

The decontextualized language explanation for school failure is very compelling, and it contains some important truths. The first flaw is this: The explanation neglects to tell us why schools fail to teach disadvantaged students decontextualized language (and the different practices in which it is recruited) and why decontextualized language does not thereby catch them up with their more advantaged peers. The second flaw is this: There is no such thing as decontextualized language. Dealing with the second flaw (obviously a serious one with the decontextualized language explanation for school failure) will help us deal with the first one, as well. We will see that all language, including all written language, is contextualized in terms of the many "conversations" (other texts and talk about those texts) that any piece of language assumes for its full comprehensibility. Therefore, all "texts" (oral or written) need to be taught as part and parcel of those conversations, not in isolation from them.

Social Languages

Speech and writing are never just in English (or some other language) "in general." Rather, any talk or text is in a specific style of language (or a mixture of styles). Let's, then, distinguish between vernacular styles of language and nonvernacular styles (Labov, 1972a, 1972b). Except in the case of massive social disruption, every human being acquires (with biological support) a native language in his or her early years. People use their native language initially and throughout their lives to speak in the vernacular style of language, that is, the style of language they use when they are speaking as "everyday" people and not as "specialists" of various sorts who engage in specialist language practices (e.g., specialists such as biologists, street gang members, lawyers, video game adepts, postmodern feminists, etc.).

Nearly every person comes to acquire nonvernacular styles of languages later in life, styles used for special purposes such as religion, work (e.g., a craft), government, or academic specialties. Let us call all these different styles of language "social languages" (Gee, 1996, 2005; they are sometimes called "registers") and say that, although every person acquires a vernacular social language (a different dialect for different groups of people) connected to his or her native language (e.g., English), people usually go on, as well, to acquire different nonvernacular social languages connected to different social groups. For example, one person may become adept at the language of Christian fundamentalist theology and someone else at the language of modern mathematics. It is important to realize that every later nonvernacular social language that a person acquires, whether this is the language of Christian fundamentalist theology or nuclear physics, builds on the grammatical resources of one's vernacular.

Acquiring different social languages—that is, different styles of language for different social purposes—is a cultural process that goes well beyond the support human biology gives all humans for the basic grammatical apparatus (the "core grammar") of their native language (Gee, 2001). In fact, acquiring any social language (including originally our vernacular dialect) requires one to learn how to recognize certain patterns of lexical and grammatical resources and how to match them to certain communicative tasks or social practices. To make matters clearer, consider the two sentences below:

1. Hornworms sure vary a lot in how well they grow.

2. Hornworm growth exhibits a significant amount of variation.

The first sentence is in a vernacular style of language. The second sentence is in a nonvernacular, or an academic social language (that is, one of a variety of different styles of language connected to academic disciplines and associated with school; see Schleppegrell, 2004). How does one know that sentence 2 is in a different style than (or is a different social language from) sentence 1? Sentence 2 does not contain any grammatical devices that are not part of anyone's vernacular dialect. What sentence 2 does that distinguishes it from sentence 1 is that it combines grammatical resources of a certain type in a certain characteristic way for certain characteristic purposes.

Sentence 2 uses a particular style of language in which verbs naming dynamic processes (e.g., *grow* and *vary*) are regularly turned into nouns naming abstract things (e.g., *growth* and *variation*). This style of language (in sentence 2) does not use affective markers like the adverb *sure* in sentence 1 (such markers express an emotion or attitude). In this style of language a phrase like *a lot* must be replaced by one like *significant variation* (where *significant* has a fairly precise definition in areas such as biology). In this style, too, subjects of sentences are very often not simple nouns (like *hornworms*), but nominalizations (like *hornworm growth*) expressing a whole clause's worth of information (i.e., hornworms grow) as an abstract concept. But what is crucial is that these linguistic features, in fact, tend to go together—to pattern together—in this specific form of language.

Let me give an analogy here. I may own coats, pants, shirts, ties, and shoes of all different sorts. These are my resources (like my linguistic resources). But I may not know, for a given event or situation, how they are supposed to go together, that is, what coat, pants, shirt, tie, and shoes I should wear together to be "accepted" as having dressed "correctly" for the event or situation. Of course, what counts as acceptable and correct in terms of either clothes or styles of language is a matter of social convention (and can change).

The patterns of grammatical elements that a social language uses are functional in the sense that they are used to carry out certain communicative functions or engage in certain social practices in a given domain or area (Halliday, 1994). Thus, in many branches of science nominalizations (like *growth* and *variation* instead of *grow* and *vary*) are used, because these branches of science (for better or worse) often study dynamic and ever-changing processes (like growing and varying) by turning them into abstract things (like growth and variation). In turn, these branches of science go on to study the abstract relationships that exist among these abstract things (Halliday & Martin, 1993). This is why relational and copula-like verbs (verbs like *exhibits*) are so common in this style of language. At the same time, these branches of science claim objectivity and mark this, in part, by eschewing the use of affective markers (like *sure*).

What this means, then, is that people can acquire the grammar of a certain social language, like the one in sentence 2, only if they come to recognize how certain grammatical devices and patterns of those devices correlate with certain sorts of communicative functions, social practices, and even attitudes and values in a given domain or area owned and operated by a certain discourse community (i.e., a group of people who share and police these functions, practices, attitudes, and values). Put another way, what this means is that a sentence like number 2 is

Characteristics of Vernacular Versus Nonvernacular Language

Vernacular Language	Nonvernacular
Affective markers are used (e.g., the adverb *sure*).	Verbs are nominalized to name abstract concepts (e.g., *growth, variation*).
Less precise language (e.g., *a lot*) is used.	More precise language (e.g., *significant*) is used.
Subjects of sentences are often simple nouns (e.g., *hornworms*).	Subjects of sentences are often nominalizations that convey large amounts of information.

understood—and can only be understood—by being contextualized within the functions, practices, attitudes, and values of the discourse community that uses the sort of social language of which sentence 2 is a part.

Understanding How All Language Is Contextualized Language

Using the previous example sentences 1 and 2 about hornworms, I first illustrate how both the vernacular style contextualized language, as well as language traditionally considered to be decontextualized, draw their meanings from context and therefore cannot be considered decontextualized. Sentence 1—the vernacular sentence—is the type of language that is often said to be contextualized. Sentence 2 is the type of language that is often said to be decontextualized. But in reality, both sentences draw much of their meaning from contextualization, though the process works somewhat differently in the two cases. Let us compare the phrase *vary a lot in how well they grow* in sentence 1 with the phrase *significant amount of variation* in sentence 2.

Vary a lot in how well they grow in sentence 1 must be understood in relation to a standard set by the activities of the speaker. This is the context against which this phrase must be understood or contextualized. The speaker, let us say, has done a school project on hornworms. As part of this activity, the speaker has taken some hornworms as prototypes of "well grown" hornworms (perhaps ones that develop fast into big hornworms). The hornworms the speaker has taken as prototypes of good growth, we assume, are ones almost anyone else in U.S. culture would have taken as prototypes (e.g., the fast-growing big ones and not, say, the ones with the biggest eyes). Compared with these hornworms, others are "less good." The speaker is saying there are lots of hornworms that develop more slowly or grow less than the prototypes. The speaker need not say any of this. It can, in many situations (though, of course, not all), be taken for granted as shared background knowledge.

Now let's consider the phrase *significant amount of variation [in growth]* in sentence 2, the supposedly more explicit sentence. This phrase too must be understood in relation to a standard, but here the standard is not set by the speaker's activities alone but by the activities, norms, and values of a particular discourse community—in this case, a community of a particular type of biologist. What counts as the sorts of variation worth measuring (in regard to growth) and what counts as being significant and how significance is measured (e.g., statistically) are settled by appeals to how a particular discourse or social practice community (a discipline) does things. Biologists of a certain sort have decided that certain things are worth measuring in certain ways. None of this is likely to be explicitly stated in a report, say, in which sentence 2 might figure, whether that report was uttered or written by a student or a professional. It is all part of the taken-for-granted context in which a sentence like number 2 is uttered or written and against which it must be understood. Therefore, both sentences need to be contextualized to be understood. Neither is decontextualized.

Furthermore, all language can be shown to be contextualized because language of the sort that is held to be decontextualized is, in fact, very often more contextualized—even more vague—than vernacular language of the sort that is held to be contextualized. There are good reasons for this. To see them, consider the sentence below (adapted from Halliday & Martin, 1993, p. 77):

3. Lung cancer death rates are clearly associated with an increase in smoking.

A whole bevy of grammatical features mark this sentence as part of a distinctive academic social language (Gee, 2004, 2005). Some of these are the ways in which a heavy subject (lung cancer death rates), deverbal nouns (*increase, smoking*), a complex compound noun (*lung cancer death rates*), a low transitive relational predicate (*are associated with*), passive or passive-like voice (are associated), the absence of agency (no mention of who does the associating), an abstract noun (*rates*), and an assertive modifier to the verb (*clearly*) pattern together in the sentence.

However, sentence 3 is no more explicit than vernacular language. It is no less contextualized. It is simply inexplicit and contextualized in a different way. Though we tend to think of academic writing and speech as clear, unambiguous, and explicit in comparison with speech, sentence 3, in fact, has many different possible meanings. However, most people who are reading sentence 3 (at least most in U.S. culture) hit on only one of these possible meanings without any overt conscious awareness that the others are perfectly possible.

How can sentence 3 have so many meanings? This fact is due to the grammar of the sentence. The subject of sentence 3 (lung cancer death rates) is a complex compound noun. There are a number of ways in which such a compound noun can be parsed (that is, in which its parts can be put together). Does it mean [lung-cancer] [death-rates], that is, death-rates from lung-cancer, where *rates* can mean the number of people dying or the speed of death from the disease? Or does it mean [lung] [cancer-death-rates], that is, cancer-death-rates for lungs, where once again *rates* can mean the number of (this time) lungs dying from cancer or the speed with which they are dying from cancer? This way of parsing the phrase is analogous to the most obvious reading of pet cancer death rates (i.e., cancer-death-rates for pets, that is how many/how fast pets are dying from cancer). Of course, most people who are reading this chapter probably interpreted lung cancer death rates in the first and not the second way, despite the second way being perfectly possible (and grammatical).

Now consider the verbal phrase *are clearly associated with* in sentence 3. Such verbal expressions are ambiguous in two respects. First, we cannot tell whether *associated with* indicates a relationship of causation or just correlation. Thus, does sentence 3 say that one thing causes another (e.g., smoking causes cancer) or just that one thing is correlated with another (smoking and cancer are found together, but, perhaps, something else causes both of them)? It is even possible that the writer did not want to commit to a choice between cause and correlate.

Second, even if we take *associated with* to mean *cause*, we still cannot tell what causes what. We may know that smoking causes cancer, but sentence 3 can perfectly mean that lung cancer death rates *lead to* increased smoking. "Perhaps," as Halliday remarks, "people are so upset by fear of lung cancer that they need to smoke more in order to calm their nerves" (Halliday & Martin, 1993, pp. 77–78).

Now, let's finish with the phrase *increased smoking*. This is a nominalization, reducing the information of a whole sentence ("smoking increases") into a noun phrase. Does it mean people smoke more (smokers are increasing the amount they smoke), or more people smoke (new smokers are being added to the list of smokers), or is it a combination of the two, meaning more people smoke more?

We can also ask, in regard to the death rates and the increased smoking taken together, if the people who are increasing their smoking (whether established smokers or new ones) are the people who are dying from lung cancer or whether other people are dying as well (e.g., people who don't smoke, but who are "associated with" smokers). Finally, we can ask of the sentence as a whole whether it is represents a "real" situation (*because* more people are smoking more people are dying) or just a hypothetical one (*if* more people were to smoke we know more people would die)?

All of these meanings are perfectly allowed by the grammar of sentence 3. And yet most people who are reading this chapter hit on just one of these many meanings and the same one (or at worst, considered a very few of the possibilities). Why? We all hit on only one (and the same one) of all the possible meanings because we have all been part of—we have all been privy to—the ongoing discussion or conversation in American society about smoking, disease, tobacco companies, contested research findings, warnings on cartons, ads that entice teens to smoke, and so on and so forth through a great many complex details.

Given this conversation as background, sentence 3 has one meaning. Without that conversation—with only the grammar of English in one's head—the sentence has a great many meanings. Obviously, however important grammar is, the conversation is more important. It leaves open one meaning (or a small number of possibilities, like allowing that sentence 3 also includes people getting lung cancer from secondary smoke). Such language is not decontextualized: to be understood it must be fully contextualized within a set of societal conversations.

Writing like that in sentence 3 is not "bad" writing. In fact, it contains grammatical structures that are absolutely typical of academic prose and for this reason: In academic domains—and other specialist domains—people want to assume that readers have been part of the earlier conversation in the domain. They don't want to always begin again, but would rather accumulate knowledge and move on from more and more advanced parts of the conversation. People write from the middle of the conversation, writing nominalized subjects like "the spin of electrons," leaving the reader to unpack what this means, and in the process, the reader must add back in a large piece of the domain conversation that is left inexplicit in the writing.

Conclusions

Learning any new social language, whether this is the style of language connected to particular sorts of literacy practices or the style of language connected to a particular domain in science, requires three key things. First, it requires the learner to learn how certain ways with words, or patterns of grammar, match up with certain communicative functions and social practices. Why and where does one appropriately say "Hornworm growth exhibits a significant amount of variation" rather than "Hornworms sure vary a lot in how well they grow"? In turn, this requires immersion in the communicative functions and social practices of people who use this sort of language.

Second, people who use language like "Hornworm growth exhibits a significant amount of variation" take on certain sorts of attitudes, values, norms, interests, expectations, and even passions. This amounts to what we can call a "socially situated identity." Any social language involves such a socially situated identity, because when anyone speaks or writes in a given social language, to understand that person, we need to know *who* is speaking or writing, in the sense of what sort of person with what sorts of values and attitudes (e.g., a scientist, gang member, or policeman) and *what* that person is doing, in the sense of what sort of function or social practice is that person trying to bring off (Gee, 1996; Wieder & Pratt, 1990). Learners cannot learn the socially situated identity that goes with a social language and its associated social practices if such an identity is not coherently developed for them.

In the end, many students fail in school because schools fail to create meaningful contexts. Some students get these contexts and their concomitant socially situated identities at home or otherwise outside school, some do not. The problem of school failure is not that certain students fail to master decontextualized language. It is that, for some students, language at school is decontextualized.

Recommendations for Educators and Classroom Applications

1. Teach overtly—talk about and reflect on—academic language, that is, the styles of language used in content learning in school.
2. Contextualize language in activities, experiences, and inquiries so that it gets connected to images, interactions, actions, goals, values, and dialogue.
3. Compare and contrast different styles of language (e.g., different ways of talking and writing about the same, similar, or related topics).

4. Have students read—for clear goals (that the students understand and accept)—lots of nonnarrative text types, not just narrative texts.

5. Pay attention to oral language—to students learning to speak in academic styles (in their oral forms)—and not just written language; make as many connections between the two as you can.

6. Give students a chance to talk about what they have read and the activities and inquiries in which they have engaged with each other and with adults.

7. Discuss how language works in the world with students—where it works well and where it is used to lie or confuse.

REFERENCES

American Educator. (2003). The fourth-grade plunge: The cause. The cure [Special issue]. Spring. Retrieved May 22, 2008, from www.aft.org/pubs-reports/american_educator/spring2003/index.html

Brandt, D. (1990). *Literacy as involvement: The acts of writers, readers, and texts.* Carbondale: Southern Illinois University Press.

Chall, J.S., Jacobs, V., & Baldwin, L. (1990). *The reading crisis: Why poor children fall behind.* Cambridge, MA: Harvard University Press.

Cummins, J. (1984). *Bilingualism and special education: Issues in assessment and pedagogy.* Clevedon, England: Multilingual Matters.

Dickinson, D.K., & Neuman, S.B. (Eds.). (2006). *Handbook of early literacy research* (Vol. 2). New York: Guilford.

Gee, J.P. (1996). *Social linguistics and literacies: Ideology in discourses* (2nd ed.). London: Taylor & Francis.

Gee, J.P. (2001). Progressivism, critique, and socially situated minds. In C. Dudley-Marling & C. Edelsky (Eds.), *The fate of progressive language policies and practices* (pp. 31–58). Urbana, IL: National Council of Teachers of English.

Gee, J.P. (2004). *What video games have to teach us about learning and literacy.* New York: Palgrave Macmillan.

Gee, J.P. (2005). *An introduction to discourse analysis: Theory and method* (2nd ed.). London: Routledge.

Goody, J., & Watt, I.P. (1963). The consequences of literacy. *Comparative Studies in History and Society, 5*(3), 304–345.

Halliday, M.A.K. (1994). *An introduction to functional grammar* (2nd ed.). London: Edward Arnold.

Halliday, M.A.K., & Martin, J.R. (1993). *Writing science: Literacy and discursive power.* Pittsburgh, PA: University of Pittsburgh Press.

Havelock, E.A. (1986). *The muse learns to write: Reflections on orality and literacy from antiquity to the present.* New Haven, CT: Yale University Press.

Heath, S.B. (1983). *Ways with words: Language, life, and work in communities and classrooms.* New York: Cambridge University Press.

Labov, W. (1972a). *Language in the inner city: Studies in the black English vernacular.* Philadelphia: University of Pennsylvania Press.

Labov, W. (1972b). *Sociolinguistic patterns.* Philadelphia: University of Pennsylvania Press.

Miller, L.S. (1995). *An American imperative: Accelerating minority educational advancement.* New Haven, CT: Yale University Press.

Olson, D.R. (1977). From utterance to text: The bias of language in speech and writing. *Harvard Educational Review, 47*(3), 257–281.

Olson, D.R. (1996). *The world on paper: The conceptual and cognitive implications of writing and reading.* Cambridge, England: Cambridge University Press.

Schleppegrell, M. (2004). *The language of schooling: A functional linguistics perspective.* Mahwah, NJ: Erlbaum.

Scollon, R., & Scollon, S.W. (1981). *Narrative, literacy, and face in interethnic communication.* Norwood, NJ: Ablex.

Sénéchal, M., Ouellette, G., & Rodney, D. (2006). The misunderstood giant: On the predictive role of early vocabulary to future reading. In D.K. Dickinson & S.B. Neuman (Eds.), *Handbook of early literacy research* (Vol. 2, pp. 173–184). New York: Guilford.

Snow, C.E. (1986). Conversations with students. In P. Fletcher & M. Garman (Eds.), *Language acquisition* (2nd ed., pp. 69–89). Cambridge, England: Cambridge University Press.

Snow, C.E. (1991). The theoretical basis for relationships between language and literacy in development. *Journal of Research in Childhood Education, 6*(1), 5–10.

Snow, C.E., Burns, M.S., & Griffin, P. (Eds.). (1998). *Preventing reading difficulties in young children*. Washington, DC: National Academy Press.

Street, B. (1984). *Literacy in theory and practice*. Cambridge, England: Cambridge University Press.

Taylor, D. (1983). *Family literacy: Young students learning to read and write*. Exeter, NH: Heinemann.

Wieder, D.L., & Pratt, S. (1990). On being a recognizable Indian among Indians. In Carbaugh, D. (Ed.), *Cultural communication and intercultural contact* (pp. 45–64). Hillsdale, NJ: Erlbaum.

SUGGESTIONS FOR FURTHER READING

Gee, J.P. (2004). *Situated language and learning: A critique of traditional schooling*. London: Routledge.

Schleppegrell, M.J., & Colombi, M.C. (Eds.). (2002). *Developing advanced literacy in first and second languages: Meaning with power*. Mahwah, NJ: Erlbaum.

Zamel, V., & Spack, R. (Eds.). (1998). *Negotiating academic literacies: Teaching and learning across languages and cultures*. Mahwah, NJ: Erlbaum.

CHAPTER 3

"O Say, Do You See?": Using Critical Race Theory to Inform English Language Arts Instruction

Arlette Ingram Willis and Kimberly N. Parker

Most readers of this book have said or have heard another teacher say, "I don't see Black, White, Asian, green, pink, or polka dot students. I just see kids." The intent in such declarations is to convey the notion of colorblindness. It is another way of saying, "I am not racist." However, it is unrealistic to believe that anyone living in a racist society is not affected in some way by assumptions about race, racism, and power. We all notice race, know about racist acts (both individual and institutional), and bring a history of unstated and often unexamined racial assumptions about people who are different from us to every situation, including classrooms. Whether or not someone decides to acknowledge racial differences is a choice. It is a choice that we believe teachers must address in a forthright manner for it will affect their perceptions, interactions, and expectations of students as well as their curricular choices and instructional strategies. Spina and Tai (1998) caution that, "not seeing race is predicated on not seeing White as race and denying Whiteness as a focus of critique and analysis. Ignoring the racial construction of Whiteness reinscribes its centrality and reinforces its privilege and oppressive position as normative" (p. 37). Those who have benefited from racism are likely to use the resources that they have historically controlled to prevent the existence of racism from being recognized or addressed. Specifically, while people possess the ability to "see" racial differences, many make a conscious suggestion that they do not see race, which implies that only one race, the White race, is of value. O say, do you see?

In this chapter, we present an overview of the evolution of Critical Race Theory (CRT) that is not intended as a comprehensive review. We then discuss how CRT is linked to education and explain how it informs our English language arts methods course specifically. In doing so, we encourage all teachers to consider informing their conceptualizing, decision-making, and curricular choices using CRT.

Review of Related Literature

In the late 20th century, legal scholars of Color sought to "reexamine the terms by which race and racism have been negotiated in American consciousness, and to

Breaking the Silence: Recognizing the Social and Cultural Resources Students Bring to the Classroom, edited by Catherine Compton-Lilly. © 2009 by the International Reading Association.

recover and revitalize the radical tradition of race-consciousness among African-Americans and other peoples of Color" (Crenshaw, Gotanda, Peller, & Thomas, 1995, p. xiv). They acknowledged that the concept of race is socially constructed and is not a biological or scientific fact while simultaneously understanding that this construct operates as "fact" within the United States where race is visible, tangible, and omnipresent. They maintain that racial categories are built on the acceptance of two fundamental untruths: (1) People can be distinguished on the basis of phenotype and physical markers, and (2) Whites are the superior racial group and Whiteness is the norm.

The centrality of race, in CRT, is not limited to a Black/White binary but includes the concerns of Latino/a, African, Asian, and Native Americans. Ladson-Billings (2005) observes, "the real issue is . . . the way everyone regardless of his/her declared racial and ethnic identity is positioned in relation to Whiteness" (p. 116). CRT acknowledges intersectionality or multiple forms of oppression—class, gender, sexual orientation, nationality, ethnicity, language, and immigration rights—that exists and are experienced among people of Color. Further, it addresses the intersection of accent, culture, ethnicity, land sovereignty, and surname (Lawrence, Matsuda, Delgado, & Crenshaw, 1993; Yosso, 2005). CRT also helps to clarify how multidimensional identities are formed and needed for survival within and outside of our communities. Scholars draw from multiple racial and ethnic epistemologies to situate their work and ask questions that challenge preconceived notions about beliefs, values, knowledge, and ways of making meaning used by people of Color.

Among the first educational researchers who have adopted CRT are Ladson-Billings and Tate (1995) and Tate (1997). They adopted CRT to more adequately address the historical and present-day contexts of race, racism, and oppression. In terms of literacy education, CRT helps to reveal the importance of literacy in the lives of people of Color and illustrates how these literacies are distinctive from, and related to, Western Eurocentric thought (Willis, 2008). When applied to literacy, CRT helps to validate that people of Color are "holders and creators of knowledge" (Delgado Bernal, 2002, p. 108), in part by dismissing deficit notions promoted in the mainstream about people of Color and highlighting the literacies used by people of Color. Moreover, CRT's connection to literacy involves acknowledging and valuing the cultures, knowledges, languages, and abilities of students of Color.

CRT scholars produce counterstories to the way race, culture, language, and the lived experiences of people of Color are depicted in mainstream research, herein, language and literacy research. CRT scholars use autobiography, biography, parables, stories, testimonio, and voice (infusing humor and allegory) to expose hidden truths and to explicate and situate race, racism, privilege, and power. These narratives are exceptionally detailed to help capture the richness of contexts, experiences, and explanations from the vantage points of those who have experienced oppression and to contradict or oppose the assumptions and beliefs held by many White people. Inherent in the narrative forms are voice, that is, the ability of group members to articulate their experience in ways unique to them (Delgado & Stefancic, 2001). The idea of voice carries with it the notion that the voices of people of Color are especially qualified to tell their own stories and do not need to be translated or interpreted by White people. Solórzano and Yosso (2001) have applied CRT to teacher education, emphasizing how necessary it is for all teachers to understand the relationships among race, racism, privilege, and power in historical and contemporary settings.

CRT demonstrates the interwoven nature of language and literacy as multidimensional, multicontextual, and multifaceted forms of communication used by people of Color. Scholars value the lived experiences and reflections on experiences shared by people of Color as essential to understanding the effects of racial inequality.

Applying CRT to English Language Arts Instruction

We have used CRT to help frame our English language arts undergraduate methods course, but we encourage all teachers to consider and discuss its tenets in planning for English language arts instruction. The importance of these discussions cannot be understated, as Harris (1992) argues,

> Literacy functions in an oppressive manner . . . when curricular materials, educational philosophy, and pedagogical techniques combine to inculcate an ideology that denigrates a group, omits or misrepresents the history and status of a group, or limits access to knowledge that would enable the individual or group to participate in all cultural institutions. (p. 277)

Pendergast's (2002) study, for instance, documents linkages between U.S. Supreme Court legislation and notions of Whiteness and literacy as the property of Whites in the United States. Moreover, discussions of race and racism, unless explicitly and specifically addressed, tend to be given short shrift and are replaced by a focus on educational jargon that shields racism under the concepts of normativity, values, and objectivity.

In the next sections we describe and illustrate two strategies (with accompanying activities) that are inspired and informed by CRT and that we use with our preservice teachers to ensure that race, racism, intersectionality, oppression, and power are clearly and explicitly addressed in English language arts instruction. We invite all educators to think about the ways race and privilege historically and contemporaneously pervade education and literacy curricula, materials, and instruction as they reflect on these activities.

English language arts teachers, for instance, can rethink how they introduce a novel to students by creating activities that allow students to adopt a sociohistoric lens to understand the context in which the author wrote the novel as well as the sociohistoric period described in the novel. Leistyna, Woodrum, and Sherblom (1996) define a *sociohistoric lens* as working "from the assumption that we are never independent of the social and historical forces that surround us. . . . [W]e all inherit beliefs, values, and ideologies that need to be critically understood and transformed where necessary" (p. 343). Although the technique works with any text, several examples from popular middle school literature selections are *Dragonwings* by Laurence Yep, *Roll of Thunder, Hear My Cry* by Mildred D. Taylor, *Taking Sides* by Gary Soto, *The Circuit* by Francisco Jiménez, and *The Watsons Go to Birmingham–1963* by Christopher Paul Curtis. Several examples from popular high school literature selections are *Ceremony* by Leslie Marmon Silko, *Ragtime* by E.L. Doctorow, *The Adventures of Huckleberry Finn* by Mark Twain, *The House on Mango Street* by Sandra Cisneros, *The Joy Luck Club* by Amy Tan, *Things Fall Apart* by Chinua Achebe, and *To Kill a Mockingbird* by Harper Lee, among others.

Autobiography/Memoir: Understanding the Reality and Social Construction of Race in the United States

Our students reflect the U.S. trend in preservice teacher education: They are predominately White, female, heterosexual, from upper-middle income and homogenous backgrounds. Each fall semester we begin our preservice English language arts methods course with an exploration of personal understandings of race, racism, privilege, and power. We strongly recommend that all teachers read widely culturally specific/conscious literature that challenges their thinking on issues of race, racial relations in the United States, and social justice to inform their instruction of English language arts. Like Nieto (2003), we believe that highly qualified language and literacy teachers must understand and address these issues in their own lives, historically and contemporaneously. We use autobiography and memoir to address racial, ethnic, and linguistic diversity in society and to help create a sense of community. Purposively, we select readings by scholars and authors of Color that center on their experiences as racialized beings and that are accurate, authentic, respectful, and positive but realistic. The readings are a starting point for conversations about how to deconstruct and demystify issues of race, racism, privilege, and power at work—in society in general and education specifically. However, we strive to avoid ethnocentrism by offering a balanced reading list of all major racial groups in the United States. We use these readings to highlight how society and the educational system privileges White people in an effort to retain power and control and to disprivilege people of Color. There are four specific activities in this portion of the course: (1) writing personal memoirs, (2) autobiographic poetry performances, (3) creating an autobiography/memoir webpage, and (4) class discussions of scholarship written by researchers of Color and selective autobiographies and memoirs written by authors of Color.

During the first two activities (writing personal memoirs and autobiographic poetry performances) White students seldom mention race. When race is mentioned, Whiteness is not critically deconstructed and more often than not it is accompanied by gender, sexual orientation, and religious affiliations. McIntyre (1997) explains that "White people's lack of consciousness about their racial identities limits their ability to critically examine their own positions as racial beings who are implicated in the existence and perpetuation of racism" (p. 16). Generally, their autobiographic information describes forms of ethnicity that can be characterized as "individualistic, symbolic, ethnic identity" (Waters, 2004, p. 433). That is, they embrace their ethnic identity/ies when called upon but do not live lives that reflect ethnic knowledge (of course, this does not apply to all White preservice educators). Waters points out that White people want to believe "all ethnicities mean the same thing, that enjoying the traditions of one's heritage is an option available to a group or an individual, but that such a heritage should not have any costs associated with it" (p. 438). It is difficult for many White students to understand that people of Color hold a "socially enforced and imposed racial identity" (p. 433) that is not optional or valued (by the mainstream).

When we recenter class discussion on race, there is an accompanying shift in the classroom discourse because these discussions often engender feelings of shame, sadness, guilt, resistance, and for some, transformation (Helms, 1992; Tatum, 1998). By way of contrast, our preservice teacher educators of Color are apt to foreground race as part of their identity, understanding that their racial identities are socially imposed and structure and inhibit their lives. We mention this phenomenon here because the latter two activities (creating an autobiography or memoir webpage and class discussions of research and autobiography and memoir) make clear that there are costs associated with racial categorization for people of Color.

Our students are required to read select autobiographies and memoirs because we believe they help students to enter worlds where race, racism, privilege, and power have affected the lives of the authors. We encourage our preservice teacher educators to understand the importance of helping students make connections between the texts and their lives. Further, we use this same literature to help students think about and plan curricula and lessons to teach in schools that have become increasingly racially, ethnically, and linguistically diverse. We point out how students of Color bring understandings to the text that may differ from their own but that are nonetheless valid. CRT fosters this type of awareness about the rich complex racial, ethnic, and cultural lives we all live. We encourage all teachers to be mindful of how necessary it is to reflect on and engage with activities presented in this chapter. Inservice teachers can use culturally specific/conscious autobiographies and memoirs as powerful personal narratives that describe from an emic perspective the reality and effects of individual and institutional racial discrimination, as well as the effects of power and privilege in the United States.

To illustrate this point, we turn to a narrative by Dowdy (2002) who situates her story in the sociohistoric events, migratory history, and genetic influences of Trinidadians whose genetic roots and linguistic routes stem from the coast of West Africa and include language patterns from Europe, India, and Asia. She reveals, "the spirits of her ancestors occupy a chamber in her consciousness that make it easy to reach back, unself-consciously, to the deeper inspiration of her linguistic culture" (p. 7). She recalls that her mother and teachers encouraged her to use formal English. To do so, she admits that in school "we had to play to a White audience . . . we had to remember that there was a White way, and that was the right way" (p. 4). Retrospectively, Dowdy observes that the pressure to adopt formal English meant that "Your job, as a survivor of the twenty-odd generations of slaves and indentured workers and overseers, is to be best at the language that was used to enslave you and your forebears. It is a painful strategy for survival" (p. 7). Her narrative artfully articulates the tensions she experienced by forced/coerced language and cultural dominance. We use her story to make clear that many students of Color are working hard to engage in school discourse as well as literature, as they may draw from very different languages, cultures, and experiences.

It is at this point in the semester that we help preservice teachers think about how they might use decision making, curricula, and materials to break strongholds of privilege and power through the selection of authentic multicultural and multiethnic literature. We suggest that practicing teachers periodically review their reading lists to ensure that their literature selections include culturally specific/conscious multicultural and multiethnic literature that is balanced in the portrayal of all racial groups. This step is particularly helpful for teachers whose student population is homogenous as it extends and applies critical discussions of race to classroom instruction. We believe that it is important for preservice teachers to learn how to select, engage, and interrogate literature, especially multicultural/multiethnic literature. Specifically, we require preservice teachers to construct literacy units that acknowledge historic and contemporary issues of access, equity, and justice for people of Color. Every teacher can apply the rich models of CRT awareness to their own lives and their own teaching.

Selecting Culturally Specific/Conscious Multicultural and Multiethnic Children's and Young Adult Literature

The English language arts consists of many communicative acts, but the centerpiece of most curricula is literature. Teachers who seek to incorporate multicultural/multiethnic literature in their classrooms face the challenge of deciding how to select appropriate texts as well as how to engage the literature in unit and lesson planning. We address two possible approaches to text selection through the lenses of Bishop (1992) and Johnson (2006) and then suggest how a teacher might evaluate a text through this framework.

Bishop (1992) makes a powerful argument for texts written by people of Color about members of the same culture. These "cultural insiders" possess a unique ability to document their experiences as a person of Color in ways that outsiders simply cannot. Bishop's three categories for multicultural children's literature include "Culturally specific/conscious," "Generically American/socially conscious," and "Culturally neutral/melting pot." Although Bishop has used different language to identify these categories (1982, 1992, 1997), the ideas that define the categories remains consistent. Culturally specific/conscious books "illuminate the experience of growing up a member of a particular, non-White cultural group" (Bishop, 1992,

p. 44). People of specific cultural groups might recognize familiar patterns (language, family relationships, etc.) within the books that might increase their affinity to those texts. However, culturally specific/conscious books are not exclusionary, Bishop notes. Culturally specific/conscious books have the potential to increase the understanding and appreciation for those not of the culture. People of the culture they are depicting write books in this category.

Generically American/socially conscious books are typified by Bishop (1992) as "feature[ing] characters who are members of so-called minority groups, but they contain few, if any, specific details that might serve to define those characters culturally" (p. 45). In these books, the assumed audience is White, and the themes presented in these books, though considered "universal," actually depict White/European American cultural activities and values. Illustrations within these books do not attempt to be culturally specific, and as Bishop notes, "have been criticized for their very lack of cultural specificity" (p. 45). Characters in illustrations can be stereotypical. Culturally neutral/melting pot books are described by Bishop as books that "feature people of color, but are fundamentally about something else" (p. 46). Within these books "cultural authenticity is not likely to be a major consideration" (p. 46). The latter two categories pose the greatest challenge for CRT because they do not interrogate Whiteness, privilege, or racism. If students consistently read texts that fail to depict people of Color in authentic ways, there is no potential to challenge their own thinking or move toward understanding and appreciating difference. Whiteness is the norm in these books and people of Color are placed in opposition to Whiteness.

Examples of Culturally Specific/Conscious Multicultural Literature

The following list of children's and young adult books can serve as a starting point for further inquiry for the study of multicultural and multiethnic literature.

Cofer, J.O. (1995). *An Island Like You: Stories of the Barrio*. New York: Puffin. Twelve stories about Puerto Rican American teenagers and their friendships, family traditions, and community life.

Draper, S.M. (1996). *Tears of a Tiger*. New York: Simon and Schuster. An African American basketball player faces the aftermath of the death of his friends in a drunk driving accident in this multigenre novel.

Erdrich, L. (2002). *The Birchbark House*. New York: Hyperion. An Ojibwa girl encounters a smallpox epidemic in 1847.

Jiménez, F. (1997). *The Circuit: Stories From the Life of a Migrant Child*. Albuquerque, NM: University of New Mexico Press. A young Mexican immigrant boy moves from place to place with his family as they search for work in this autobiographical account.

Soto, G. (2003). *Taking Sides*. New York: Harcourt. A Latino basketball player moves from a poor neighborhood to one more affluent and must negotiate tensions between his old friends and new friends as the big game approaches.

Yang, G.L. (2006). *American Born Chinese*. New York: First Second. A boy who is the only Chinese American at his school tries to belong but struggles against stereotyping and his own identity in this graphic novel.

CRT is best reflective of Bishop's culturally specific/conscious children's books because it validates the experiences of people of Color, through the "counternarrative" or "counterstory." Delgado and Stefancic (2001) write,

> The hope is that well-told stories describing the reality of black and brown lives can help readers bridge the gap between their worlds and those of others. Engaging stories can help us understand what life is like for others, and invite the reader into a new and unfamiliar world. (p. 41)

In our teacher education courses, we use culturally specific/conscious books because they are the most appropriate multicultural and multiethnic books for teachers to select and share with students. We suggest that teachers read the research of Bishop and others who have studied multicultural and multiethnic literature for children and young adults.

Using the Diversity Wheel to Identify Conscious Multicultural Literature

We have used a diversity wheel (Loden, 1995; see Figure 3.1) as a useful bridge to instantiate concepts examined in our autobiography and memoir portion of the course and as a connector between Bishop's categories of multicultural literature because it is helpful in determining the appropriateness of a text. The wheel requires users to work within two concentric circles. In the first (inner) circle, users identify themselves by age, ethnicity, gender, physical ability, sexual orientation, and race. Then, users move to the second (outer) circle to identify their education, geographic location, income, marital status, military experience, parental status, religious beliefs, and work background (Loden & Rosener, 1991). First, preservice teachers use the diversity wheel, as explained by Johnson (2006), to examine their own lives before applying the diversity wheel to characters in a text, authors, and illustrators. This initial encounter helps to encourage students to make reference to their personal selves and to develop familiarity with the wheel's purposes and concepts. Second, preservice teachers apply the characteristics of the diversity wheel to characters, and they look for specific culturally specific/conscious examples within texts that support a decision to use the text. Finally, preservice teachers apply the diversity wheel to authors and illustrators. Likewise, inservice teachers can use this same strategy for a self-examination of diversity and to engage their students' racial identity.

Johnson (2006) cautions that after completing the diversity wheel, one might comment that the wheel does not include internal insights or history; however, the wheel "does say a lot about the social reality that shapes everyone's life in powerful ways" (p. 14). Interestingly, characters in texts exist in these social realities as well.

Determining how those social realities contribute to the development of a character, as well as portrayals of race and equality (or inequality) enables teachers to locate a text within a CRT framework and thus begin to make informed decisions about the most appropriate texts to include within their curriculum. To extend preservice teachers' understanding and appreciation for the personal and institutional racism that are part of the lives of people of Color, we turn to a young adult novel.

Figure 3.1. The Diversity Wheel

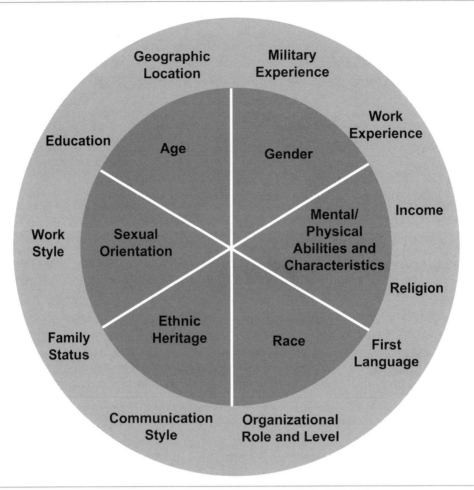

From Loden, M. (1995). *Implementing Diversity.* New York: McGraw-Hill. Reprinted with permission of The McGraw-Hill Companies.

Applying CRT to a Culturally Specific/Conscious Text: *Monster*

Monster (Myers, 1999) is about Steve Harmon, a 16-year-old young Black man who is an aspiring filmmaker. Steve is falsely accused of being the lookout in a robbery and murder of a drugstore owner. The novel is written as a screenplay and includes snippets of Steve's life at home and school as well as graphic details of the violence that surrounds Steve in the detention center where he remains throughout the trial. The novel grapples with the larger issue of Steve's attempts to proclaim his innocence within a system that has no interest in that innocence and instead trades heavily in racist perceptions of him (and his fellow inmates) as guilty before his trial begins and throughout the trial. *Monster* also integrates images within Steve's screenplay that include a photo of a young Black man sitting in a prison cell, that same young man in a police car, and the young man's mug shot. In Table 3.1, we chart Bishop's points about cultural specificity and consciousness and aspects of

Table 3.1. Applying the Diversity Wheel to the Culturally Specific/Conscious Text *Monster*

	Main character: Steve Harmon	Author: Walter Dean Myers
Age	16	60
Race	Black	Black
Ethnicity	African American	African American
Gender	Male	Male
Physical abilities/qualities	Nondisabled	Nondisabled
Sexual/affectional orientation	Heterosexual	Heterosexual
Culturally specific examples	• The White female prosecutor calls Steve "monster" during her opening comments. (p. 5) • Steve's detention center echoes with "voices [that] are clearly Black or Hispanic" males. (p. 7) • Steve's White female defense attorney commands him to pay attention during the trial and present himself seriously. (p. 13) • Steve's attorney explains to him that her "job" is to "make you a human being in the eyes of the jury." (p. 16) • Court proceedings are a formality: Judges and attorneys (all White) discuss their holiday and recreational plans, and a guard explains, "It's a motion case. They go through the motions; then they lock them up." (p. 14) • During the trial, Steve's lawyer worries that too many men of Color will ruin Steve's attempts to be seen as innocent: "She was afraid that the jury wouldn't see a difference between me and all the bad guys." (p. 116) • Steve includes a newscast featuring then-mayor of New York City, Rudy Guiliani, who says, "The idea that we're just trying to stop crime in White or middle-class areas is nonsense. Everyone living in the city deserves the same protection." (p. 138) • Steve is found not guilty and attempts to hug his lawyer, who "stiffens" and turns away from him. (p. 276)	

Loden's diversity wheel to illustrate how the novel is an example of a culturally specific/conscious text that should be read using a CRT lens.

Monster is a culturally specific/conscious text through which teachers can interrogate issues from a CRT perspective. Myers creates the protagonists and voice of Steve Harmon, who has a stable home life and loving parents and attends a school with teachers who think of him highly. Within that context, Myers characterizes Steve's attempts to remain human in the eyes of a judicial system that presumes him guilty before his trial starts and a penal system that is overwhelmingly populated with men of Color. He is branded as a "monster" for his alleged role in a murder. As the novel unfolds, Steve struggles to maintain his humanity against the prosecutor's—and even his own defense attorney's—attempts to dehumanize him. The process of dehumanization extends beyond the courtroom and into the detention center where Steve fears that he might be the victim of sexual assault, and he resists showing any vulnerability. He learns quickly that his guilt is implicated by his Blackness when his attorney tells him, "Half of those jurors, no matter what they said . . . believed you were guilty the moment they laid eyes on you. You're young, you're Black, and you're on trial. What else do they need to know?" (Myers, 1999, p. 79).

Steve's struggle throughout the novel invokes the larger problems of the justice system as related to Black men. At the end of 2005, there were 3,145 Black males sentenced to prison per every 100,000 Black men (United States Department of Justice, 2006). The lack of law enforcement in neighborhoods of people of Color also is highlighted in *Monster* by a press conference featuring then-mayor of New York City Rudy Giuliani openly calling for the end of violence in areas that are not White or middle class.

Steve's experience is an example of how negative perceptions—dominant beliefs about Black men—can influence the potential life sentence of a 16-year-old boy: Steve entered the drugstore only for some mints. Once he is imprisoned, his innocence does not matter. Despite his lawyer's orders for Steve to "believe in himself," (Myers, 1999, p. 24) few sources exist from which Steve can draw any inspiration, other than his parents. The White people in the judicial system around him, even his attorney, are convinced that he is guilty. There are moments that Steve even considers himself guilty and contemplates suicide so he will not have to serve a life sentence in prison. Irrespective of the attempts to dehumanize him, enough to believe himself a monster, Steve resists. Myers' attempts to humanize Steve are difficult given the world within which he lives and we live. It is a world constructed on perceptions, however false, about young Black men, that play out in the novel. Steve's guilt is a foregone conclusion, it seems, because the White characters, who have the ability to influence his fate, have already convicted him. It is difficult to be optimistic about Steve's future, particularly given that he feels he "already [has] 'Monster' tattooed" on his forehead" (Myers, 1999, p. 61).

Myers, who also is a Black male, constructs a counternarrative in this text that rejects dominant, negative perceptions of young Black men. He portrays Steve as a young man who is sensitive, caring, and talented and who attends an academic high school. Informed by spending time with incarcerated youth, Myers articulated a desire and need to write works that construct young Black men positively:

> You want to see a book with your experiences. When you don't see your experiences, you don't feel positive about who you are. I believe it's up to people like me to take the African American experience and humanize it. (Myers as interviewed by Williams, 2005, pp. 39–40)

Myers holds out hope for Steve, and after he is found innocent, Steve resumes filmmaking because he feels the need to reconstruct himself as human.

Applying CRT to this novel requires a deeper critical and conscious reading to understand the intersecting oppressions in Steve's world. He is incarcerated because police officers assumed that, as a young Black man near the store during the crime, he is guilty. The White judicial system employees and jurors (sans the Black female juror) assumed Steve was guilty before the trial began. In the detention center, Steve is housed with inmates who are predominantly men of Color in a violent environment. Finally, his past, in which he is a high school student and a filmmaker, slips further away.

To illustrate our point, we share two difference sets of responses to *Monster*. First, in a graduate class in library and information sciences, there was a discussion about the novel that included a number of White women (graduate students, librarians, and classroom teachers). The participants articulated how disturbed they were because Steve was exonerated. In their reading of the novel, they claimed that Steve was "clearly guilty," and they felt the justice system was "wrong" for not finding him guilty. Taking a step back from this encounter, we wonder about what systems of power, privilege, and racism exist that allow these women to rail Steve's innocence and denounce the judicial system. Further, what is it about these women's own privilege that prevented them from even seriously contemplating Steve's innocence? Second, in a discussion following the reading of *Monster* with a group of Black and biracial middle school boys, we note they did not automatically assume Steve was guilty. In fact, they discussed how the judicial system was "biased anyway" (against males of Color). Further, they "read the word and world," albeit fictional, in which Steve lived. Moreover, they visibly expressed relief at the novel's conclusion when Steve was found not guilty. These boys were informed by their own experiences as young Black and biracial men living within a racist society, as well as personal experiences of family members in the judicial system.

We have interpreted these experiences to illustrate that teachers preparing to use *Monster* must interrogate race, racism, privilege, and power in their own lives as well as how it is presented in this novel. For example, it should be deeply troubling that the judge, attorneys, and most of the jurors are White, while Steve and the other men convicted of the murder are men of Color; a fact that must be acknowledged and addressed when teaching this book. The lack of seriousness displayed by the judge and attorney (who spend more time discussing their holiday plans rather than trial-related formalities) and Steve's attorney's desire for him to concentrate on presenting himself as innocent, are equally disturbing. In addition, Steve's experience inside the detention center speaks to the larger condition of incarceration as dehumanizing. Teachers must consider statistics from sources such as the statistics from the Bureau of Justice that clearly outline the disparities between the number of Black males in prison as compared with the overall population (an idea that also should include a review of their school, city/ town, county, and state use of physical incarceration of males of Color compared with White people. Further, teachers must consider how they will guide students to critically analyze Steve's position in the novel, other characters with whom he interacts, and the institutional racism that is illustrated within the judicial system. Teachers also can encourage students to engage in conversations around Meyer's decision to use the term *monster* (by the prosecutor) to label Steve. How is that label used as a euphemism to represent a larger unvoiced fear of young Black men, and how do such assumptions, perceptions, and fears affect the lives of people of Color? Moreover, how can teachers find ways to change these assumptions, perceptions, and fears within their own understandings, classrooms, schools, and school districts?

Conclusions

A focus on race, racism, power, and privilege—whether at the academic or practical level—makes people uncomfortable, in part, because discussions imply blame for social inequities. Failing to explicitly address these issues, however, serves to normalize Whiteness and reproduce inequities that leave the needs and strengths of students of Color on the periphery. Our framework for teaching an undergraduate English language arts methods course from a CRT perspective includes the use of autobiography and memoir and the reading of culturally specific/conscious multicultural literature. Specifically, race, racism, privilege, and power are foregrounded in theory, approach, and materials, whereby traditional views of race and racism are challenged through the activities and materials that place people of Color, their lived experiences, and their knowledges, at the center of discussions. This approach can be used by all educators to work through their personal and societal responses to race, racism, privilege, and power.

Recommendations for Educators and Classroom Applications

1. Learn to acknowledge your race and racism in society and education as well as your power to make positive social change. It is not enough to acknowledge race, racial discrimination, power, or privilege without also actively working for equity and social justice.

2. White teachers must understand their unmerited privilege in U.S. society. All teachers must understand how race, racism, and power has privileged Western Eurocentric ideologies, pedagogies, and assessments that normalize Whiteness. One way to demystify Whiteness is to adopt a CRT perspective and include culturally specific/conscious multicultural/multiethnic literature as an integral part of your curriculum.

3. Locate yourself within systems of privilege in your life, using the diversity wheel as a guide. Recognize how your location on the diversity wheel has influenced decisions you have made, opportunities you have had (or have not had), and then envision how you can work for change by addressing areas on the diversity wheel where you notice a disparity or inequality.

4. Commit to using culturally specific/conscious literature in your curriculum. Select literature that is written by cultural insiders and make sure the literature is of high quality by drawing on many of the award-winning books (look to the American Libraries Association, www.ala.org, yearly winners of ethnic awards—the Coretta Scott King Award, the Pura Belpré Award, etc.).

5. Compile a list of easily accessible resources and add bookmarks such as www.oyate.org, a site for Native American Literature and the Cooperative Children's Book Center website www.education.wisc.edu/ccbc as a portal for publishing statistics and recommended lists of multicultural literature.

6. Create a classroom where students feel safe to look at bigger issues presented (or not presented) in the texts they read. Challenge "givens." If a particular book is required in your curriculum, evaluate it for cultural authenticity.

7. Predict areas that can begin discussion with students about intersections of ability, class, ethnicity, gender, immigrant status, language, race, and sexual orientation in ways that challenge them to work from points of their own identity and privilege to understand author and character motivations for a work of literature.

REFERENCES

Bishop, R.S. (1982). *Shadow and substance: The Afro-American experience in contemporary children's fiction.* Urbana, IL: National Council of Teachers of English.

Bishop, R.S. (1992). Multicultural literature for children: Making informed choices. In V.J. Harris (Ed.), *Teaching multicultural literature in grades K–8* (pp. 37–53). Norwood, MA: Christopher-Gordon.

Bishop, R.S. (1997). Selecting literature for a multicultural curriculum. In V.J. Harris (Ed.), *Using multiethnic literature in the K–8 classroom* (pp. 1–20). Norwood, MA: Christopher-Gordon.

Crenshaw, K.W., Gotanda, N., Peller, G., & Thomas, K. (Eds.). (1995). Introduction. In K. Crenshaw, N. Gotanda, G. Peller, & K. Thomas (Eds.), *Critical race theory: The key writings that formed the movement* (pp. xiii–xxxii). New York: New Press.

Delgado, R., & Stefancic, J. (Eds.). (2001). *Critical race theory: An introduction.* New York: New York University Press.

Delgado Bernal, D. (2002). Critical race theory, Latino critical theory, and critical raced-gendered epistemologies: Recognizing students of Color as holders and creators of knowledge. *Qualitative Inquiry, 8*(1), 105–126. doi:10.1177/1077800402008001007

Dowdy, J.K. (2002). Ovuh Dyuh. In L. Delpit & J.K. Dowdy (Eds.), *The skin that we speak: Thoughts on language and culture in the classroom* (pp. 3–13). New York: New Press.

Harris, V.J. (1992). African American conceptions of literacy: A historical perspective. *Theory Into Practice, 31*(4), 276–286.

Helms, J.E. (1992). *A race is a nice thing to have: A guide to being a white person or understanding the white persons in your life.* Topeka, KS: Content Communications.

Johnson, A.G. (2006). *Privilege, power, and difference* (2nd ed.). New York: McGraw-Hill.

Ladson-Billings, G.J. (2005). The evolving role of critical race theory in educational scholarship. *Race, Ethnicity and Education, 8*(1), 115–119. doi:10.1080/1361332052000341024

Ladson-Billings, G.J., & Tate, W.F. (1995). Toward a critical race theory of education. *Teachers College Record, 97*(1), 47–68.

Lawrence, C.R., III, Matsuda, M.J., Delgado, R., & Crenshaw, K.W. (1993). Introduction. In M.J. Matsuda, C.R. Lawrence, III, R. Delgado, & K.W. Crenshaw (Eds.), *Words that wound: Critical race theory, assaultive speech, and the first amendment* (pp. 1–16). Boulder, CO: Westview Press.

Leistyna, P., Woodrum, A., & Sherblom, S.A. (Eds.). (1996). Glossary. In P. Leistyna, A. Woodrum, & S.A. Sherblom (Eds.), *Breaking free: The transformative power of critical pedagogy* (pp. 333–344). Reprint Series No. 27. Cambridge, MA: Harvard Educational Review.

Loden, M. (1995). *Implementing diversity.* New York: McGraw-Hill.

Loden, M., & Rosener, J. (1991). *Workforce America! Managing employee diversity as a vital resource.* Homewood, IL: Business One Irwin.

McIntyre, A. (1997). *Making meaning of whiteness: Exploring racial identity with white teachers.* Albany: State University of New York.

Nieto, S. (2003). Challenging current notions of "highly qualified teachers" through work in a teachers' inquiry group. *Journal of Teacher Education, 54*(5), 386–398. doi:10.1177/0022487103257394

Pendergast, C. (2002). The economy of literacy: How the Supreme Court stalled the Civil Rights Movement. *Harvard Educational Review, 72*(2), 206–229.

Solórzano, D.G., & Yosso, T.J. (2001). From racial stereotyping and deficit discourse toward a critical race theory in teacher education. *Multicultural Education, 9*(1), 2–8.

Solórzano, D.G., & Yosso, T.J. (2002). Critical race methodology: Counterstorytelling as an analytic framework for education research. *Qualitative Inquiry, 8*(1), 23–44. doi:10.1177/1077800402008001003

Spina, S., & Tai, R. (1998). The politics of racial identity: A pedagogy of invisibility. *Educational Researcher, 27*(1), 36–40, 48.

Tate, W.F. (1997). Critical race theory and education: History, theory, and implications. *Review of Research in Education, 22*(1), 195–247. doi:10.3102/0091732X022001195

Tatum, B.D. (1998). *"Why are all the black kids sitting together in the cafeteria?" and other conversations about race.* New York: Basic.

United States Department of Justice. (2006). *Bureau of justice statistics.* Retrieved April 14, 2007, from www.ojp.usdoj.gov/bjs

Waters, M.C. (2004). Optional ethnicities: For whites only? In M.L. Andersen & P.H. Collins (Eds.), *Race, class, and gender: An anthology* (pp. 418–447). Belmont, CA: Thomson Wadsworth/Learning.

Williams, G.L. (2005). At their level: Seasoned children's author is at it again. *Black Issues Book Review, 7*(7), 39–40.

Willis, A.I. (2008). Critical race theory and literacy. In B.V. Street & N.H. Hornberger (Eds.), *Encyclopedia of language and education Vol. 2: Literacy* (2nd ed., pp. 1–14, 15–28). New York: Springer Science.

Yosso, T.J. (2005). Whose culture has capital? A critical race theory discussion of community cultural wealth. *Race, Ethnicity and Education, 8*(1), 69–91. doi:10.1080/1361332052000341006

LITERATURE CITED

Myers, W.D. (1999). *Monster.* New York: HarperCollins.

SUGGESTIONS FOR FURTHER READING

Chapman, T.K. (2007). Interrogating classroom relationships and events: Using portraiture and critical race theory in education research. *Educational Researcher, 36*(3), 156–162. doi:10.3102/0013189X07301437

Delgado, R. (1995). *Critical race theory: The cutting edge.* Philadelphia: Temple University Press.

Dixson, A.D., & Rousseau, C.K. (2006). *Critical race theory in education: All God's children got a song.* New York: Routledge.

Yosso, T.J. (2002). Toward a critical race curriculum. *Equity & Excellence in Education, 35*(2), 93–107. doi:10.1080/713845283

"First, Do No Harm": A Cautionary Consideration of Classroom Research From a Sociocultural Perspective

Deborah Appleman

Most of us are familiar with the first line of the physician's Hippocratic oath: "First, do no harm." That statement is applicable to teachers and teacher researchers as well. Recent qualitative research on literacy teaching and learning has emphasized the significance of the rich social context in which learning takes place, and the complex collection of factors that contribute to that context. Much of this research is ethnographic and draws significantly into the heart of classrooms, deeply implicating teachers and students as both participants and observers. While university researchers were often "outsiders" to the classroom and previously conducted most classroom research, in the last two decades, the role of teacher research has grown significantly in forwarding our understanding of the complex processes of literacy learning (Cochran-Smith and Lytle, 1999.) Now classroom teachers more frequently find themselves as both teachers and researchers, contributing significantly to what we know about the sociocultural context of literacy learning.

On the whole, the growing phenomenon of teachers as researchers has contributed significantly to improving literacy teaching and learning (Lewis, Enciso, & Moje, 2007). As literacy teachers, we want to improve our classroom practice to ensure the best literacy education possible of all students. We engage in classroom-based research with noble intentions. Yet the very act of "doing" research further complicates the dynamics of teaching and learning. At the very least we must make certain that our research practices, methodologies, and subsequent publications do not inflict harm on the very populations we hope to serve. As a teacher who researches and a researcher who teaches, I have learned that in the research process it is possible to do harm, however unintentional. The purpose of this chapter is therefore to consider, through cautionary tale and confessional, how we can, as a research community, consider ways to do no harm.

Using Teacher Research to Examine Classroom Practices

Recent sociocultural theory has helped both teachers and researchers recognize the incredible complexity of classroom spaces and of teacher–student relationships

Breaking the Silence: Recognizing the Social and Cultural Resources Students Bring to the Classroom, edited by Catherine Compton-Lilly. © 2009 by the International Reading Association.

both in and out of the classroom. Sociocultural theory requires that we situate our students' learning, that we consider "the relationship between human mental functioning, on the one hand, and cultural, historical, and institutional setting, on the other" (Wertsch, 1995, p. 56). More recent iterations of sociocultural theory have focused on issues of agency, identity, and power relations in literacy learning (Lewis et al., 2007). To more fully understand these complex dynamics, literacy researchers have moved in the last two decades toward teacher research. Teacher research can involve the investigation of classroom practices and allow teachers to recognize the existence of social and historical practices that exist in their own classrooms. It can also help us to analyze and revise those practices. It can offer a local view.

Yet as Brandt and Clinton (2002) have written, there are "limits to the local." Even as teacher researchers we can still animate those positions of power and privilege both through our work with young people and in the words we write about them, especially when dealing with marginalized students, or students who do not share our background and experiences.

Is Ethnographic Research Really Better?

To improve our literacy teaching to best serve all our students, both classroom teachers and literacy researchers have turned increasingly to ethnographic or qualitative research. Using this methodology, we create inquiry designed to improve the literate lives of the young people we serve as well as the literacy practices that guide our teaching. We reject the traditional approach of empirical, Western scientific research. We readily admit there is not one objective truth to be discovered in our research. We reject the overtly hierarchal nature of a researcher–subject relationship that ultimately subjugates and objectifies those subjects under scrutiny. We recognize that qualitative research helps us situate our studies within the rich sociocultural contexts of schools. We recognize that, prima facie, qualitative research appears to be less hierarchical, less imperial, less manipulative, and better able to capture the nuances of the research than more traditional quantitative forms of research. Teacher research also eliminates that pesky middleperson, the university researcher, from the equation. At its best, such research can be transformative. It can help the researcher understand implicit power relationships and inequities and serve to correct them by interrupting them. It can empower the underserved by giving voice to their needs. It can agitate for institutional change.

Yet despite these obvious advantages, ethnographic research poses some thorny problems for the researcher, ranging from the political to the ethical. Ironically, the deeply situated and contextual nature of such research can easily lead to what ultimately constitutes an abuse of preexisting relationships. What follows is a brief explication of some of the dangers that such research can pose. I share the late Alan Peshkin's (2000) assertion that "To be forthcoming and honest about how we work as researchers is to develop a reflective awareness that, I believe, contributes to enhancing the quality of our interpretive acts" (p. 9).

The Dilemmas of Ethnographic Research

In her poignantly titled book *The Vulnerable Observer: Anthropology That Breaks Your Heart*, Behar (1996) reminds us that by embarking on the study of the lives of others, we are sure to break hearts—the hearts of those we study as well as our own, the vulnerable observers. Behar's conclusion, of course, is "that anthropology that doesn't break your heart just isn't worth doing anymore" (p. 177). Yet the source of the heartbreak for Behar lies not in methodological flaws or ethical lapses but in the ultimately heartbreaking realities we are doomed to uncover as we explore the foundational dilemmas of the human condition. Unfortunately, there are ways that our methodologies can break hearts as well.

A couple of summers ago, the president of the faculty at the small liberal arts college where I teach had a brilliant idea for a faculty retreat. We would discuss the challenges and excitement of our increasingly diverse student body. As the faculty mentor to Carleton College's second "Posse"—a national organization that recruits underserved public school students to college and universities by providing full scholarships, a cohort structure, training, and a faculty member—the faculty president asked me to jot down some of my thoughts. My experiences as a mentor had been full of challenges that could serve as cautionary tales for the institution, and I wrote a heartfelt piece chronicling some of the challenges that my advisees had faced in what I thought was an honest and forthright manner. I decided to write only about students who had already withdrawn from the college and to write about them without any reference to their names, ethnicity, or background. I wrote about our collective joys as well as our sorrows and thought I had a created a provocative think piece for our faculty discussion and an accurate representation of my students' experiences. In my reflection, I tried to present a sociocultural perspective of the institutional and cultural factors that were at play.

It wasn't exactly research; it was summer, and I wasn't even sure how to contact the three students I focused on because they had already withdrawn (or had been withdrawn) from the college. I guess for these two reasons as well as my own carelessness, I didn't ask the students for permission to share their stories.

We held the faculty retreat, and I delivered my talk. Most of my faculty colleagues praised me for my candor, though one thought I was "airing dirty laundry." Weeks passed, and I didn't think again about the piece until one late fall afternoon when one of the remaining Posse students came to my office with the piece in her hand, telling me that I had betrayed her, her fellow Posse members, and the program and that she would never trust me again.

Most of the Posse members disagreed with her assessment and seemed to understand why I had written what I did. They even agreed with the points I was trying to make and understood that I was making an argument on their behalf, not against them. Still, one of my staunchest supporters whispered to me, "Why didn't you at least ask us about this?" Good question. The very act of writing about students I cared for betrayed that trust even though I had theoretical, pedagogical, and even ethical reasons to make the points I did and to make them public. This regrettable experience has made me wary and skeptical of the possibility of producing ethnographic research situated in classroom contexts that is not, in the end, fundamentally exploitive.

Things to Consider Before Conducting Teacher Research

1. Come clean about your motives for doing the research. What do you hope to accomplish? Whose interest would it serve?

2. Consider your relationship to the participants. What potential harm could the research cause to the relationship? Is there any way that the research could enhance the relationship?

I am a teacher researcher, like so many others who have contributed to this volume, like so many of you who are reading it. Yet I've come to believe that that dual identity or aspiration is a vexed one. On the basis of my own experiences and miscalculations of writing about the young people I teach, I'm beginning to wonder if it is possible to serve young people well and responsibly within the context of the classroom, and in addition, use them as focal points for our research.

This is only the most recent case of ethnographic dilemmas that I've experienced. Several years ago, I received a phone call from a graduate student in composition who had been assigned a piece from *College Composition and Communication* that I coauthored, called "Mapping the Elusive Boundary Between High School and College Writing" (Appleman & Green, 1993). The piece used student writing from the summer program I directed to map the boundaries and transition between high school and college writing. It was, I thought, an appropriate piece of teacher research, one that interrogated the instructional practices we had used and considered the developmental context of the learning. The student, five years out of the program, called to say, "I could be wrong, but aren't you talking about me and my writing in this piece?" She was right; I was. Although I collected permission slips to copy and quote from student work, I had never bothered to inform the student, long gone from my ephemeral three-week interaction with her, that I was indeed writing about her or that the article had been accepted for publication.

Similarly, I received a phone call last fall from another young woman about whom I had written (Appleman, 1999). Using my one-to-one interactions over the space of two years, I developed a case study of an underachieving urban student to understand the complex sociocultural factors that were contributing to her academic disengagement (see Figure 4.1). This student was calling, as it happily turned out, to reconnect and to get some advice about teacher education programs after her recent graduation from college. But still, why did my heart flutter and my palms sweat when I first heard her voice? Did I somehow think that I had wronged her with my prose, that she had finally realized it after all these years and was calling to take me to task about it?

I recently took myself to task over similar sins of research, ranging from what might be benevolently called blind carelessness to an unethical, and perhaps—at least in the case of one Posse student—unforgivable refusal to acknowledge the complexities of choosing to write about the young people I teach (Appleman, 2003). I've learned several hard lessons, and in this chapter I share those lessons in the hope that our collective research efforts are guided and informed by a deeply contextualized understanding of the relationship between the researcher and the researched in classroom spaces.

Figure 4.1. Excerpt From Alice, *Lolita*, and Me

Meeting Alice

This story will surprise those who believe that if literary theory is to be taught to secondary students, it would be most appropriate with college preparatory students. I met Alice during her sophomore year when I was teaching a class on multicultural literature at her high school. In previous work I described Alice in the following way:

Alice is the middle child and only daughter in a split-apart family of five. She idolizes her two older brothers, both of whom are still remembered by teachers at her urban Minneapolis high school as being "brilliant" but troubled. Alice's oldest brother is a recovering heroin addict. She lives at home with her two younger brothers and her single mother, a full time graduate student.

Alice favors the look of studied castoff casualness sported by the "alternative" crowd. Her hair changes colors frequently (though always with a wash and not a dye). Alice has an offbeat kind of fashion flair; she can make Doc Martens work with a dress. Lavender is her favorite color and she sports silver rings on most of her fingers, including her thumbs. As a present to herself, Alice got her tongue pierced on her eighteenth birthday, a decision met with horror by her mother who considered it a defiling of Alice's natural and honest beauty.

Alice was a remarkably unremarkable student. She moved uncritically through her required reading, wrote nearly illegible essays, hated her journal and perfected the pout of the reluctant learner. Her classroom participation was regular and sometimes brave, but hardly ever fully engaged. Between independent studies and college classes at the local university, Alice generally manages to never spend an entire day in school (Appleman, 1997, p. 283).

During her junior year, long after our time together in class was over, Alice asked me if we could do an independent study project as an alternative way of earning her English credits. She said she simply couldn't find any English classes she could tolerate. She seemed restless, unsatisfied, hungry for something not on the school menu. When asked what she wanted to study with me, she replied, "Women's studies. I'm not sure what it is, but I think I'd like it."

From Appleman, D. (1999). Alice, *Lolita*, and me: Learning to read "feminist" with a tenth-grade urban adolescent. In L. Alvine & L. Cullum (Eds.), *Breaking the cycle: Gender, literacy, and learning* (pp. 71–88). Portsmouth, NH: Heinemann. Reprinted with permission.

Role of the Researcher

The role of the researcher in ethnographic research is both compromised and complicated, especially so when the researcher inhabits other roles with regard to the participants. This is especially true when the researcher is also the classroom teacher. At the most basic level, a teacher researcher is a participant-observer, one whose dual roles complicate the process of inquiry and the relationship of all participants. Although neutrality or the elusive objectivity is clearly not within the reach of the ethnographer's grasp, we all too often in the face of that admittance, fail to address the complexities of the relationship of the researcher to the researched.

As Delgado-Gaitan (1993) points out, critical theory encourages us to interrogate "the interaction between researcher and researched in the context of the researched community" (p. 389). Peshkin (2000) reminds us that the act of research can both echo and reproduce systems of power, especially when one works with socially disenfranchised groups. Considerations of already established power dynamics are of critical importance to researchers who enter classroom spaces. In those contexts, it is easy for the researcher to exploit the power differential that already exists between student and teacher or between those who live outside the research community and those who live within it. Teacher researchers need to acknowledge the power dynamics that already exist within the relationship and to guard against requests or situations that subjects have little recourse to refuse.

The Relationship Between the Researcher and the Researched

A central issue that emerges in a critique of qualitative or ethnographic research is the issue of the relationship between the researcher and the researched. As Stacey, quoted in Duncombe & Jessop (2002) points out,

> The irony I now perceive is that the ethnographic method exposes subjects to far greater danger and exploitation than do more positivist, abstract and masculinist research methods. The greater the intimacy, the apparent mutuality of the researcher/re-searched relationship, the greater is the danger. (p. 21)

Duncombe and Jessop (2002) warn of the dangers of "doing rapport" or "faking friendship" that researchers may fall into a trap of creating a falsely friendly or encouraging atmosphere. According to the authors, this may be especially true of female researchers, who are more likely to attempt to create a relationship between the researcher and the subjects. Duncombe and Jessop (2002) warn us that an encouraging and empathetic approach to the subjects may inadvertently lead them into mistaking the relationship for being something that it is not. This kind of dilemma is particularly vexing because it can turn a good thing (creating a trusting and a meaningful relationship with the subjects) into a bad thing (creating the opportunity to be able to exploit those subjects or mislead them because of that very relationship).

This kind of misunderstanding can be manifested differently within the context of classroom relationships. Although it is less likely that the parameters of friendship would be overstated in a student–teacher relationship, it is very possible that the relationship between student and teacher can be muddied, compromised, or, at the very least, troubled by a conflict of interest and positions. Teaching and researching can require us to situate ourselves differently toward our subjects. Teaching requires empathy and a commitment to put the needs of the students at the center of our efforts. Research requires a once-removed stance and putting inquiry at the center of our efforts. The students' learning, in some ways, becomes a means to an end, rather than an end in itself. Ironically, even though our research is ultimately designed to improve our pedagogy, it often distracts us from it.

The collection, analysis, and the ultimate interpretation of data can jeopardize the often-vulnerable relationships that are at the heart of teaching. In classroom spaces that I think I am ultimately going to write about, I sometimes find myself leaving the teaching moment that I am in with students and assessing the importance of that moment to the research. When I do that, no matter how hard I try to stay present, I remove a part of myself from my students and from the act of teaching. And in the end, that compromises the teaching by subordinating it, even momentarily, to a different end.

The Issue of Informed Consent

More than 25 years ago, noted scholar Barrie Thorne (1980) raised the question of informed consent. While she explored the legal issues of informed consent, she presciently predicted that ethical issues would also be raised as ethnographers relied increasingly on (a) methods of data collection that affect the setting under study, and (b) the vexed role of participant-observers and the subsequent "objective" interpretation of the data. Thorne points out that informed consent is a necessary but not sufficient condition to ensure the sound ethics of a research project. She asserts, "The doctrine of informed consent does not take account of ethical dimensions of the knowledge a researcher may seek" (p. 293).

The concept of informed consent is compromised in classroom research by the power differentials that already exist between teacher and students and by the question of whether our students/subjects are really *informed* about what they are consenting to. Miller and Bell (2002) problematize the issue of informed consent by noting that one's subjects often do not know what they are consenting to. They argue that "'consent' should be on-going and re-negotiated between researcher and researched throughout the research process" (p. 53).

Unschooled in the problematics of representation or the vagaries of publishing academic research, students might easily agree to participating in an activity or to having their work quoted or their picture taken, without fully understanding either the possible objectification of themselves or their work and the permanent ramifications that might result. Thorne (1980) warns, "Special populations who are vulnerable or subordinated populations (deviants, ethnic minorities, prisoners, students) may need special protection against possible exploitation by researchers" (p. 293).

The Writing Up, or the Representation

The complexities of researching private lives and placing accounts in the public area raise multiple ethical issues for the researcher that cannot be solved solely by the application of abstract rules, principles, or guidelines (Birch, Miller, Mauthner, & Jessop, 2002).

It is often in moving the research to the public arena, through publication and presentation, that the greatest damage is inflicted. This is because we are driven to reshape our data into clear and compelling narratives. Thus there are at least two main problems with writing and publishing our research on the young people we teach. They are problems of interpretation and of presentation. Our research is marked indelibly with a perspective, a point of view, a stance, a position. That positioning can fuel our argument, but it can also color our interpretations of our data. We see what we need to see, expect to see, imagine we would see, based on our expectations and our positions. And our qualitative data are so malleable that we can bend it, almost unconsciously, into the stories we think need to be told.

The presentation of that data are usually in our published work. Even an unofficial publication, such as the Posse paper I produced, brings the work into what Peshkin (2000) called "the court of public discourse" (p. 9). We permanently freeze our subjects, fossilize them with our words. We need to be more vigilant about those representations, guarding against the likelihood that we may indeed be reinscribing both power and caricature in the words we choose.

Potential Solutions of the Dilemmas Encountered With Ethnographic Research

A simple yet ultimately unsatisfying solution for us, as teacher researchers, is to be more willing to make hard choices. Sometimes we might need to forfeit potential research opportunities for the greater good of our students. Sometimes we can't be both teachers *and* researchers. If the most important thing to do with a particular student or group of students is to teach them in an unfettered way, then perhaps that is what we should do. And when we make that choice, we should do so happily and without resentment.

On the other hand, there may be research opportunities in which we remain the observer and refrain from being a participant observer. We may see a particular phenomenon or question that we want to pursue in our own classrooms that we might more fruitfully do with other people's students.

Perhaps these two suggestions seem cowardly. But there are times when we cannot reconcile the often competing and contradictory demands or roles of the teacher with that of the researcher.

Another possibility, anathema I'm certain for those in the publish-or-perish world of academia, is to sometimes choose to *not* write about or publish certain research projects. I've given some conference papers about my Posse, sometimes with a couple of the members present so that they might represent themselves, but I have vowed—especially after the experience with which I opened this chapter—never to publish an academic article or paper about them. It simply isn't worth the risk.

Making space for subjects to represent themselves, through their own writing or in public, is another way to avoid or correct potential dangers of interpretation (Peshkin, 2000). Now, whenever possible, I try to let the students speak for themselves. I include their words in what I write, whether it be through transcripted conversations or their own writing. For example, in a recent book about book clubs, I have extended transcripts of student talk, transcribed from videotape and unedited. I invite students to present with me at conferences, whenever that is possible. I try to limit the degree to which I am mediating, or in the worst case, colonizing their self-representation.

Finally, the researcher always needs to be mindful of the power differentials that are inherent in both teaching and research and to ward against abusing that power. The first step of course is to acknowledge that power to ourselves. Thorne (1980) writes,

It has often been observed that to be powerful is to be able to guard ones interests, to protect one's self from unwanted intrusions. The literature of the social sciences bears out this fact: the bulk of research has been on the less powerful, to whom researchers have greater access. (p. 294)

Conclusions

These days, in addition to my usual college teaching and occasional but sustained teaching gigs at area high schools, I teach a literature course at a maximum-security prison every Wednesday night. There are 28 inmates in the class, ranging in age from their early 20s into their 60s. Because their individual prisoner numbers are on my attendance sheet, I could easily look up why they are incarcerated. I have vowed not to do so during the course of the class. I am their literature teacher now. Period.

Yet after over 20 years of scholarship, my data-collecting habits are almost instinctual. I copy their papers, with their permission, before I return them. I am preparing photographic releases and catch myself thinking simultaneously about the amazing power of this teaching experience as well as about what a great article the experience would make.

From the perspective of sociocultural research, the lure of such data-rich contexts is nearly impossible to ignore. Surely our field of literacy research could be usefully informed by a critical examination of the complex collisions of language, culture, text, and context? The question is, Whose interests would I serve in writing the article? And perhaps, that is the ultimate barometer for us teacher researchers as we weigh the relative advantages and disadvantages of research that implicates our students, be they squirmy eighth graders or convicted felons.

Perhaps in the end, our responsibilities as teachers trump our responsibilities as researchers. Put another way, our responsibility to individual people trumps our responsibility to an abstract good. Although it is true that our literacy research aims to understand the sociocultural context in which learning occurs so that we can better serve young people we haven't met, perhaps the immediacy of human relationships should help guide the decisions we make in our research. In addition, Lewis and her colleagues (2007) call for a rethinking of sociocultural theory, one that "accounts for these larger systems of power as they shape and are shaped by individuals in particular cultural contexts" (p. 9). Only through vigilance and self-reflection as participants in the discourse communities of our students will we, as researchers and teachers, be able to follow our own version of the Hippocratic oath: "First, do no harm."

Recommendations for Educators and Classroom Applications

1. Make certain that you have permission from your participants to describe them, quote them, and represent them. Despite its limitations, informed consent is a must. You have a responsibility to your subjects in all cases, but if, as we have discussed previously in this chapter, your subjects are your students, it is even more important to secure their permissions as well as the permission of the school and the students' families.

2. Review your original research goals, and see if the projects need to be modified in the face of what you are discovering. The sociocultural perspective requires that we realize that teaching and learning occur within a complex nested network of social and cultural factors. As you learn more about the contours and complexities of that context, you may be surprised at what you discover, and you may need to rethink your research goals.

3. Don't be afraid to abandon the project to preserve relationships if you feel as if you need to do so. Sociocultural research on literacy calls into question issues of identity, agency, and power (Lewis, et al., 2007.) If your inquiry strains the relationships you have with fellow teachers, administrators, or your students and their families, you may need to abandon the project to protect your long-term teaching goals.

4. Triangulate your data by supplementing your field notes with either audio or video records. Remember, your interpretation of data are just that—your interpretations. It is often both powerful and advisable to let the data speak for themselves without your mediation, a mediation that is inevitably marked by traces of both power and privilege.

5. In a similar vein, invite a third party to view your notes and your final version of your report or article. Ask them to describe the context based on what they read. See if you are conveying the context in the way you intended to.

6. Check in regularly with your informants as your research project changes, noting that it might be necessary to renegotiate consent. Classroom research is a dynamic process. Informed consent also means that you need to keep your subjects informed as your research project changes.

7. Whenever it is possible, let your participants read what you have written. Subtle descriptive words or variations in tone can shade or distort the meanings of even the most able writers. Let your subjects sit with the portrait of them that you have rendered to see if they are comfortable with it. Remember that the act of writing about someone is ultimately an exercise of power, one that cannot be abused.

REFERENCES

Appleman, D. (1999). Alice, *Lolita*, and me: Learning to read "feminist" with a tenth-grade urban adolescent. In L. Alvine & L. Cullum (Eds.), *Breaking the cycle: Gender, literacy, and learning* (pp. 71–88). Portsmouth, NH: Heinemann.

Appleman, D. (2003). "Are you makin' me famous or makin' me a fool?" Responsibility and respect in representation. In S. Green & D. Abt-Perkins (Eds.), *Making race visible: Literacy research for cultural understanding* (pp. 71–85). New York: Teachers College Press.

Appleman, D., & Green, D. (1993). Mapping the elusive boundary between high school and college writing. *College Composition and Communication, 44*(2), 191–199. doi:10.2307/358838

Behar, R. (1996). *The vulnerable observer: Anthropology that breaks your heart.* Boston: Beacon.

Birch, M., Miller, T., Mauthner, M., & Jessop, J. (2002). Introduction. In M. Mauthner, T. Miller, M. Birch, & J. Jessop (Eds.), *Ethics in qualitative research* (pp. 1–13). Thousand Oaks, CA: Sage.

Brandt, D., & Clinton, K. (2002). Limits of the local: Expanding perspectives on literacy as a social practice. *Journal of Literacy Research, 34*(3), 337–356. doi:10.1207/s15548430jlr3403_4

Cochran-Smith, M., & Lytle, S. (1999). The teacher research movement: A decade later. *Educational Researcher, 28*(7), 15–25.

Delgado-Gaitan, C. (1993). Researching change and changing the researcher. *Harvard Educational Review, 63*(1), 389–411.

Duncombe, J., & Jessop, J. (2002). "Doing rapport" and the ethics of "faking friendship." In M. Mauthner, T. Miller, M. Birch, & J. Jessop (Eds.), *Ethics in qualitative research* (pp. 107–122). Thousand Oaks, CA: Sage.

Lewis, C., Enciso, P., & Moje, E. (2007). *Reframing sociocultural research on literacy: Identity, agency, and power.* Mahwah, NJ: Erlbaum.

Miller, T., & Bell, L. (2002). Consenting to what? Issues of access, gate-keeping and "informed" consent. In M. Mauthner, T. Miller, M. Birch, & J. Jessop (Eds.), *Ethics in qualitative research* (pp. 53–69). Thousand Oaks, CA: Sage.

Peshkin, A. (2000). The nature of interpretation in qualitative research. *Educational Researcher, 29*(9), 5–9.

Thorne, B. (1980). "You still takin' notes?" Fieldwork and problems of informed consent. *Social Problems, 27*(3), 284–297. doi:10.1525/sp.1980.27.3.03a00040

Wertsch, J.V. (1995). The need for action in scoiocultural research. In J.V. Wertsch, P. del Río, & A. Alvarez (Eds.), *Sociocultural studies of mind* (pp. 56–74). New York: Cambridge University Press.

SUGGESTIONS FOR FURTHER READING

Hubbard, R.S., & Power, B.M. (1999). *Living the questions: A guide for teacher-researchers.* York, ME: Stenhouse.

MacLean, M.S., & Mohr, M.M. (1999). *Teacher-researchers at work.* Berkeley, CA: National Writing Project.

Sunstein, B.S., & Chiseri-Strater, E. (2002). *FieldWorking: Reading and Writing Research.* New York: St. Martin's.

CHAPTER 5

Cultural-Historical Approaches to Literacy Teaching and Learning

Mariana Pacheco and Kris Gutiérrez

In this chapter, we discuss the contribution of a cultural-historical approach to literacy in designing productive learning environments for all students. We believe that a cultural-historical approach to learning and development is a particularly robust theory, as it focuses on the relation between an individual's development and the contexts of development of which the individual student has been a part. From this perspective, to understand a student's literacy practices, we would want to know as much as we could about the student's history of involvement in literacy practices across all the contexts of his or her everyday life. For example, bilingual children of immigrant parents often serve as translators for their parents across a range of institutional practices, including medical, educational, and business transactions. These same children might also participate in religious, social, cultural, and political activities that involve various language and literacy practices. These children also participate in schooling activities.

Taken together, participating in these practices provides opportunities for children to develop a literacy toolkit with resources that can help them navigate the intercultural exchanges of everyday life. We refer to the toolkit acquired by a person's history of involvement in practices as their "repertoires of practice" (Gutiérrez & Rogoff, 2003). In other words, the concept of repertoires of practice refers to people's ways of engaging in activities stemming from their participation in a range of cultural practices. This perspective requires attention to people's history of engagement in practices of the cultural community of which they are a part. We attribute cultural differences, then, to variations in people's involvement in the common practices of particular cultural communities.

In the classroom, a focus on students' repertoires of practice helps us understand better what students know and also moves us away from deficit explanations of students' performances in which students' differences in language and literacy practices are attributed to students' membership in particular cultural communities. By *cultural community*, we mean a group of people who share a history of some traditions and understandings in common, extending across several generations. Further, a cultural-historical approach assumes that individual development and

Breaking the Silence: Recognizing the Social and Cultural Resources Students Bring to the Classroom, edited by Catherine Compton-Lilly. © 2009 by the International Reading Association.

disposition must be understood in (and not separate from) cultural and historical contexts, which are always embedded in social-political relations and struggles. In other words, we talk about patterns of students' approaches to given situations without reducing the explanation to a claim that they do what they do because they are immigrants or English-language learners (ELL), for example. This cultural-historical view advances a dynamic notion of culture in which culture is not equated with categories of race and ethnicity, a common but unfortunate tendency among educators and practitioners.

In educational contexts, conflating race and ethnicity with culture can lead to stereotypical or essentialist notions about communities and their members. As we have written previously (Gutiérrez & Correa-Chavez, 2006; Gutiérrez & Rogoff, 2003), reductive or narrow notions of culture that are linked to social categories such as race and ethnicity can affect the assumptions we make about students' learning potential. All too often, "cultural learning styles" are attributed to students on the basis of racial and ethnic categories. Instead, educators should focus on understanding the relation of individual learning and the practices of the students' cultural community. The challenge for educators is to reexamine their working notions of culture, how their views influence the ways learning is organized in their classrooms, and whether extant views of culture lead to viewing cultural differences as deficits.

The Role of Culture in Learning and Development

Understanding the role of culture in learning requires understanding what is actually "cultural" about students' learning. For this reason, the focus of this chapter centers on culture and the mediating role it assumes in human activity. A cultural-historical theoretical approach to learning and development is particularly useful here, as it is the only theory of learning and development in which culture is not treated as a variable; rather, culture is central to this view of learning and human development in which culture is said to mediate human activity. From a cultural-historical perspective, human beings interact with their worlds primarily through mediational means, such as cultural artifacts, tools, signs, and symbols (including language). Instead of conceiving of culture as a totalizing concept, it is more useful to think about culture as that which mediates an individual's relation to the social world, as depicted in Figure 5.1.

In this way, culture is indexed in our everyday practices—as Moll (1990) has said, the way we live *culturally*. *Culture* is also defined as our social inheritance, as we are born into a world that is filled with tools (also known as artifacts) designed by previous generations to help facilitate everyday life. As Cole (1996) notes,

> Culture . . . can be understood as the entire pool of artifacts accumulated by the social group in the course of its historical experience. In the aggregate, the accumulated artifacts of a group—culture—is then seen as the species-specific *medium* of human development. It is "history in the present." The capacity to develop within that medium and to arrange for its reproduction in succeeding generations is *the* distinctive characteristic of our species. (p. 110, emphasis in original)

Figure 5.1. Cultural Mediation of the Social World

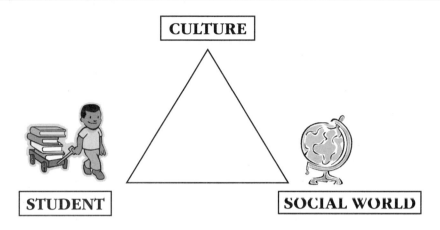

We are all implicated in dynamic cultural processes, as we organize our lives around particular material tools (such as alarm clocks) and social constructions (such as notions of time) that we did not necessarily create but are, in essence, "borrowing" from previous generations, and in many ways, "lending" to future generations. Moreover, according to Cole (1996), the organizing principle of the cultural-historical school of thought is "that the structure and development of human psychological processes emerge through culturally mediated, historically developing, practical activity" (p. 108). Through the processes of enculturation or socialization, human beings organize life for new and future generations to rediscover and appropriate mediating artifacts.

Over time, human beings accumulate, use or reject, and transform the various tools or resources available to us. These cultural tools and artifacts include both material artifacts—such as computers, pens, books, and recipes—and ideational artifacts—such as theories, ideologies, belief systems, and the like. Institutions, including schools and households, for example, are artificially organized settings in that they are far from "natural"; rather, our institutions are culturally constructed, historical in origin, and social in context. Of course, because generations before us have created these artifacts for us, we can begin to understand how culture can be considered to be both enabling and constraining.

Cultural artifacts can facilitate or mediate our existence in the social world, but they can also enhance or limit the ways we accomplish everyday tasks with others. Imagine what everyday life for many people would be like without a computer, television, microwave oven, telephone, or cellular phone. We know, for example, that computers have changed people's writing processes and that the Internet has enhanced access to information previously unavailable or difficult to access in a reasonable amount of time. However, although technology has enhanced the ways we communicate, electronic mail (or e-mail) in particular contexts has become constraining, as its abundance has radically altered the way we work, oftentimes demanding substantial portions of our workday designated for other tasks.

Within cultural communities, participants have varied roles across practices, and continual change among participants as well as transformation in the community's practices means that individuals regularly acquire, develop, and expand their knowledges and capacities, or their repertoires of practice. Across culturally mediated practices, adults and children take up different roles that extend beyond the static view of children as learners or "novices" and adults as teachers or "experts." In everyday settings, such as doctors' offices or the local arcade, children—including students we perceive as underachieving, low-performing, "at-risk," and so on—employ a variety of language and literacy practices and regularly shift their participation as novices or experts. Educators and practitioners should recognize that all children engage in schooling activities with a history of participation in a broad range of language and literacy experiences that reflect their cultural communities. Too often, deficit views of students have ignored children's active participation in the social and cultural activities that characterize their everyday lives.

The funds of knowledge approach that Moll and his colleagues (Moll, Amanti, Neff, & González, 1992) implemented has explicitly used students' participation in the social and cultural activities of their families and communities as a central construct for helping teachers and researchers rethink, and hence, redesign classroom literacy activities. Teachers and researchers documented the funds of knowledge—or the social and cultural resources—that households used to sustain their families. For example, teachers documented that households used and distributed their resources in agriculture and mining (e.g., knowledge of minerals), business economics (e.g., knowledge of building codes), household management (e.g., budgeting), material and scientific knowledge (e.g., construction, automobile repair), medicine (e.g., midwifery, folk veterinary cures), and religion (e.g., Bible studies). Teachers then worked collaboratively to design thematic curricula that built specifically on the social and cultural activities that mediated families' everyday lives and in which their students had a history of ongoing participation.

Retheorizing Teaching, Learning, and Curriculum

Clearly, a cultural-historical theoretical perspective that emphasizes the everyday cultural practices in which school-aged children develop an expanded repertoire of languages and literacies can powerfully inform discussions about teaching, learning, and curriculum. This view of the role of culture in learning and development challenges us to rethink how we build on what our students already know in classroom teaching. Inherent to this discussion is a reframing of what it means to be a teacher: that is, to engage in new and alternative ways to use the knowledge and capacities of students implies new ways of learning about, from, and with our students. Although our current reform and accountability contexts perhaps limit alternative approaches to literacy curriculum, a cultural-historical view challenges us to learn from our students and to reorganize learning contexts that build strategically on the social, cultural, linguistic, and intellectual resources of the increasingly diverse students and families we serve.

The unfortunate reality is that more often than not, despite some grass-roots efforts across local and professional communities, learning is often socially and culturally organized to ignore the kinds of literacies students acquire and develop throughout their everyday lives. We believe contemporary testing apparatuses used to judge achievement, effectiveness, and success are narrowing ways that teachers approach literacy teaching and learning and institutionalizing reductive literacies that fail to prepare children for participation in—and potentially, for the social transformation of—increasingly complex, multimodal, and shifting globalscapes.

We use a series of classroom examples to help us illustrate how classrooms, too, are cultural communities organized through particular schedules, ways of talking, spatial arrangements, ways to accomplish tasks, and routines. Although classrooms are, of course, complex, consider for a moment the cultural practices we find almost exclusively in schools. Students line up, desks are arranged in rows or in groups, everyone eats and takes breaks at the same time, a teacher manages a majority of classroom activities, teachers engage in ongoing evaluation of students' talk and work, and classroom discourse is limited to immediate classroom tasks. We fail to recognize that a range of cultural practices exist in the classroom across our students' experiences, but that teachers and students also jointly construct and participate in the culture of the classroom (Gallego, Cole, & Laboratory of Comparative Human Cognition, 2001).

A cultural-historical perspective emphasizes that participation in cultural practices with others has consequences for individuals' learning and development. In other words, how students participate and engage in meaning-making activities depends largely on how adults and teachers socially and culturally organize those activities. Discourse patterns are one way to describe the social organization of talk in classrooms, and these discourses have implications for how students participate and perhaps contribute to meaning making. Although classrooms likely reflect a range of discourses across activities, researchers have documented that the Initiation-Response-Evaluation (or I-R-E) pattern reflects the overwhelming character of classroom talk wherein a teacher initiates (I) a question, a student or students respond (R), and the teacher evaluates (E) the response with an utterance such as "That's right!" (Mehan, 1979).

Obviously, classroom discourse is varied and complex, but there are nevertheless considerable consequences to the overwhelming use of I-R-E in learning contexts. These discourse patterns limit the potential for expanded ideas and understandings, as the teacher's evaluation of students' contributions ostensibly constrains opportunities for new and different modes of sense making. These patterns of interaction, however, also reveal assumptions about who possesses the knowledge that counts in classroom learning, how knowledge is constructed, and whose knowledge counts.

We have a history of examining these issues in various contexts—English-only and bilingual classrooms in low- and high-performing schools, after-school computer clubs, summer high school programs, and literacy coaching contexts. However, we believe classroom examples in particular best illustrate some cultural-historical theoretical constructs for a teaching audience who seeks to deepen its understanding of how the social-cultural organization of literacy practices has consequences for students' literacy learning opportunities. These classroom examples show how talk, social interaction, roles, and the use of cultural tools and artifacts affect the kind of knowledge that is acquired and how students and teachers jointly contribute to meaning making—or how they are limited in this respect.

Cole and his colleagues (Cole, 1996; Cole & Griffin, 1983) have applied cultural-historical theoretical perspectives to a conceptualization of reading as "interpretation of the world" that emphasizes meaning making, rather than to "bottom-up" approaches oriented toward discrete reading skills and subskills. They acknowledge the social and cognitive processes involved in reading that in effect mediate humans' interpretations of the world. This mediation is accomplished through representations, the textual organization of graphic symbols (i.e., the alphabet), images, perceptions, ideas, concepts, and so on. For many practitioners, struggling readers in particular provoke calls for innovative methodologies that might help these students, many of whom include ELLs and students from low-income communities. For struggling readers especially, Cole and Griffin (1983) extend the notion of *re*-mediation. From their perspective, the organization of reading is a matter of *re*thinking, *re*arranging, *re*structuring, and *re*organizing the social systems that constitute reading practices rather than relying on *remedial*, skills-based instruction that rarely facilitates the kinds of reading we value across academic institutions. This view of reading, then, challenges us to *re*-mediate the social contexts that facilitate the teaching and learning of reading, instead of relying on reductive strategies and remedial approaches often used with struggling readers.

Exploring Reading "Discussion"

The following literacy event example illustrates how the social organization of reading discussion in this particular context facilitated one aspect of the "reading as interpretation of the world" process—vocabulary development—at the expense of expanded meaning making. We documented this literacy event in a third-grade Spanish–English bilingual/transition classroom with mostly Latino/a ELLs in a "high-achieving" school, according to state measures. According to the district's bilingual program model, third-grade ELLs were "automatically" transitioned from mostly Spanish instruction with some English to English-only instruction in all content areas.

We use the classroom example that follows to illustrate three points. First, through the overwhelming use of the I-R-E discourse pattern, the teacher's cultural organization of discussions was oriented toward next-step learning strategies (Griffin & Cole, 1984), or assistance aimed at getting to the "next steps" involved in accomplishing the task—defining the words *trunk* and *attic*. Second, although we might agree that vocabulary expansion is productive in helping ELLs improve their reading comprehension abilities, this example shows how talk during whole-group reading discussions was ostensibly oriented toward vocabulary rather than sense making. In essence, the questions *were* the task; that is, the focus on vocabulary diminished opportunities for reading as interpretation of the world. Third, we hope to show how the teacher was nonetheless strategic about building on her students' expanding lexicons, drawing on the text as a resource for obtaining the correct answers to her questions, and building on her students' cultural and experiential knowledge about trunks and attics.

The whole class sat in a large circle and participants held an English-language anthology in their laps, which they were reading aloud and in silence, regularly referencing the texts to participate in intermittent discussions facilitated by their teacher, Ms. Lucero (all research participants' names, except the researcher's, are pseudonyms). The students had just read a paragraph to themselves about a young girl who is rummaging through her grandmother's trunk, which is in her grandmother's attic. As was often the case, Ms. Lucero asked a simple recall question about the most recent paragraph. Though it was unclear why she focused on the words *trunk* and *attic*, it is possible she believed these words were unfamiliar to her ELLs.

Ms. Lucero:	And where did she get—she got some accessories or extra things to put on, like earrings and bracelets and necklaces? [motions toward her ears, wrist, and neck] Where did she get those from? Ramiro?
Ramiro:	In a trunk.
Ms. Lucero:	In a trunk. Now, what is a *trunk*? What is a trunk? I know about the elephant's trunk and the tree trunk and—Karina?
Karina:	Um, the back of a car.
Ms. Lucero:	The back of a car is part of a trunk. Uh-huh?
Salvador:	And it could be the attic?
Ms. Lucero:	Okay, that mentions that, something about the attic, doesn't it? Let's find that sentence. It's about the middle of it. Let's read that sentence together. It says, "The old bracelet—"
Students:	[reading out loud from their anthologies] "The old bracelet . . . in the attic jingled noisily . . ."
Ms. Lucero:	Stop right there. So she found them in a trunk in the attic. Okay, that's two words that we need to discuss right there. *Trunk* and *attic*. Now, trunk. A trunk is part of a car. [pause] But is a car in the attic?
Students:	No.
Ms. Lucero:	And what is an attic?
Jose:	Somewhere where you put old things.
Ms. Lucero:	Somewhere where they put old things. Where can you find an attic?
Eduardo:	Up your house. [points upward]
Ms. Lucero:	In some houses that are maybe two stories or more [motions structural levels], there's a little area up where the roof [makes an A-shape in the air] is at. There's a little room [motions a structural level]. It's called an—
Students:	Attic.
Ms. Lucero:	Sometimes they [people] use it just to put junk in there. Sometimes they fix it up, and you even use it as a room. In her house, I think they're using it as a place to put what?

Students:	Junk.
Ms. Lucero:	Junk or maybe things they're not using, like we use our garages. Where do you put things? Where does mom and dad put things that they're not using?
Students:	The garage.
Ms. Lucero:	The garage. Well, they have an attic. So there was a trunk in the—
Students:	Attic.
Ms. Lucero:	Now what do you think trunk is? [pause] Now, remember, what did she find? They found—she found bracelets and earrings in the trunk? What could it be?
Nayeli:	Uhmm . . . .
Salvador:	Oooh! [waving his right hand]
Ms. Lucero:	What would you put bracelets and earrings in?
Isel:	A box.
Salvador:	In a box?
Ms. Lucero:	In a box! A trunk is like a—
Students:	Box.
Ms. Lucero:	A BIG box. Sometimes they're like this big [leans over to show width of a big box] and you open 'em up like this [motions the opening of a treasure chest lid]. It's like a treasure chest.
	There's a—oh! How many of your parents have like a big suitcase? [pause] That's like a big box? [leans over to motion toward an imaginary box] And sometimes you open it up [motions the opening of a treasure chest lid] and it looks like a treasure chest or like—a trunk. A trunk is a what? A big box where you put things. Do any of your families have a trunk? Any big trunks? [several students raise their hands]
	Yeah. And they're pretty heavy to carry.
Students:	Yeah.
Marcos:	Yep.
Ms. Lucero:	Especially filled with lots of things. Alright.

Certainly, Ms. Lucero was quite strategic about building on her students' current understandings of trunks and attics, specifically drawing on their cultural practices and knowledge—car trunks, jewelry (i.e., earrings, bracelets), jewelry "boxes," garages, houses, treasure chests, suitcases, junk, and storage containers. Rather than provide students with the definition of *trunk* and *attic*, she proceeds through an elaborate sequence of connections to arrive at a potentially more concrete understanding of what these words mean in the context of the story.

Although she uses the I-R-E pattern of talk, she does, for example, build on students' prior knowledge of suitcases ("There's a—oh! How many of your parents have like a big suitcase?") to liken a big suitcase to a trunk. Ms. Lucero also uses logical deductions ("Now, a trunk is part of a car, but is a car in the attic?") and context cues from the text ("Now, remember, what did she found? They found—she found bracelets and earrings in the trunk?") to mediate students' ability to arrive at the correct definitions, especially because *attic* and *trunk* have multiple meanings. Finally, Ms. Lucero uses bodily gestures to motion different structural levels in a house, represent an A-shaped roof, a large box, and motion the opening of a treasure chest and suitcase.

From a cultural-historical perspective, Ms. Lucero used a variety of tools (i.e., talk, cultural knowledge, gestures, comparisons, and text) to help expand her students' lexicon, as these vocabulary words were central to the narrative they were reading. Nevertheless, Ms. Lucero and her students were oriented toward vocabulary building: Even though they spent a substantial amount of time discussing these keywords, the focus was clearly not based or initiated by students' meaning making of the story. Consider that in fact Ms. Lucero and not the students instigated the discussion about *attic* and *trunk* after Ramiro correctly answered her initial question, which included the word *trunk* ("In a trunk. Now, what is a *trunk*?"). This particular practice illustrates how Ms. Lucero oriented "discussions" toward vocabulary development and raises concerns about how an overemphasis on vocabulary compromises the broader sense making these ELLs will need across their academic trajectories. Recall that these ELLs were making the transition from mostly Spanish reading to English-only reading so that we might expect them to need ongoing, strategic assistance unpacking text meanings, particularly through key vocabulary words in English.

A cultural-historical perspective urges us to question whether the social organization of reading practices promote "the image of reading as a whole" so that skills like vocabulary development matter as they pertain to joint (re)interpretations of the world. These questions are further complicated by our concern for the number of bilingual students who are perhaps fluent Spanish readers but formally encounter English-only reading practices in school contexts where their reading fluency in Spanish is undermined through skills-based practices. In Ms. Lucero's classroom, for example, how often are "discussions" based on defining vocabulary words? How often do students instigate sense making around particular texts? How are students encouraged to draw on the languages and literacies they develop through their participation across cultural communities to develop the meaning making and critical thinking we value across formal academic contexts?

We have deliberately examined some of these questions across formal and informal learning contexts. Next, we share our participation and research in one bilingual middle school classroom that drew specifically on Latino/a students' languages, literacies, and social-political sensibilities, which provided an opportunity to explore how these practices affected the academic capabilities that matter in and beyond formal school contexts.

Facilitating Sociocritical Literacies

In this section, we draw on research that explored the translation practices of Chicano/a and Latino/a bilingual youth. Rather than remediating the academic "deficiencies" that standardized tests and prepackaged curricula tend to substantiate, we used the powerful social critiques these appartuses ignore to *re*-mediate a curriculum unit (Cole & Griffin, 1983). In other words, we shifted our focus toward the set of skills and capabilities these students *already* possess. This unit was developed as part of a larger effort to leverage bilingual youths' translation experiences for the development of academic literacies (Orellana & Eksner, 2006; Orellana & Reynolds, 2008; for a fuller discussion of the curriculum, see Martínez, Orellana, Pacheco, & Carbone, in press). For example, this past research documented how English–Spanish bilingual youth help their Spanish-speaking families and community members negotiate important social exchanges in grocery stores, doctor's offices, and schools, for example (Orellana, Reynolds, Dorner, & Meza, 2003). For the purpose of this analysis, we focus on how the research team created critical discursive spaces where these youth built on local knowledge and social critiques to engage in critical social thought, or what we have called sociocritical literacies (Gutiérrez, 2002, 2007).

To be clear, these students do not engage in these practices because of their race or ethnicity, because we know Chicano/a and Latino/a students differ in their bilingual capacities and participate in various cultural communities. From a cultural-historical perspective, these students expand their strategic use of language varieties, genres, registers, codes, and scripts through participating in cultural practices across a range of social and community contexts.

During our curriculum unit, we held ongoing discussions about the range of translation experiences of these sixth-grade students and designed a culminating writing task in which students "translated" their stance on one social issue to two distinct audiences. We specifically designed tasks that helped students unpack these translation experiences and practices, and our in-class discussions revealed the socioculturally complex dimensions of this everyday practice. Even as children, they recognized how adults (and society) constantly positioned them across translation encounters as novices, experts, nuisances, and so on. For example, Pablo shared a particularly unnerving encounter in which he negotiated between his monolingual English-speaking principal and his monolingual Spanish-speaking mother.

The angry principal called the family home to let Pablo's mother know that he suspended Pablo's older brother, César, for a school violation. In César's presence, Pablo had to help both the angry principal and his distressed mother reach some mutual understanding about the matter. Pablo's challenges during the encounter illustrate child translators' awareness of social context and of power differentials, including the ongoing consequences of their ongoing decision making. Pablo and his peers unpacked the social-cultural dimensions of this familiar experience by identifying the following challenges that Pablo faced during this situation:

- Maintain some neutrality in his discussions with an angry principal
- Advocate effectively on behalf of his mother as she voiced questions, concerns, and a defense of her son to the principal
- Preserve his loyalty to César while he essentially carried out César's punishment
- Maintain his composure as he mediated between the principal's frustration, his mother's palpable concern, and César's anxiety

For Pablo and his peers, translation was not just about relaying a message across two languages—these students were adept at interpreting context and power through language use, word choices, tones, gestures, facial expressions, and body movements. We facilitated students' use of this sociocultural knowledge in their final essays (e.g., how to express particular tones and emotions in their writing).

Of relevance, our discussions about translation coincided with the latest manifestation of the (im)migration "debates" in the United States that occurred after the House of Representatives passed HR 4437 (The Border Protection, Antiterrorism, and Illegal Immigration Control Act of 2005). We share one specific discussion to highlight how, despite their documented "underperformance" and "underachievement," these Chicano/a and Latino/a sixth-grade students engaged in social critique that challenged the dispositions promoted through curriculum-based approaches to learning. In our work, we explored how these diverse forms of knowledge served as resources for expansive learning and for the development of sociocritical literacies in particular.

Given the social-political context, we found strategic ways to address the (im)migration issue that so impassioned these sixth graders' transformative acts of resistance (i.e., student-led walkouts), and at the same time facilitated their critical thinking about translation as a benign social practice. We used the road sign depicted in Figure 5.2 to reflect critically on both the (mis)representation of (im)migrant communities in broader U.S. discourses, as well as the perceived accuracy of translated messages.

In cultural-historical terms, semiotic signs like the one depicted in Figure 5.2 mediate particular messages or representations of the world; in turn, we interpret and reconstruct these messages in particular ways. For example, the semiotic sign depicted in Figure 5.2 might overtly caution drivers to watch for pedestrians crossing the road, but this sign also could be interpreted as fossilizing an image of historically and economically diverse Latino/a communities as "border crossers." We encouraged students to deconstruct the sign with which many of them were already so familiar. They immediately noticed a discrepancy: although the word *caution* is purportedly translated into Spanish as *prohibido*, in actuality the sign sends the message of *prohibited* to speakers and readers of Spanish. We used this discrepancy to engage students in considering why this sign might depict two very distinct albeit politicized messages to two language-specific audiences who represent unique categories of people in the U.S. sociopolitical and economic landscape.

Exploring Semiotic Signs

Our everyday lives are saturated with semiotic signs—in the streets of our communities and in virtual worlds, for example. These signs construct particular social relations that reify the world as it is. Educators and practitioners can draw on these signs as an opportunity for students to express their critical readings, or develop critical readings, of these social relations with respect to their own material realities. Moreover, students and teachers could use *historical thinking* to interrogate the social circumstances that gave rise to these semiotic signs and to explore the potentially transformative power of ones that promote a socially just world.

Figure 5.2. Thinking Critically About Signs

Photo by Sean Biehle. © 2002 by Sean Biehle.

To extend students' analytic thinking around semiotic signs, we showed our students a video clip produced by a well-known Latino/a comedian who examined how "people on the street" interpreted this freeway sign. The clip included an interview with a representative of the Department of Transportation (DoT) about what specific group of people is depicted in the sign. When the comedian claims to turn off the camera (and hence interviews the individual under the pretense of confidentiality), the DoT representative states, "Who's the sign for? [pause] Wetbacks." The word *wetback* had a particularly palpable affect on our Chicano/a and Latino/a students, even though the DoT representative was unclear about how the sign was specifically supposed to mitigate "wetbacks" crossing the freeway. To be clear, we meant to use this video clip to facilitate discussions about translation and semiotic signs and how these tools/artifacts together shape and are shaped by broader social-political concerns (e.g., [im]migration). However, the discussion that ensued demonstrated first how students applied their various forms of knowledge and second how students developed their current thinking about this issue.

In the classroom dialogue that follows, we present a portion of students' elaborations on the (mis)representation of the Latino/a (im)migrant community in the signs and symbols that permeate our everyday lives. One of the authors

(Mariana) facilitated students' application of their cultural, historical, and political knowledge to articulate their social critiques about the treatment of (im)migrants in the United States and the race-based discourses that inevitably characterize the (im)migrant experience. These elaborations were supposed to provide an example of how students could begin to organize their final essay—the culminating task—which required them to identify a social issue (like [im]migration) and "translate" their stance on the issue to two different audiences.

Maritza: Why do they put the sign up for immigrants if the people that put the sign up are immigrants themselves? The U.S. belonged to the Natives so everyone is an immigrant.

Mariana: Did everybody—can somebody else repeat the question that Maritza asked? A little bit louder.

Students: [inaudible]

Mariana: A little bit louder.

Osvaldo: That aren't the white immigrants too because the Native Americans... [were here first]?

Mariana: OK, that's a very good question that you would ask to the man from the Department of Transportation or other people right? Right? That would be a very excellent question, if you would write a letter to him and if you were going to write about how there's racism in this country against the immigrants. That would be one really, really good point, a question that you would make to somebody like the guy who was calling [(im)migrants] wetbacks, who was saying that the sign is for wetbacks. That's one very good question. Anthony?

Anthony: I don't want to say it out loud.

Mariana: Just say it out loud. We're all friends.

Anthony: Then, why do they call White people "White trash"?

Mariana: Why do they call White people White trash? Who wants to take a—

Rolando: Mexicans. They [Whites] kept calling them [Mexicans] wetbacks so they started calling them White trash.

Mariana: We [Mexicans] wanted a name to call them [Whites]? OK, Maritza?

Maritza: Um, I wouldn't write it to that guy. I would write it to [President] Bush.

Mariana: So Maritza says, "I wouldn't write it to that guy." She would go straight to the top, and she would write it to somebody like President Bush, right? Is there somebody else you could write it to?

Students: Arnold [Schwarzenegger]. . . . The Governator . . .

This particular exchange emerged during our analysis of highway sign and the DoT representative's claim that it was intended for "wetbacks." It is clear from the excerpt that students used "they" to index a political power structure that was largely determined by the actions and decisions of "White people," and that "they" referred to "Mexicans." The relevance of this exchange lies in how the cultural organization of discourse built on students' varied knowledges, rather than engaged students in knowledge reproduction or in lengthy skills-driven interactions (as in the example from Ms. Lucero's class). Surely, these Chicano/a and Latino/a students need some skills-based instruction, perhaps not unlike many sixth graders across ethnic and socioeconomic groups throughout the country. Nevertheless, our ongoing tasks were strategically oriented toward facilitating students' thoughtful, analytic construction of a final essay.

Through this discussion, students applied their historical knowledge of European and non-European (im)migration to the United States (i.e., "aren't the Whites immigrants too," "The U.S. belonged to the Natives so everyone is an immigrant"), historical knowledge of Native American exploitation (i.e., "Native Americans were here first"), awareness and interpretations of race-based discourses (i.e., "wetbacks," "White trash"), and powerful critiques of political figures they perceived as anti-(im)migrant (i.e., "the Governator"). In the interaction, Mariana was doing very little "teaching" and instead taking up students' views and encouraging them to engage one another's ideas ("Why do they call White people White trash? Who wants to take a . . .") in preparation for their final essay.

The cultural organization of discourse extended I-R-E patterns but more important, the social context created the discursive space for students to take risks and create new discursive trajectories based on their own musings, as illustrated through Anthony's question. It is clear that Anthony was apprehensive about even articulating his question: perhaps this hesitancy reflected his years of schooling during which student-initiated questions are limited, especially questions related to such politically charged topics like race and power. Moreover, Mariana refrained from answering the question and instead redirected it back to the class. Rolando inevitably answered the question, only for Maritza to revisit the audience who she believed most needed to hear her stance—President Bush.

In short, this example illustrates one way we built on students' cultures in the service of academic and sociocritical literacies. We drew on the knowledge and critiques students developed through their participation in various cultural contexts, including but not limited to schools, and facilitated literacy goals that expanded students' interpretations, views, and readings of the world. Given these students' social-political sensibilities, they also articulated their perception of the ways the world reads *them* as Chicanos/as and Latinos/as who are either (im)migrants or the descendants of (im)migrants, and ways to transcend—and perhaps transform—current social arrangements.

It is important to emphasize that even this class of Chicano/a and Latino/a students reflected a broad diversity of cultural experiences, languages, knowledge, understanding, and sociocritical literacies, because we do not wish to replace one supposition about low-income nondominant students with another. In this case, not all students felt strongly about the (im)migration debate and only a quarter of the class actually participated in the walkouts that the school's students organized to voice their opposition to HR 4437. Nonetheless, we based our modifications to the translation-based curriculum unit on what we learned from students as social actors that traverse various cultural communities in their everyday lives and on the social-political dynamics at play within and beyond the classroom walls.

Conclusions

A cultural-historical theoretical approach to literacy emphasizes the relationship between human learning and development and the social contexts that foster this development. This perspective places culture "in the middle," as culture provides us with the resources to realize varied and hybrid ways of being, believing, valuing, knowing, and learning. Put another way, the capabilities we develop across various cultural contexts are essentially our "cultural capabilities." This view challenges contemporary approaches to culture and cultural differences that essentialize students based on working assumptions about race, ethnicity, language, religion, class, sexuality, or group histories, especially those students who are deemed "different" (which inevitably renders Whiteness the norm). Based on a view of culture as the accumulated tools and artifacts that mediate our everyday activities across cultural communities, we believe this theory has powerful implications for reexamining students' literacy learning in classrooms. We also believe cultural-historical theory has equally powerful implications for imagining new kinds of classroom learning organized around the social, cultural, intellectual, and political knowledge of students aimed at facilitating sociocritical literacies.

Our classroom examples illustrate the usefulness of this theoretical approach for reexamining how social contexts—the organization of talk, classroom discourse, space, texts, ideas, tools, and artifacts (signs and video), for example—affect the development of students' literacy toolkits. Ms. Lucero used similar discourse patterns that nevertheless enhanced students' coconstruction of vocabulary definitions. Still, she managed an exchange that was ostensibly oriented toward skills that are necessary but not sufficient for the kind of meaning making we value across academic contexts. In the sixth-grade class, on the other hand, we organized popular cultural tools and discussions around the sociocritical literacies students already embodied so that discussions were patterned but not limited to a predetermined outcome (like information recall or defining a word). So, what can we learn about culture from these examples?

Current approaches to literacy learning are perhaps ignoring the resources available through the repertoires of (literacy) practices students develop across their cultural communities. To capitalize on these resources, however, educators and practitioners will need to expand their curricular methods and approaches to learn about, from, and with their students, especially students whose communities and histories are least familiar to us. We make some recommendations for teachers here, although we recognize that a cultural-historical approach to literacy teaching and learning emphasizes the unique social, cultural, and historical contexts embedded in the cultural community of the classroom. We believe a cultural-historical theory that emphasizes culturally specific ways of being, believing, valuing, knowing, and learning provides powerful constructs for reimagining how we might better assist our students, particularly our historically underperforming students, across their long-term life trajectories in and out of schools.

Recommendations for Educators and Classroom Applications

Cultural-historical perspectives that emphasize the socially and culturally mediated nature of learning and development can help practitioners reconceptualize what (and how much) students know and how to build on those cultural capabilities. Educators and practitioners can promote a view of literacy that seeks to expand students' repertoires of practice if they hope to enhance the academic potential of all students, and ELLs and nondominant students in particular. Students have developed particular literacies in their families and communities (e.g., translating and other funds of knowledge). The school-based literacies we organize in classrooms (e.g., summarizing texts, vocabulary development) add to this repertoire, which continues to expand during and well beyond school. However, these teaching and learning practices must lead to expanding students' repertoires of literacy. For example, while Ms. Lucero built on what and how much students knew about trunks and attics, an overwhelming focus on vocabulary development for ELLs diminished their participation in critical sense making.

Specifically, cultural-historical perspectives promote a view of teaching and learning that is oriented toward the ongoing *re*-mediation, or *re*organization, of the social configurations and tools and artifacts that facilitate reading and literacy. Teachers can seek to mediate and *re*-mediate a range of social contexts that provide multiple opportunities for students to construct knowledge and develop understanding, rather than depend on remedial approaches that continue to fail nondominant students especially. For example, teachers should alter *how* students participate in literacy activity through a combination of dyads, small groups, whole groups, cross-age and cross-grade groups, joint writing, and joint virtual activity. This range of social configurations facilitates multiple and ongoing literacy learning opportunities. Moreover, a broader range of tools and artifacts can enhance these literacy learning opportunities, especially when they reflect students' lived realities. These tools and artifacts might include documentaries, curriculum programs, music, supplemental texts, popular cultural tools, virtual and digital worlds, e-mail exchanges, guest speakers, community outings, and video. For example, the sixth-grade translation-based curriculum unit described earlier made use of a familiar but contentious highway sign to help students think critically and to explore their sociopolitical sensibilities in the service of academic literacy.

Too often, classrooms position students as "learners" when in actuality, they can participate as "teachers" in contexts that build on their knowledge and understandings. Educators and practitioners can hence organize for ongoing shifts in the roles students play in the classroom through varied opportunities as novices and experts as well as teachers and learners across a range of literacy tasks. For example, Pablo was able to share his expertise as a translator and participated in the class's unpacking of the cultural capabilities embedded in this everyday literacy practice in his family and community. Moreover, in our implementation of the unit, the class was able to "teach" us about their community-based knowledge that was unfortunately ignored in the district's language arts curriculum.

To build on what our students know, teachers can look to families and communities as ongoing sources of expertise about students' everyday practices and as potential contributors to classroom literacy learning. The funds of knowledge approach Moll and his colleagues (1992) implemented has been a particularly productive model of deliberate examinations of the cultural resources available in students' families and communities. This approach challenges us to also learn about students' participation in out-of-school, after-school, alternative summer school, and community-based contexts, for example, where learning is organized around the application of literacy (e.g., digital storytelling [Nixon & Gutiérrez, 2007]), rather than literacy skills per se. Deepening our learning about students' literacy experiences beyond the classroom might foster more complex, nuanced understandings of their experiences and challenge us to continually reject deficit-oriented views and static notions of our students' communities and worlds.

Finally, we encourage literacy educators, practitioners, and researchers to engage with colleagues in a deliberate reexamination of the literacies we currently foster through our classroom cultural communities. Together, we must consider how our current literacy practices inadvertently affect our historically underserved students and perpetuate their academic vulnerabilities in the long-term. Moreover, we must consider the extent to which school-based literacies reflect the "real" reading and writing adults do across everyday contexts (as citizens, consumers, community members, activists, professionals, etc.). These dialogues could potentially transform the ways educators and practitioners reconceptualize literacy teaching and learning to explore ways to learn about our students, from our students, and with our students to expand the power of their lived knowledge and sensibilities.

Acknowledgments

This research was supported by grants from the University of California Linguistic Minority Research Institute (UC LMRI) under the UC LMRI Grants Program and from the University of California All Campus Consortium On Research for Diversity (UC ACCORD). Opinions reflect those of the authors and do not necessarily reflect those of the grant agencies. The authors would also like to thank the collaboration and insights of Marjorie Faulstich Orellana, Ramon Martinez, Paula Carbone, and Rosa Jimenez.

REFERENCES

Cole, M. (1996). *Cultural psychology: A once and future discipline.* Cambridge, MA: Harvard University Press.

Cole, M., & Griffin, P. (1983). A socio-historical approach to re-mediation. *The Quarterly Newsletter of the Laboratory of Comparative Human Cognition, 5*(4), 69–74.

Gallego, M.A., Cole, M., & Laboratory of Comparative Human Cognition. (2001). Classroom culture and culture in the classroom. In V. Richardson (Ed.), *Handbook of research on teaching* (4th ed., pp. 951–997). Washington, DC: American Educational Research Association.

Griffin, P., & Cole, M. (1984). Current activity for the future: The zo-ped. In B. Rogoff & J. Wertsch (Eds.), *Children's learning in the "zone of proximal development." New directions for child development* (No. 23, pp. 45–64). San Francisco: Jossey-Bass.

Gutiérrez, K. (2002, November). *Rethinking critical literacy in hard times: Critical literacy as transformative social practice.* Paper presented at the annual conference of the National Council of Teachers of English, Atlanta, GA.

Gutiérrez, K. (2007). Commentary on a sociocritical approach to literacy. In C. Lewis,

P. Enciso, & E. Moje (Eds.), *Identity, agency, and power: Reframing sociocultural research on literacy* (pp. 115–120). Mahwah, NJ: Erlbaum.

Gutiérrez, K., & Correa-Chavez, M. (2006). What to do about culture? *Lifelong Learning in Europe, 11*(3), 152–159.

Gutiérrez, K., & Rogoff, B. (2003). Cultural ways of learning: Individual traits or repertoires of practice. *Educational Researcher, 32*(5), 19–25. doi:10.3102/0013189X032005019

Martínez, R., Orellana, M.F., Pacheco, M., & Carbone, P. (2008). Found in translation: Connecting translating experiences to academic writing. *Language Arts, 85*(6), 421–431.

Mehan, H. (1979). *Learning lessons: Social organization in the classroom*. Cambridge, MA: Harvard University Press.

Moll, L.C. (1990). Introduction. In L.C. Moll (Ed.), *Vygotsky and education: Instructional implications and applications of sociohistorical psychology* (pp. 1–27). Cambridge, MA: Cambridge University Press.

Moll, L.C., Amanti, C., Neff, D., & González, N. (1992). Funds of knowledge for teaching: Using a qualitative approach to connect homes and classrooms. *Theory Into Practice, 31*(2), 132–141.

Nixon, A.S., & Gutiérrez, K. (2007). Digital literacies for young English learners: Productive pathways toward equity and robust learning. In C. Genishi & A.L. Goodwin (Eds.), *Diversities in early childhood education: Rethinking and doing* (pp. 121–135). New York: Routledge.

Orellana, M.F., & Eksner, H.J. (2006). Power in cultural modeling: Building on the bilingual language practices of immigrant youth in Germany and the United States. In J.V. Hoffman, D.L. Schallert, C.M. Fairbanks, J. Worthy, & B. Maloch (Eds.), *55th Yearbook of the National Reading Conference* (pp. 224–234). Oak Creek, WI: National Reading Conference.

Orellana, M.F., Reynolds, J., Dorner, L., & Meza, M. (2003). In other words: Translating or "para-phrasing" as a family literacy practice in immigrant households. *Reading Research Quarterly, 38*(1), 12–34. doi:10.1598/RRQ.38.1.2

Orellana, M.F., & Reynolds, J.F. (2008). Cultural modeling: Leveraging bilingual skills for school paraphrasing tasks. *Reading Research Quarterly, 43*(1), 48–65. doi:10.1598/RRQ.43.1.4

SUGGESTIONS FOR FURTHER READING

Duffy, J.M. (2007). *Writing from these roots: Literacy in a Hmong-American community*. Honolulu: University of Hawaii Press.

Gee, J.P. (2004). *Situated language and learning: A critique of traditional schooling*. New York: Routledge.

González, N., Moll, L.C., & Amanti, C. (2005). *Funds of knowledge: Theorizing practices in households, communities, and classrooms*. Mahwah, NJ: Erlbaum.

Hedegaard, M., & Chaiklin, S. (2005). *Radical-local teaching and learning: A cultural-historical approach*. Aarhus, Denmark: Aarhus University Press.

Hooks, B. (1994). *Teaching to transgress: Education as the practice of freedom*. Oxford, England: Routledge.

Hull, G., & Schultz, K. (2002). *School's out! Bridging out-of-school literacies with classroom practice*. New York: Teachers College Press.

Moll, L.C. (1990). *Vygotsky and education: Instructional implications and applications of sociohistorical psychology*. Cambridge, MA: Cambridge University Press.

Muspratt, S., Luke, A., & Freebody, P. (1997). *Constructing critical literacies: Teaching and learning textual practice*. Cresskill, NJ: Hampton.

Samway, K.D. (2006). *When English language learners write: Connecting research to practice, K–8*. Portsmouth, NH: Heinemann.

Santa Ana, O. (2004). *Tongue-tied: The lives of multilingual children in public education*. Lanham, MD: Rowman & Littlefield.

Zentella, A.C. (2005). *Building on strength: Language and literacy in Latino families and communities*. New York: Teachers College Press.

PART II

Working With Diverse Students and Families

Unpacking the Science Fair: Sociocultural Approaches to Teaching English-Language Learners

Margaret Hawkins and Kathleen Nicoletti

Mr. Mogley enters his fourth-grade classroom with great excitement. Today he will talk to his class about the upcoming science fair. The science fair is an institution at Kennedy School; all the classes participate, and last year one of Kennedy's fifth graders went on to participate in the state science fair, walking away with the third-place ribbon for his project on nanotechnology.

After the bell sounds and the students begin to quiet down, Mr. Mogley begins. "OK everyone, settle down. We have a lot of exciting stuff to do this morning. I don't know if you've all heard or not, but the Kennedy School Science Fair is on May 2. That's only two months away! Each of you will create and display a science project in the fair. What you do it on is totally up to you. I'll give you some class time to get started, but other than that, all the work on the project needs to be done outside of class. I have a handout for you; it contains all the information you need about the fair: important dates, as well as all rules and project requirements. Be sure to share this with your parents so that they can mark their calendars, because your parents are all invited to attend the fair!"

"This morning I am going to show you a slide show of some of last year's winning projects. We'll take a quick look at those projects so that you get an idea of the kind of quality projects Kennedy expects at its fair. After that, the school librarian, Ms. Grinnel, will be waiting for us in the library. She has set aside a bunch of science books that you can look through for project ideas. In addition, you are welcome to use the library's computers to search for ideas. Ms. Grinnel has compiled a great list of websites that she thinks you might find helpful. We'll have about 25 minutes in the library, and then we'll return to the classroom where you'll have about 5–10 minutes to ask any questions you might have. OK, if there are no questions, let's take a look at this slide show!"

The preceding fictional scenario represents a typical teacher's introduction to a common elementary and middle school phenomenon: the science fair. Odds are that you have participated in at least one of these as a student, a teacher, or a parent. Because science fairs have a long history as part of schooling, they are often taken for granted as "normal" and "typical" school events; however, such events are not always familiar or accessible to many learners. This chapter is devoted to looking at schooling, and school practices, for one particular group of learners: those whose first, or home, language is not English. We will identify some principles of culturally and linguistically responsive practices that offer English-language learners (ELLs) access to participation in schools, examine the above scenario in detail to uncover implications for ELLs in light of those principles, and along the way, question whether "normal" and "typical" school practices, such as the science fair, offer equal access to education for all learners.

Understanding the Role of Language in Schooling

There are a number of clear differences between mainstream students—those who come from the dominant society of the place where the school is located—and ELLs. The most obvious, perhaps, is English-language proficiency. It is, quite reasonably, difficult for those who are not proficient in English to participate in classrooms where the language of instruction, texts, and interactions is English. However, language does not stand alone. Sociocultural theory tells us that language is so deeply integrated with other things—such as cultures, lived realities, identities, and social relationships—that these things are fundamentally inseparable. Language use, including what languages people speak and which specific forms and varieties of those languages they use, reflect who people perceive themselves to be in specific situated interactions, who people perceive others to be, what people perceive the place to be and the interaction to be about, and what people want to accomplish. It also reflects the histories and experiences participants in the interaction bring with them and the relationships they have with each other. Importantly, language use not only reflects these factors, it is shaped by them. So what does this mean for teaching ELLs? And what implications does it have for helping them to participate successfully in events such as the science fair?

Using Multiple Forms of Language

We all speak multiple forms, or varieties, of language. Even if English is the only language we speak, we code-switch in daily interactions; that is, we go back and forth between different genres and registers (see Chapter 2 for further discussion on language and differing contexts for language use). We can speak more formally or less formally. Some of us can speak "street slang," or "academic-ese," or "baby talk," depending on the situation and who we're interacting with. Within the field of ESL, a distinction was made by Cummins (1986) between Basic Interpersonal Communication Skills (BICS) and Cognitive Academic Learning Proficiency (CALP). Cummins claimed that BICS is the language students might use for informal social interaction, such as when they are at lunch, or on the playground, while CALP is the academic form of language needed to succeed in school. Although sociocultural theory offers us a different lens—a view of learners being socialized into multiple different forms of language, with none necessarily more developed or advanced than others, and all tied to social relations and identity work—it is clear that there are school-based forms of language that students who arrive with limited prior experience with schooling may not have. And it is language that is only available in schools or from experiences with formal learning. So in Mr. Mogley's class, for example, for newcomers from other language backgrounds, simply having books and websites on offer may not be enough support. If the students don't know the language of science, which includes not only specific vocabulary words and certain sorts of grammatical structures (such as "if . . . then" constructions, passive voice, etc.), but also specific ways of developing and stating hypotheses, structuring experiments, displaying results, and making knowledge claims, then these students cannot successfully engage in this activity. So how do we offer access to ELLs?

The Importance of Social Interaction to Language and Learning

If students need to know the language of school to succeed in school, then activities must be designed such that they can learn it. A fundamental tenet in instructional design is that new language and new concepts are learned through the negotiation of meaning in social interaction. That is, hearing (or reading) a new word or a new idea may offer exposure, but it does not ensure comprehension (not even with an explanation attached), nor does it enable ELLs to appropriate words and ideas and use them for their own purposes. ELLs must not only encounter new language and concepts, but they also must encounter them in authentic contexts (to understand situated usages and applications) and have the chance to explore them and try them through interactions with others. As meanings are negotiated, often through trial and error, ELLs come to "own" the language and ideas and feel confident using them to make meaning with others. Thus, Mr. Mogley's presentation of the science fair was not well executed; he simply stood in front of the students and talked at them instead of using nonverbal support for what he was saying or enabling discussion of the information he was presenting, and he gave a handout, which again provided information in school-based ways with no meaning cues and no opportunity for discussion. As a side note—Mr. Mogley erred as well in his presentation by not using appropriate comprehension checks. Simply asking if anyone has questions does not begin to adequately serve ELLs (nor most likely others as well). Students who already feel different from their mainstream peers may not want to draw attention to the fact that they do not understand and can't keep up. Further, in some cultures it is disrespectful, and perhaps even insulting, to question the teacher, as it may imply that the teacher has not explained sufficiently. Children in many cultures are taught not to question their elders and that learning is done by listening. Thus asking for clarification or help may be culturally inappropriate. If, instead of talking at students and then asking if there are questions, teachers were to offer students chances to interact using new language and concepts, they would then be able to evaluate students' emerging

Attention to Participation Patterns

What sorts of participation patterns are used in your classroom? Do students engage in pair work? Group work? Individual work? Teacher-fronted instruction or lecture? When is each used, and for what purpose? Try to track the participation of ELLs in the classroom during each sort of instructional pattern as you use it to see how often they actively make use of language during lessons.

understandings and ensure that all students understand the information and are able to engage with it.

Perhaps more important, however, Mr. Mogley's instructional design was flawed in that he expected the science fair activities to be done individually and in isolation. Students were to leaf through books and access websites to find ideas and prepare the projects on their own outside of school time. This not only disadvantages students without strong English skills because it creates hurdles to accessing information necessary to design the projects, but it also sets up barriers to mastery of the science concepts by denying students the opportunity to negotiate content meaning with others.

Building on What Students Bring to School

ELLs, especially immigrant and refugee children, often (perhaps usually) come to school with significantly different histories and experiences than mainstream children. These histories and experiences are what they use to make sense of new language, experiences, and practices (as we all do). Unfortunately, in many cases, while considering gaps between what ELLs bring and what is expected in school, ELLs may come to be viewed as *deficient*—that is, as coming to school without good language skills, knowledge, or experience. However, sociocultural theory helps us understand that all ELLs come embedded in rich language and cultural practices. These practices may be different than those of mainstream students, but they are no less valuable or valid. Thus, the question becomes, How can we recognize and recruit what ELLs know and bring to support classroom learning for all students? Teachers must understand what it is that ELLs bring, ensure that it is represented and valued in the curriculum, classroom, and school environment, and use it as building blocks to facilitate learning.

In the case of Mr. Mogley's class, his method of presenting the science fair project would likely cause significant problems for ELLs. Odds are that they have no prior exposure to science fairs. These are part of the school culture in the United States but not necessarily elsewhere. Imagine, for example, the daughter of a rural Thai farmer. Her parents have never attended school, don't speak English, and are not literate in any language. This child did not attend school before arriving in Mr. Mogley's class; she was needed to help on the farm so that her family could survive. She has had no access to technology, much less exposure to the discipline of science. She would not know what counts as science, and certainly not what a science project consists of, nor what a science fair looks like. This is not to say that she knows nothing about science. She may well have significant knowledge of weather patterns, crop growth, animal husbandry, and many other things that would fall within the disciplinary realm of science. It is Mr. Mogley's responsibility to discover what his students know and bring so that he can find ways to connect instruction to prior knowledge and experiences and enable learners to use what they know to engage in learning. So for this student, he might help her identify a topic for her project that she already knows something about, thus giving her interest, motivation, and a solid foundation to build on, as well as validating her prior experiences and letting her know that they have worth in this environment.

Even if ELLs can use what they know for language, literacy, and content learning, if they have little understanding of what sorts of performances count for success in school (How do you ask a research question or frame a hypothesis? How do you go about finding answers? How do you display your work to represent what you've done and learned?), then success in the science fair is out of reach. ELLs may know quite a bit about the content but not know what sorts of knowledge count here or how to demonstrate what they know, especially if they are expected to demonstrate it in English. Although Mr. Mogley was on the right track in showing slides of last year's project, offering some visual support for what a project might look like doesn't bridge the gap that might exist for ELLs encountering science projects and fairs for the first time, nor those without sufficient language skills to access and display information. The pictures show the product, but they don't unpack the process.

Families' Roles in Schooling

Families and caregivers play a key role in providing early language and literacy experiences that socialize their children into specific usages and understandings of language and literacy processes. Thus, educated, literate, mainstream families often mirror at home many of the practices and expectations of school. Their children, for example, come to school with preliteracy skills (such as knowing the directionality of print and the function of illustrations, being able to make intertextual connections, and to predict and analyze story lines). These students also may have an advantage in the case of the science fair project because their parents also likely have introduced their children to things like ant farms, magnets, and other phenomena within the realm of science. These parents have at-hand resources to support their children's emerging research and presentation skills. They know what science fairs are and what it takes to create a successful project. If their children need ideas, or materials, or information, they are available to help. They also understand the importance within schools of succeeding and even "winning" in events such as these. Thus, they impart values and information and serve in many ways as resources for their children.

Immigrant and refugee children often lack these resources. Their homes may not be equipped with computers, software, dictionaries, and the like. Their parents may not know what a science fair is or how to design a project. They may not have transportation to take their children to the library or knowledge of how libraries work, and they may not be able to afford materials. In some cases, these families may simply not have the English or literacy skills to guide their child through the process or to answer questions. Thus, a project such as this, assigned to be done out of school, sets up an unequal playing field. Children who come to school already privileged because the resources and practices in their homes are compatible with those valued in schools can draw on these to shine, while others, often those from differing language, culture, educational, or socioeconomic backgrounds, fail. In addition to academic consequences, there are social ones as well. Activities such as science fairs often serve to make visible to the children as well as the adults the lines between the "haves" and the "have nots."

To illustrate this point, we juxtapose the words of two parents with children in the same fourth-grade class in school. These are quotes taken from an interview project. One parent, Jaime (all names are pseudonyms), is from Mexico. He and his wife both work double shifts, believing that they must do everything they can to provide for their family. Jaime speaks English, although not fluently, but his wife does not. He was schooled in Mexico through the eighth grade; she has a third-grade education.

Margaret (coauthor): So when he was having trouble reading . . . did you work with him and the school in any particular way with that?

Jaime: No, not so much. Because aah . . . it is not my aah . . . I was trying to teach him to read but it is difficult for me to teach him to read in English. So I would tell him you just have to slow down pretty soon it is gonna come out by itself you just have to listen to the teacher . . . the teacher say this is what we think is good for Tonio.

Jaime is telling us that although he values schooling for his son, he is unable to offer academic support. He and his wife rely on the teacher to do what's best for Tonio. We will contrast this with Amy, an Anglo, middle class, native-English–speaking mother, speaking about her two daughters, one of whom is in Tonio's class.

Amy: I am much more involved in both of their education than I ever thought I would be. Just monitoring and making sure or helping them. I mean, I have the sixth grader coming now with math that isn't being taught to her. She's working ahead. And so Peter and I are expected to teach her. Something . . . base four, which is just sending us into camps. [laughs] So we went out and bought a textbook. The arrangement I have now with math for Hanna (the fourth grader) . . . the teacher actually told me, "We don't like having the kids work ahead in fourth grade, because what are we gonna do with them in fifth grade?" I was flabbergasted. And I said, "Can we worry about it in fifth grade? She's doodling." And she said, "Yeah, by the end of the month—because I'll have some student teachers, and we'll be done with this unit—we can let Hanna work ahead in the textbook at her own pace when I'm teaching to the class. But if she has any questions, and she can't get a student teacher to help her, she's gonna have to come home and ask you." OK, that's fine.

Amy and her husband actively monitor their children's classrooms and academic development and take on a teaching role. They do not trust the teacher to do what is best for their children and feel that, left to teachers' devices, their children would be undereducated and would act out in school. An additional point is that Amy has direct communication with the teacher about what she wants for her children and how she thinks they ought to get it. Jaime and his wife are not even aware that this sort of involvement and advocacy are possible for parents. It is, perhaps, too easy to imagine the different ways in which the two families would react to, and be involved with, their children's science projects at school.

The Family Connection

What sorts of relationships do you have with the families of your students? How do you learn about their families? How do you ensure that all families can be involved in your classroom and with their children's learning?

In the example of Mr. Mogley's classroom, in addition to designing a project that ensures unequal support for his students, he erred by instructing the students to share the assignment sheet with their parents and insisting that parents will want to come. If parents are not literate, or do not speak English, how will they even access the information on the sheet?

It is true, in our experience, that all parents want their children to succeed in school. However, parents' understanding of their roles in supporting that success may differ from schools' expectations of families' involvement. As discussed, not all parents can facilitate and scaffold their children's academic work in the same ways. Availability may differ, too. In families where both parents work double shifts to provide food and a roof over their children's heads, taking time (and pay) off to attend the science fair may not be first priority or even be possible. Transportation may be an issue, as may be the care of siblings. If parents don't speak English or have not themselves attended school, they may feel uncomfortable or even embarrassed to attend. Jaime, in fact, says that he can't attend school events because he doesn't have the time; both he and his wife work. And because he is unfamiliar with U.S. cultural models of schooling, he does not understand that this is one of the many expectations that schools have about how parents are "supposed" to be involved in their child's education. We do, however, want to include a note of caution here. Jaime and his wife have limited educational backgrounds and live in poverty. We must not assume that this is true for all families of ELLs in schools; family circumstances and experiences vary as widely for ELLs as they do for native English speaking children. And many of the issues we've highlighted may be equally relevant for native English speaking families who live in poverty or have limited educational backgrounds and literacy skills. However, inability to access information because of limited English and differing cultural models of schooling (and families' roles in schooling) are common occurrences for immigrant and refugee families who are not proficient in English.

Conclusions

What we can see, in exploring the science fair scenario, is that access and engagement for ELLs is about more than "learning English." It is about understanding that there are different forms of English, used in different places with different people for different purposes, and having the ability to switch among them. It is about understanding how schools work, what sorts of activities and performances are valued, and how to do them. It includes understanding the roles that schools expect students and parents to play. And it is especially about social interactions and meanings that are negotiated and messages that are conveyed in those interactions, among students, and between students and school staff, students and parents, and parents and school staff. The social and interactional aspects cannot be divorced from the linguistic and academic ones. Thus, designing and implementing good curriculum and classroom environments must be premised on offering students opportunities to interact (using new language and concepts) on an equal playing field, with sufficient and appropriate support available, making sure that students' diverse histories and experiences are represented, respected, and valued.

Does this mean abolishing science fairs? No, it doesn't. The science fair is one of many activities in which students must be able to competently participate to succeed in North American schools. So how might Mr. Mogley support all of his students to do that? The following is a revised scenario in which Mr. Mogley introduces the science fair in a way that aligns with sociocultural principles:

Mr. Mogley enters his fourth-grade classroom with great excitement. Today he will begin to lay the groundwork for involving all of his students in the upcoming science fair. He realizes that this will take several classes and can't be done in one period. He is dressed in a long white lab coat with a paper hat on his head with the word SCIENTIST printed in large letters.

After the bell sounds and the students begin to quiet down, Mr. Mogley begins. "OK everyone, settle down. I have some exciting news for you. Today we are taking the first step toward becoming scientists!" He then points to the word SCIENTIST on his hat. He asks, "Can anyone tell me a word you think of when you think of a scientist?" After receiving and discussing a few answers, he continues, "On your desks I've placed a large sheet of paper with the word SCIENTIST written at the top and a line drawn down the middle of the paper. (He points to the large example sheet posted in front of him as he speaks.) Working with your desk partner, on the left side of the paper I would like you and your partner to write down any words that come to mind when you hear the word scientist. After you've written down all the words both of you can think of, on the right side of the paper draw pictures of anything that comes to mind when you hear the word scientist." Mr. Mogley shows an example using one of the words the class has volunteered. "You have 15 minutes to do this."

When the 15 minutes are up, Mr. Mogley asks half of the class members to tape their sheets on different walls throughout the classroom. He then instructs the two students who created the sheet to stand by it and share what they've written and drawn with two of their classmates. For the next several minutes, the students share what they have put on their paper, then the students switch, and the remaining students put their papers up and explain their words and pictures to classmates.

When everyone is finished, Mr. Mogley asks the students to return to their desks and to help him make one big list of all the words. Once the list is complete, Mr. Mogley says, "You all seem to have a really good idea of what the word scientist means. Now let's take some time to meet some scientists and see if we can get a better idea of the kinds of things they do. All around this classroom I have placed pictures of some of the world's most famous scientists. Under their pictures you will find their name, the country they are from, and a short description of what they have done that has made them famous. You will also find pictures of the things the scientists have discovered or invented. I'd like you and your partner to walk around and see who these people are. I am giving you some note cards. On each note card, write the scientist's name, the country he or she comes from, and the name of his or her invention."

Once students are seated, Mr. Mogley goes to the map on the classroom wall. He points to each scientist and has a student come up and locate the scientist's country of origin. Mr. Mogley puts the students in groups of four and assigns the following task: "For each scientist, discuss his or her invention or discovery and why it is important. What impact does it have on our lives? Put a few ideas on the scientist's note card." When students are finished with the activity, Mr. Mogley leads a class discussion of the inventions, remembering to make a list of the inventions and discoveries on a large sheet of paper that is visible to all students, with bulleted answers from the students below each invention.

In the preceding vignette, Mr. Mogley does not even mention the science fair in his introductory lesson. Before he does that, he needs to ensure that students understand the larger concepts of science and scientist. And he must do that by finding out what students already know and building upon that. He therefore begins by using the collective knowledge of the group to activate schema—to make visible to members of the classroom the knowledge they individually and collectively bring with them—to construct a definition of scientist and an understanding of what it is that a scientist does. Mr. Mogley works to overcome the potential language barrier through dressing like a scientist and providing photos of scientists and inventions, instead of just using words. Instead of just issuing verbal directions, he models what he'd like the students to do and how to do it. And he asks for pictures as well, which offers a mode of participation for students less sure of (or less proficient with) their language skills, as well as visual support for the written concepts to clarify meaning.

The students work together in pairs to generate vocabulary and concepts about science, thus offering an opportunity for ELLs—and all learners—to interact and negotiate meaning. Sharing the posters offers practice in using the new vocabulary and concepts, as well as practice in speaking and presenting to others. The class then composes a composite list of words, which both enriches the emerging understandings the partners have constructed and allows everyone to contribute.

In the next portion of the lesson, Mr. Mogley introduces famous scientists and their inventions and discoveries. This not only enhances students' knowledge of science and scientists, but through Mr. Mogley's representation of multiple ethnicities and geographic locations, it validates knowledge and knowledge-makers as being global. The note cards serve to organize the learning and cue students into the important points that they are expected to take from the display. Using the note cards also offers the opportunity for students to work together to negotiate understandings of the information. And the final task, the small-group discussions, gets to the heart of science: What is it that scientists do, and why does it matter? The students are actively engaged in constructing understandings of scientific inventions and discoveries, and the impact these have on human lives and on the world. At the end, Mr. Mogley pools the collective information and makes it accessible to the entire class.

One additional point worthy of note is that in this lesson, Mr. Mogley integrates what are referred to as the four skill areas: listening, speaking, reading, and writing. He offers many modes of support for the development of literacy as well as language skills.

Clearly this lesson only begins to unpack what science is about. And equally clear, its end point isn't yet close to having students begin to plan their science fair presentation. Teaching ELLs well—perhaps teaching all students well— requires attention to detail, laying necessary groundwork, and providing adequate scaffolding, all of which may be time consuming. However, we argue that surface coverage of concepts and "getting through" the curriculum unit and plans don't promote learning or support students' academic success. Students cannot be adequately prepared for the science fair in one lesson.

Recommendations for Educators and Classroom Applications

The recommendations that follow are a sample of the ways in which Mr. Mogley—and all teachers—might design lessons and activities aligned with the sociocultural approaches discussed in this chapter that teach students about science and prepare them to successfully create their projects.

- Have students from last year's fair visit the classroom and talk about their projects, namely, what the students did and how they did it. In this way, students get multiple real-life models from peers and the opportunity to discuss both product and process.

- Have community members in the field of science visit the classroom and talk to the students about what they do. This connects science to "real life" and students to communities. It helps to bring together the worlds of home and school, and again, promotes scientific discussions and interactions.

- Have students interview family and community members on how they use science in their lives. This provides practice in conducting interviews (something not done usually by youth outside of school); practice formulating "who," "what," "where," "when," and "how" questions; verbal interactions around science; validation of the importance of their families' and community members' voices and experiences within the academic environment; and connections between science and the "real world."

- Have students keep an illustrated journal for a week on ways that science affects or is visible in their daily lives. The journal connects home and school explicitly and supports development of writing skills, and the illustrations offer an alternative and a support for those less proficient in English.

- Send messages to parents in their home languages. The simple act of translation bridges barriers between families and schools and sends a message that home languages are recognized and have value in school environments.

- Offer parents the opportunity to attend a workshop with their children on how to create a science project (with translators available). Building on what families know and bring means meeting them where they are and offering explanation and support for schools' expectations. Soliciting input and listening to parents' ideas during the workshop is necessary to develop an authentic home–school partnership, rather than a one-way flow of information.

- Allow students to do joint projects, either in pairs or small groups. This enables students to try out new ideas and language through social interaction and to provide support for each other. It's essential to learning and to building a strong and comfortable classroom community.

- Offer class time for working on projects and mentors (perhaps older students) for help in project design and locating information. This equalizes access among students, regardless of outside resources and demands.

- Provide materials (perhaps through soliciting from community businesses and organizations). As with the previous point, this equalizes access for those who may not be able to afford materials. It also engages community businesses and organizations with the work of school.

- Take a field trip to a science museum. Many children have visited science museums by the time they are in elementary and middle school. Others, however, may not have had the opportunity to do so. This broadens students' concepts of what science is and means in the world and what it means to be a scientist. It also provides ideas for projects and bridges learning in school with the natural world.

- Have undergraduate and graduate students who are majoring in various areas of science visit the classroom and talk with students about their interests, motivations, passions, and goals. Once again, this enables interactions around science concepts and illustrates career possibilities related to the field. It provides models of (graduate) students who are excited about science and thus serves to stimulate ideas and discussion. It also provides information about career trajectories and educational processes involved.

These are just a handful of ideas, but they include ways to facilitate language and science learning, utilize and validate what children know and bring, locate appropriate support, and involve families and communities. In this way, all children can deepen their knowledge of the discipline of science and learn school-based ways of engaging in knowledge work, as well as create a successful project for the fair. We believe that this, ultimately, is the goal of teaching in schools: to provide equal access to and engagement with the discourses of school for all learners.

REFERENCES

Cummins, J. (1986). Empowering minority students: A framework for intervention. *Harvard Educational Review, 56*(1), 18–36.

SUGGESTIONS FOR FURTHER READING

Fradd, S., & Lee, O. (1999). Teachers' roles in promoting science inquiry with students from diverse language backgrounds. *Educational Researcher, 28*(6), 14–20.

González, N., Moll, L.C., & Amanti, C. (2005). *Funds of knowledge: Theorizing practices in households, communities, and classrooms.* Mahwah, NJ: Erlbaum.

Hawkins, M.R. (2005). ESL in elementary education. In E. Hinkel (Ed.), *Handbook of research in second language teaching and learning* (pp. 25–44). Mahwah, NJ: Erlbaum.

Toohey, K. (2000). *Learning English at school: Identity, social relations and classroom practice.* Clevedon, England: Multilingual Matters.

Valdés, G. (1996). *Con respeto: Bridging the distances between culturally diverse families and schools.* New York: Teachers College Press.

CHAPTER 7

Posing, Enacting, and Solving Local Problems in a Second-Grade Classroom: Critical Literacy and Multimodality in Action

Melissa Mosley and Rebecca Rogers

A s critical literacy teachers—teachers who are interested in the power of literacy to construct more just spaces—we struggle with the productive tension between talk and action. One cause for tension is finding the time to address big social issues and take action within the constraints of curricular time. When time is short, as it always is when teaching for literacy acceleration within a critical framework, we find ourselves struggling with the dilemma of action. On one hand, we want our students to identify problems and see themselves as social actors who can use multiple tools to solve these problems. On the other hand, we know that not all problems can be solved through classroom curriculum. Like other critical literacy teachers, we wrestle with the dilemma of what constitutes action.

As a teacher and researcher in a second-grade classroom, I (Melissa) began to reflect on how I could engage with students' concerns and ideas in ways that would empower students to take action and make differences within their communities. With my students, I studied freedom and the U.S. Civil Rights movement, and through books, discussions, and projects, the students built understandings of how oppression and injustice are changed through collective action. During our class discussions and small reading groups, students brought tools and actions from the Civil Rights movement to solve their present-day problems.

Then, after reading several articles and talking about the place of action in a critical literacy classroom, Rebecca, my coteacher researcher and literacy professor, encouraged me to learn about what specific social issues were of concern to my students. Inspired by the prompts of Comber, Thomson, and Wells (2001), we asked the students questions such as What worries you? and What do you want to change about the world? I opened the discussion to our concerns about freedom and rights in our own neighborhood and community. Rebecca was our scribe, writing ideas on a piece of flipchart paper. One student began, "Teenagers put Cheetos in my mailbox." The class giggled, then offered more examples. "Some people throw toilet paper in the trees and you can't clean it up." They reported that "ding-

Breaking the Silence: Recognizing the Social and Cultural Resources Students Bring to the Classroom, edited by Catherine Compton-Lilly. © 2009 by the International Reading Association.

dong ditching" often occurs, a prank that usually carries racial meanings, in which someone rings the doorbell of a house (or knocks loudly as if it were the police) to scare the person who opens the door, and then runs away. Another student stated, "Something worse happened to my house," and told the class that someone threw a rock at her window. Having an intimate knowledge of this racially diverse working class community, having grown up there myself, I knew these were issues that related to family life, economics, and social relationships. My challenge was to integrate the students' concerns about social issues into the curriculum while still attending to their needs as literacy learners.

The answer to this challenge came in the form of a play about social issues in the community and taking action on these issues, written and performed by students in the class. Using multimodal literacy as a form of action, this play—videotaped and shown to community members—served as the students' way of communicating their messages to a broader audience. In our viewing of the play, we noted places where status quo performances of race, gender, and class were reproduced within the context of performance and places where students' words did not match their actions. To explore what constitutes action, we looked to both language and nonverbal modes to see how the second graders called upon a set of tools to create a performance. We intend to guide the reader to understand *how* action might be understood by examining the multiple modes of literacy learning—such as writing, discussion, performance, and reading—that students use to make meaning. We describe how meaning making is distributed across modes; for example, we examine movement and the layout of the physical space as well as the social identities as indicated by the dress and language and movement. This method also allows us to see how social action in the classroom is part of larger stories that the students tell about their lives (Norris & Jones, 2005). In this chapter, we consider the following questions:

- In the dramatic play of students in this classroom, what phrases, objects, and actions construct the meaning of the dramatic play? What are the histories of these tools?

- What are the threads that weave through the dramatic play, and how are those threads woven together?

- How are multimodal resources used to introduce conflicts and propose solutions in the plays? How might we read the actions associated with each performance?

- How do the students use phrases, objects, and actions together to construct particular identities in the performance of the play?

- How do the students individually and collectively manage the play-acting in the scenes? What gender, race, and class roles are the girls and boys taking in the scenes?

Mediated discourse analysis (MDA), the method we used, emerges from critical discourse studies, the study of mediated action, and sociocultural theory. In our description of the play and the modes engaged in the performance, we show

how the students made meaning using tools of physical and mental action—tools that have a history and cultural meanings (Wertsch, 1998). Reading action in this way is part of a practice referred to as MDA (Scollon, 2001). Scollon (2001) writes, "Social actions are called mediated actions within MDA (mediated discourse analysis) to highlight the idea that all social actions are mediated by cultural tools or mediational means" (p. 143). Using this method, we examine talk and action as tools that students use in dynamic ways to make meaning.

Pedagogy: Critical Literacy and Multimodality

Critical literacy is a set of approaches designed to engage students in literacy practices such as questioning the author, proposing and identifying multiple perspectives, and making connections between history and other social practices when reading texts (Comber et al., 2001; Lewison, Flint, & Van Sluys, 2002; Vasquez, 2003, 2004). Like other sociocultural approaches to literacy pedagogy, critical literacy practices place language in social contexts as the center of attention. If you were listening to what critical literacy sounds like in a classroom, you might hear students ask each other questions that reach deeply into texts, such as "Why was the book/news report/movie written/performed this way?" or "What is the author's position on this topic?" Critical literacy approaches rub against the grain to ask, How else might this idea be represented? Using the tools of critical literacy, students design new versions of old stories that somehow change the playing field or reenvision who may benefit from the wealth or privilege our society has to offer.

When we think about what critical literacy is like in a classroom, we begin to consider how meaning is made using many different modes (Kress, 2003; Kress & van Leeuwen, 2001). Modes are semiotic tools, or tools used to make signs, such as spoken language or bodily movements. Sound is also a mode, as are the images in a picture book. Modes are used in different combinations to make a single message; for instance, the body can be used along with written words to convey a story. Cueing students into how both language and nonverbal action are used in social spaces to make meaning, we further envision new possibilities for reading and creating narrative texts in a digital society. We can imagine, for example, a group of students creating a photostory or short film on the computer to expose a local injustice, such as a lack of safe playground space in the community (Mahiri, 2006). Incorporating the language of multimodality into our pedagogy further supports students in using critical literacy practices. Students learn to recognize the power of their words in conjunction with images and other actions to construct new possibilities for themselves and their communities.

In our class, students wrote and performed a play about vandalism and social injustice in their neighborhood. The students transformed the written text of the play into the performed action of the play (Siegel, 2006). They made a variety of choices in representing the script of the play, using their speech as well as their bodies in motion as signs. For example, one set of signs, the dialogue and stage directions, was transformed into spoken text and embodied action of a particular character. These actions were mediated by the use of cultural tools including the text of the script and the students' bodies, voices, and props (Gal'perin, 1989; Wertsch, 1991).

We recognize that in choosing tools to mediate, some messages get performed in particular ways, and other messages are left out. Some students' ideas are taken up, others eliminated. Such is the enactment of power and control within the negotiations of signs. We chose to use this play as an example of the pedagogical work that we do as teacher researchers, often on the spot, as we help students make choices about how to represent themselves and others while moving from talk to action.

MDA: A Method for Describing Action and Talk

After viewing the videotaped version of the play several times and taking notes on language and action, we focused on the narrative structure of the plays. We noted how each of the plays included elements of narrative structure—an introduction, conflict, resolution, and coda, or ending (Labov & Waletzky, 1967). Next, we looked at the plays using a set of tools associated with MDA. We examined both the mental and physical action of the students as well as the cultural tools that made that action possible or mediated the action. For example, we might imagine a teacher using a marking pen to scribe ideas on a large piece of paper. The action (scribing, which is a physical tool) is mediated by language (a mental tool) as the teacher restates a student's idea. Then words, the teacher's body, and the marking pen mediate the teacher's action of scribing. Discourse, in MDA, refers to the broad range of approaches that discourse analysts draw from as well as the understanding of how language makes certain actions, identities, and social practices possible. MDA, in contrast to other approaches to discourse analysis, allows us to move past talk, the verbal action, to the nonverbal action of the play.

MDA allowed us to focus on how students make choices to use actions to create identities and roles for themselves and others within the narrative of the play (Scollon, 2001). MDA includes tools that teacher researchers can bring to verbal and nonverbal data to examine the roles people play, ideas that are constructed, and how interactions are held together. When we used a MDA with our second-grade students, we asked ourselves the following questions:

- How would you describe the scene?
- What do you notice about the use of space? Body positioning? Gaze?
- What artifacts are being used?
- What are the potential meanings being made in this image?

We encourage the reader to use these tools to look at the illustrations of still images and descriptions of scenes that we present throughout the chapter. Keep your observations in mind as we describe the context of play writing and acting in this second-grade classroom.

List of Recommended Reading for Play Acting and Thinking About Mediated Action

Boal, A. (1985). *Theatre of the oppressed.* New York: Theatre Communications Group.

Boal, A. (2002). *Games for actors and non-actors* (2nd ed.). New York: Routledge.

Gerke, P. (1996). *Multicultural plays for children: Volume 2: grades 4–6.* Lyme, NH: Smith and Kraus.

Nelson, L., and Finneran, L. (2006). *Drama and the adolescent journey: Warm-ups and activities to address teen issues.* Portsmouth, NH: Heinemann.

Rohd, M. (1998). *Theatre for community, conflict and dialogue: The hope is vital training manual.* Portsmouth, NH: Heinemann.

Schneider, J.J., Crumpler, T.P., and Rogers, T. (Eds.). (2006). *Process drama and multiple literacies: Addressing social, cultural, and ethical issues.* Portsmouth, NH: Heinemann.

Weigler, W. (2001). *Strategies for playbuilding: Helping groups translate issues into theater.* Portsmouth, NH: Heinemann.

Play Writing and Play Acting: Critical Literacy and Multimodality in Action

In our classroom, critical literacy and multimodality came together when students examined text sets using critical literacy questions. Text sets were used by students to observe multiple perspectives and provide multimodal experiences incorporating listening, looking, and reading. The text sets included print books and audio books, relevant photographs, images, poems, and songs on a single topic. Text sets also included a list of questions such as How is this author's perspective different than another's? or Why did he or she write the book this way? Multimodality and critical literacy also came together through dramatic play.

In a classroom where we conducted a six-month long teacher-research study, second graders constructed a play script that was the culmination of months of study and classroom talk (cf. Mosley, 2009; Rogers & Mosley, 2004). The play was part of a literacy curriculum that centered guided reading, book club discussions, writer's workshop, and literacy centers within critical frameworks as the major pedagogical methods. Literacy centers in this classroom included choices such as perusing text sets, writing in writers' notebooks, practicing spelling using magnetic letters, and reading with a friend or alone. During guided reading and book clubs, groups met with Melissa or in peer-led groups to discuss texts that were chosen to relate to larger themes. Two thematic units occurred during the spring term: (1) U.S. Black History from Civil War to Civil Rights, and (2) Japan: Japanese Americans and World War II (see Rogers & Mosley, 2006, for a complete list of children's literature included in first thematic unit.) At the close of the first thematic unit, the second graders in this classroom were given a choice to perform a play that Melissa had written based on the children's book *Follow the Drinking Gourd* (Winter, 1992) or to author an original play. There was an almost unanimous vote to write an original play.

Structuring and Creating the Play

When Melissa announced that the students would write scenes for a play on civil rights, she guided the students to list problems in their neighborhood that might inform the storyline. They brainstormed problems that included vandalism, pranks, and a lack of things for teenagers to do for fun in the neighborhood. The problems related to the students' understanding of their rights to own property, to protect one's property, and to rally against those who do not respect property. This school was located in one of few communities within a larger metropolitan area where families can find affordable housing in a safe neighborhood. The people of this community were protective of their neighborhood and property because of the challenges that accompany living in a working class community, specifically the lack of resources necessary to rebuild a fence destroyed by vandalism or to pay for the child's emergency room bill when bitten by a loose dog. However, families also quietly practiced "white flight," a practice in which Whites leave neighborhoods that are racially integrated for areas that are demographically populated by a White majority. Often, these moves were in response to perceived threats to property and property value that were often based on racist beliefs.

After the identification of "neighborhood problems," the students decided to coauthor scenes for the play in small groups. Each scene included the construction of a problem, resulting action, and a resolution, and it was written and cast by the writers. As students wrote their plays, they drew on resources from the literature about the U.S. Civil Rights movement that they had read or listened to as read-alouds or on tape. The group members held a discussion to choose the cast of characters. The characters in many of their scenes were the "heroes" from Black history—Martin Luther King, Jr., Coretta Scott King, Rosa Parks, and two former presidents, George Washington and Abraham Lincoln. One student added that his father, a police officer, should be in the play, and another student added her mother, a Marine, to the list. Neighborhood kids and teenagers were also part of the cast of characters.

With eight dramatic scenes, two musical interludes, and a student-led question-and-answer session, the students constructed a thematic play. Rather than perform the play live, Melissa videotaped each scene so that the students could have multiple "takes." The resulting video was shown during a project night to parents and siblings. To witness the complexity of students' understanding of problems, solutions, and actions related to vandalism, pranks, and missing resources, we examined various modes used in the play performance. For example, we considered the clothes that students brought from home as costumes. We paid attention to the props that became part of the action of the play, such as soda cans and pizza boxes from area chain restaurants. We noted the use of stage direction and gesture to keep the scenes moving.

Handwritten signs introducing each scene were one tool used to structure the play. The students drew on other tools (e.g., language bits, names, places, means of solving problems) borrowed from the literature in text sets. There were several lines in the play that referenced the destruction of property as forms of violence and racism; these emerged from discussions of the bombing of Martin Luther King, Jr.'s home. One student echoed the strong resistance of Rosa Parks, stating, "I wouldn't give up my seat on the bus, and I won't let you play tricks on me." This student used civil disobedience to protest a present-day problem. As we will demonstrate, the students drew on a variety of resources when writing the play to capture the issues important to the students and embedded in the contours of daily practice in their community.

The play begins with a scene called "The Food Replacers." In this scene, teenagers play pranks in a grocery store. After a problem setup and resolution, a local restaurant owner provides the group with free hamburgers as a reward when the teenagers stop doing the prank. Three more scenes follow that address other pranks, such as "TPing" (throwing toilet paper into people's trees), stealing a pizza, and playing tricks such as ding-dong ditching (ringing a doorbell before running away). "The Bad Teenagers," the fourth in the series, is slightly different from the others because it addresses the consequences for working people when vandalism occurs. The family's window has been broken when we join the family. The repair will cost three hundred dollars and take two days. When the police are not able to find the teenagers, the father complains, "But they do this to the whole neighborhood!" Halfway through the performance of the plays, the whole class sings "We Shall Overcome." The play concludes with the spiritual learned in music class, "Free at Last." Similar to the "special features" section on many DVDs, the performance concludes with a question-and-answer period when the students describe the process of production.

Embodying the "Problem" and the "Solution"

We present two very different scenes from the play. We have interspersed two verbal transcripts of these scenes with still images created from a videotape of the student-written play. The sketches of the scenes assist the reader in visualizing the action that occurs in the play (drawings, rather than photographic still images of the videotaped scenes, are used to protect the identities of our students).

"Vandalism at the White House": Embodying the Problem. In "Vandalism at the White House," "Mr. Lincoln" and "Mr. Washington" as well as three teenagers enact the problem of the play: neighborhood vandalism and its effects on people.

In this scene, Brad and Sam (all names are pseudonyms), two high-achieving students who are both White, play the roles of two Presidents. Mr. Washington knocks on Mr. Lincoln's door, and Mr. Lincoln motions as if he is opening the door (see Figure 7.1a). As the two presidents have a conversation, they sit down at a table.

Washington:	I have some problems.
Lincoln:	Sit down and we can discuss your problems.
Washington:	Thank you, Mr. Lincoln.
Lincoln:	You're welcome, Mr. Washington. What are your problems?
Washington:	Some teenagers are bugging me.
Lincoln:	Do you think it will happen to me?
Washington:	I don't know, you haven't had a long life as president.

Figure 7.1. Sketches From "Vandalism at the White House" Scene of the Classroom Play

a. Washington Arrives at the White House to Visit Lincoln

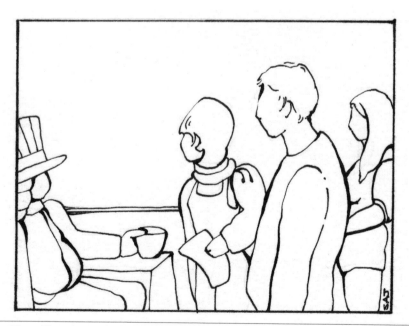

b. Teenagers Discuss Their Plans

Figure 7.1. (Continued)

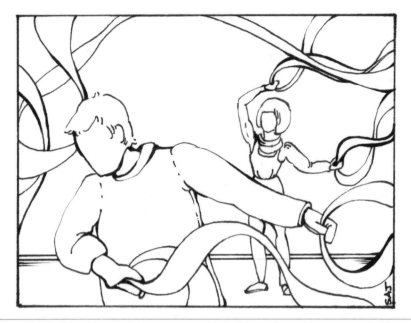

c. Teenagers TP the White House

d. The Teenagers and Presidents Discuss Vandalism

In Figure 7.1b, the three students in the right half of the frame are the teenagers. As they enter the scene, Mr. Washington turns toward them, then back to Mr. Lincoln. The conversation between the presidents continues, and they use cups of coffee as props. Simultaneously, the teenagers have their own conversation about vandalizing the White House:

Teenager 2:	Hey guys, do you want to go to the White House?
Teenager 3:	Yeah, let's go!
Lincoln:	Would you like some coffee?
Washington:	Yes.
Teenager 3:	Ding Dong.
Lincoln:	I'll get it. Come on George. Hello?

At this point in the scene, the teenagers enact the prank known as ding-dong ditch as one teenager knocks on the door, and then all three run away. Mr. Washington follows Mr. Lincoln toward the imaginary door, and when they see that nobody is there, they wave and walk away.

In Figure 7.1c, another prank is enacted, as the teenagers TP the White House. All three teenagers have toilet paper rolls, and they step into the scene. Mr. Washington and Mr. Lincoln walk outside as they are throwing toilet paper.

Teenager 3:	Let's TP the White House!
Lincoln:	Let's go outside.
	What in the world is going on?
Teenager 2:	Stop. No not yet.
Lincoln:	What are you doing?
Teenager 1:	All right, you got us.
Lincoln:	Come in the house.
Washington:	Stop this now!
Teenager 2:	All right.

The teenagers stop their actions and walk into the room toward the table and sit in the chairs. Lincoln stands up, preparing to interrogate the teenagers. The teenagers in turn put their toilet paper on the floor, scoot into the table, and sit with closed postures at the table, as evident in Figure 7.1d.

Lincoln:	Why are you doing this?
Teenager 3:	We want to have some fun.
Washington:	Well, it's not fun for us.
Lincoln:	You can have fun in a different way. You could go to a store, go to the movies, or do something else.
Teenager 3:	OK, we'll try it.
Teenager 1:	OK, we'll try it.
Lincoln:	Thank you. Now sit down and have something cold to drink.

An MDA of "Vandalism at the White House." The roles of the characters are mediated by the costumes that the actors wear and their actions within that role. The hat on Sam's head is too small to fit over his rolled white wig, and he holds it tight as he performs his physical actions. He is restricted by his costume, as is Brad, whose coat is borrowed from a grown man. The second graders comfortably take on the identities of the teenagers—and imagine themselves in that role—performing the actions of littering, TPing, and ding-dong ditching in their everyday overalls and baseball caps.

As they move into larger dramatic action in Figure 7.1c, the actors who play teenagers quite easily take up the physical activity of throwing toilet paper through the air. The students' bodies create the conflict of destroying property through the swings of their arms and the gesture of throwing rolls of toilet paper. Sandra and Katrina's movements, for example, are broad and bold as they stand in opposition to the government, swinging the toilet paper toward the imagined White House. We found ourselves examining more carefully the positions that the students assumed in each scene and how students took up roles in which actors had to resist or perform social control. In this frame, these movements can be read as moving beyond traditional gender roles for girls, roles that are constructed, enforced, and policed.

In "Vandalism at the White House," the enactment of "the problem" by the teenagers was achieved across the multiple modes of talk, artifacts, movements, use of space, and gesture. The problem was solved by verbal action that orders the bodies and bodily functions of the teenagers. The students wrote this play focusing on the problem rather than the solution. The solution comes about very quickly, and the action centers on the vandalism of the teenagers and the presidents' reaction to the vandalism.

The presidents rely on their words to make their point. They ask, "What in the world is going on? What are you doing?" Asking rhetorical questions to the teenagers, coupled with the authority of their institutional position (as president) and age, stops the conflict. Interestingly, when the teenagers were invited into the White House by the presidents and Sandra sat down (Figure 7.1d), her body language was constrained and restricted, contrasting with her earlier movements in opposition to the government in Figure 7.1c. Sandra sits in the lower right corner of this image, within the boundaries of the chair and with her hands on her lap in a very "lady like" position. We might argue that Sandra took on roles in the play that afforded her the opportunity to enact divergent aspects of her identity.

The presidents use space very differently than the teenagers. In Figure 7.1d, Washington has his legs crossed and is slouched, taking up more space than his chair allows. He freely moves his chair away from the table and is at ease interacting with both Lincoln and the vandals who were throwing toilet paper at the White House. Lincoln stands up, embodying a taller and more prominent position as he offers alternative actions for the teenagers to try out such as going to the store, or the movies, or do something else, whereas the others are seated (Figure 7.1d). The presidents also use words to control the actions and bodies of the teenagers; for example, when Lincoln states, "Now sit down and have something cold to drink."

While play acting, the second graders easily embody the problem of destruction of property. They enact two pranks that cause inconvenience rather than destruction, however, which is different than other scenes in which windows are broken by rocks. The solution is easy to design because these teenagers are "bored" rather than intentionally harming others. Sandra, in particular, embodies a passive response when invited into the house. The students showed us what it looks like, and the consequences, when one practices disobedience or obedience to the rules.

"Martin's Kids": Embodying the Solution. In the scene, "Martin's Kids," the title and the cast of characters suggest that the students propose an intergenerational solution to the problem of vandalism posed by the teenagers and presidents earlier in the play. The scene was written and performed by two Black male students, two White male students, and a Chinese American female student. This particular group represented a range of literacy skills, from the very high achieving to students who received special services for reading.

The scene begins with three Black historical figures making protest signs. For the first segment of the scene, three students position themselves in a circle around a table, their hands holding the posts of handwritten protest signs. The students make only slight rocking motions while looking at their signs, and focus the action of the scene on the verbal conversation:

Martin Luther King (MLK):	I want my sign to say no ding-dong ditching. Yeah [spoken under his breath].
Coretta Scott King (CSK):	I want my sign to say no TPing.
Rosa Parks:	I want my sign to say no littering.
Teenager 1:	We used to do that stuff, now we are helping to fight against it.
Teenager 2:	Yeah, we are helping to protest against vandalism and for equal rights.
CSK:	Yeah, we want equal rights.
Teenager 2:	No more fighting! Nonviolence and no vandalism!
Rosa Parks:	We're still fighting for equal rights even if the police stop us. We're still fighting.
MLK:	The laws don't make sense.
CSK:	It's not fair that we can't get along.

As they are making the signs, they tell us what they are writing, for example, "I want my sign to say no ding-dong ditching." The statements of what words will be on the signs mediate the actions of making the signs. One teenager pretends to write on his sign as they talk at the table. The students depart from the narrative structure of the other scenes, as here, the conflict is embedded within the solution; they address the problems of TPing, littering, and ding-dong ditching while enacting the solution of making protest signs.

Next, the students offer a narrative of redemption. "We used to do that stuff, now we are helping to fight against it." This redemption narrative is punctuated with ambiguous language such as "do that stuff" and "fight against it" without stating, explicitly what "stuff" and "it" stands for. The next student expands on this narrative. He names the "stuff" as "vandalism" and names the "fight" as "protest."

Calling on discourses from the Civil Rights literature, the character of Coretta (played by a male child) adds his intention "for equal rights." Similar to other scenes, the words that signal protest are accompanied by actions. However, in this scene, collective action rather than the control of individual bodies is part of the solution. As the scene evolves, "I" transforms into the collective pronoun "we" (e.g., "we want equal rights," "we're still fighting," "we can't get along"). Through their enactment, the students represent the idea that the community, an intergenerational group, will embody Martin Luther King's "I have a dream..." speech by working together.

An MDA of "Martin's Kids." The students' collective action is embodied in their words and actions. In Figure 7.2, there is a clear purpose and intention in the signs and the movement of bodies as they march around the table. The words "the laws don't make sense" mark the beginning of the marching. The male student playing Rosa Parks puts his hand on another student's back to keep him moving along, exercising control of the teenager's body. This parallel movement of words and artifacts embodies the meaning of the Civil Rights movement literature they have been reading, writing, and discussing. The signs, about the same size and made from cardboard, are also multimodal. They include drawings of houses and people throwing objects at houses and accompanying words such as "Stop Vandalism" and "No Littering." The students acknowledge the power of actions over words in this scene. As they march around the table, no words are spoken

Figure 7.2. Sketch From "Martin's Kids" Scene of the Classroom Play

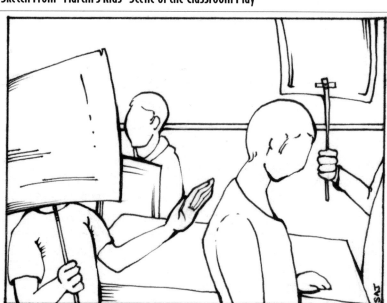

(Figure 7.2). We hear the movement of their feet as they march around the table three times and see their protest signs as they hold them up within inches of the video camera. This intentional use of space emphasizes the messages they are conveying with their signs. It is the in-synch movement among mediational tools (words, artifacts, body language, and movement) that suggests the embodiment of an idea. Nonviolent conflict resolution is represented across modes as they apply these tools to a present-day problem, and rather than passively follow the rules, the students embody collective social action.

Bringing MDA Into Critical Pedagogy

The method we used, MDA, as well as sociocultural perspectives on learning, allow us to view students' talk and social action as the building blocks of literacy practices. As Norris and Jones (2005) remind us, "it is not always possible to 'read' social actions from discourse or to expect certain forms of discourse to accompany social action" (p. 9). Therefore, as teachers concerned with learning and transformation in critical literacy classrooms, we need to focus our attention to the ways in which students act as well as the ways in which they use language, recognizing that actions are embedded within language.

As the students wrote and acted in multimodal plays, they drew on a wide range of resources. They merged the problems they had identified from their community, issues concerning property rights and vandalism, with the tools and strategies uses to solve historical problems. Traversing boundaries of time and space, the students designed answers to their problems ranging from controlling the bodies of others to collective problem solving. We learned, by focusing on action in a critical literacy curriculum, that action takes many shapes and forms. More attention might be paid to not only *what* actions are taken but also *how* they are taken.

In order for the school to understand the lived experiences of students, pedagogy might be grounded in the students' lives and a critical literacy lens must be brought to bear on the students' experiences (Jones, 2006). We can see that social, gender, racial, and class-based roles are reproduced in the texts students create. In the play, phrases came from both school-based texts and community texts that were present in students' lives. These phrases have a moral dimension and guide what is normal behavior. For example, we heard phrases such as "I like the message you sent to the teenagers." This language performs a monitoring function that is present in the school and community. The norms of the community, including the pattern of "white flight" and racist talk and action, were disrupted and reinforced in some ways. The White students in the first scene assumed that by following the rules, and eliminating vandalism, that rights could be restored. However, the interracial playwriting team in the second scene presented the idea that visible collective action is necessary to end injustice.

The value in activity and the analysis after the fact is that it raises our consciousness of how talk and action mediate performance and create certain types of characters and actors. As teacher researchers in this classroom, we might have followed Jones's (2006) advice and opened the very text of the play up to analysis by the group. We could have engaged in a Theatre of the Oppressed (Boal, 1985) to view our own performances for instantiations of power and positioning.

Hilary Janks (2000), a critical literacy theorist, challenges us to continue to explore ways to design action in critical literacy classrooms:

> Critical language awareness emphasizes the fact that texts are constructed. Anything that has been constructed can be de-constructed. This unmaking or unpacking of the text increases our awareness of the choices that the writer or speaker has made. Every choice foregrounds what was selected and hides, silences, or backgrounds what was not selected. (p. 176)

Conclusions

Critical literacy practices are tools to bring our attention, as educators, to the ways that language and other action shape social contexts. In this chapter, we have demonstrated how the pedagogical tool of mediated discourse analysis allows us to witness how meanings are constructed in the student plays. The meanings that were constructed through embodied action were both in line with community norms and worked against the status quo. The framework of critical literacy practices framed our inquiry. Our analysis of embodied action occurs along with the development of our pedagogies for critical literacy instruction.

Because we center critical literacy in our pedagogy, we could not conclude this chapter without raising lingering questions. Although we know that the two scripts, "Vandalism at the White House" and "Martin's Kids" were written collaboratively, we do not know how much of the action and movement within each play was scripted or improvised. In addition, how did the students decide which person would play which role? Did they discuss the body movements that would accompany each turn in the play?

We wondered about how problems and solutions were decided in each of the plays within a very short span of time and space. Similarly, many of the endings suggested that the problems had been completely resolved. We suspect that these structures mimic the literature that the students read in this classroom, which had simple plots and limited numbers of characters. One book that comes to mind is *The Bus Ride* (Miller, 2001). In this book, Sarah defies the city's policy of racial segregation on its public transit system, which sets in motion a chain of events that results in a policy change. Sarah and her mother participate in a boycott, but the problem is more easily solved than in the actual events of the Montgomery Bus Boycott. Many children's books written about critical social issues do not fully represent the historical background of action for racial justice (Rogers & Christian, 2007). These questions suggest the need for revising the plays in ways that allow students to linger a little longer in their consideration of the problems and solutions, expanding their understandings of possibilities and challenges.

In thinking about these questions and the goals of mediated discourse analysis, which is designed to create more socially just spaces, we might explore techniques from *Theatre of the Oppressed* and *Games for Actors and Non-Actors* (Boal, 1985, 2002). We could use these methods to create "still images" as the students act by asking them to "freeze the action." Then we could draw students' attention to the ways in which they use multiple modalities to communicate their meanings and draw their attention to their seemingly unconscious use of bodies and artifacts.

Recommendations for Educators and Classroom Applications

We encourage you to explore multimodal literacy practices and critical analysis of both written and performed texts in the classroom. It takes time to recognize and build on the complexity of multimodalities. It helps to socialize our attention to the ways in which language and literacy practices are always comprised of multiple modes. Choose a children's book or a piece of student writing or drawing. Conduct a multimodal analysis of the text, considering the following questions inspired by Janks (2000):

- How are characters and the big ideas of the story represented?
- Why did the writer/illustrator make these choices?
- What do the choices tell you about the writer/illustrator's identity?
- Whose interests are served?
- What is left out?

It is useful for educators to become aware of how their literacy practices are multimodal. Write in your journal about your own multimodal literacy practices. How do you use talk and action to design practices for yourself and your students? Take a few snapshots in your classroom of students engaged in various literacy activities. Return to the questions on page 92 to analyze the images. Finally, talk with colleagues about why attending to multimodalities in your classroom matters. What do you see as the relationship between literacy, talk and action, and the creation of more socially just classrooms and societies?

REFERENCES

Boal, A. (1985). *Theatre of the oppressed.* New York: Theatre Communications Group.

Boal, A. (2002). *Games for actors and non-actors* (2nd ed.). New York: Routledge.

Comber, B., Thomson, P., & Wells, M. (2001). Critical literacy finds a "place": Writing and social action in a low-income Australian grade 2/3 classroom. *The Elementary School Journal, 101*(4), 451–464. doi:10.1086/499681

Gal'perin, P. (1989). Mental actions as a basis for the formation of thoughts and images. *Social Psychology, 27*(2), 45–64.

Janks, H. (2000). Domination, access, diversity and design: A synthesis for critical literacy education. *Educational Review, 52*(2), 175–186. doi:10.1080/713664035

Jones, S. (2006). *Girls, social class, and literacy: What teachers can do to make a difference.* Portsmouth, NH: Heinemann.

Kress, G.R. (2003). *Literacy in the new media age.* London: Routledge.

Kress, G.R., & van Leeuwen, T. (2001). *Multimodal discourse: The modes and media of contemporary communication.* New York: Oxford University Press.

Labov, W., & Waletzky, J. (1967). Narrative analysis. In J. Helm (Ed.), *Essays on the verbal and visual arts* (pp. 12–44). Seattle: University of Washington Press.

Lewison, M., Flint, A.S., & Van Sluys, K. (2002). Taking on critical literacy: The journey of newcomers and novices. *Language Arts, 79*(5), 382–392.

Mahiri, J. (2006). Digital DJ-ing: Rhythms of learning in an urban school. *Language Arts, 84*(1), 55–62.

Mosley, M. (2009). Talking about war and freedom in critical book clubs. In R. Rogers,

M. Mosley, & M.A. Kramer (Eds.), *Professional development towards social change: A portrait of the literacy for social justice teacher research group*. New York: Routledge.

Norris, S., & Jones, R. (2005). Discourse as action/ discourse in action. In S. Norris & R. Jones (Eds.), *Discourse in action: Introducing mediated discourse analysis* (pp. 3–14). London: Routledge.

Rogers, R., & Christian, J. (2007). "What could I say?" A critical discourse analysis of the construction of race in children's literature. *Race, Ethnicity and Education, 10*(1), 21–46. doi:10.1080/13613320601100351

Rogers, R., & Mosley, M. (2006). Racial literacy in a second-grade classroom: Critical race theory, whiteness studies, and literacy research. *Reading Research Quarterly, 41*(4), 462–495. doi:10.1598/RRQ.41.4.3

Scollon, R. (2001). Action and text: Towards an integrated understanding of the place of text in social (inter)action, mediated discourse analysis and the problem of social action. In R. Wodak & M. Meyers (Eds.), *Methods of critical discourse analysis* (pp. 139–183). London: Sage.

Siegel, M. (2006). Rereading the signs: Multimodal transformations in the field of literacy education. *Language Arts, 84*(1), 65–77.

Vasquez, V.M. (2003). *Getting beyond "I like the book": Creating a space for critical literacy in K–6 classrooms*. Newark, DE: International Reading Association.

Vasquez, V.M. (2004). *Negotiating critical literacies with young children*. Mahwah, NJ: Erlbaum.

Wertsch, J.V. (1991). *Voices of the mind: A sociocultural approach to mediated action*. Cambridge, MA: Harvard University Press.

Wertsch, J.V. (1998). *Mind as action*. New York: Oxford University Press.

LITERATURE CITED

Miller, W. (2001). *The bus ride*. New York: Lee & Low.

Winter, J. (1992). *Follow the drinking gourd*. New York: Dragonfly.

SUGGESTIONS FOR FURTHER READING

Pahl, K., & Rowsell, J. (2005). *Literacy and education: Understanding the new literacy studies in the classroom*. London: Paul Chapman.

Rogers, R., & Mosley, M. (2004). Learning to be just: Interactions of white working-class peers. In E. Gregory, S. Long, & D. Volk (Eds.), *Many pathways to literacy: Young children learning with siblings, grandparents, peers and communities* (pp. 142–154). New York: Routledge.

Vasudevan, L.M. (2006). Looking for angels: Knowing adolescents by engaging with their multimodal literacy practices. *Journal of Adolescent & Adult Literacy, 50*(4), 252–256. doi:10.1598/JAAL.50.4.1

CHAPTER 8

This Is How We Do It: Helping Teachers Understand Culturally Relevant Pedagogy in Diverse Classrooms

Adrienne D. Dixson and Kenneth J. Fasching-Varner

Like every generation before us, we find ourselves in an increasingly globalized and technology driven world, informed by mass media. To situate the historic moment in which this chapter is constructed, we are in the midst of the most media-enhanced presidential preelection campaign in U.S. history; engulfed in the dangerous waters of war, political mistrust, and governmental scandal; and every single second of our lives seems to be available on websites, Internet blogs, television, and other forms of media. On the popular culture front, we have been bombarded and obsessed with the personal lives of celebrities from their marriages to their pregnancies and divorces. It seems that every channel on cable and network television has a new "reality" show, all of which are so far removed from reality that we truly experience what Baudrillard (1983) has theorized as simulacra of copies of things that have never really existed. The *Matrix* films (I, II, and III) starring Keanu Reeves and Laurence Fishburne are good examples of Baudrillard's thesis that challenges the reality of order and the order of reality.

In the midst of our "reality," we have become accustomed to quick critiques and even quicker fixes. The Learning Channel's "What Not to Wear" show is a good example. On "What Not to Wear," participants have their wardrobe critiqued by fashion experts. After a short discussion of their fashion faux pas and important "tips" on more appropriate clothing styles and colors to accentuate his or her body type and update their wardrobe, the experts send the participant off with US$5000 to "correct" their wardrobe. Similarly, professional development for classroom teachers is analogous to the "What Not to Wear" mentality of quick fixes and easy solutions to the challenges of teaching, particularly as it relates to teaching "diverse" students.

Many commercial professional development workshops encourage a "made for Monday" mentality. For example, Ruby Payne's workshops on the "Culture of Poverty" presumably help teachers to work more effectively with students who live in poverty. The workshops include untested questionnaires designed to supposedly measure one's awareness and understanding of living in poverty, being middle class, and being wealthy. At the conclusion of the workshop, teachers, with the aid of Dr. Payne's supporting workbooks, are meant to have a greater understanding

Breaking the Silence: Recognizing the Social and Cultural Resources Students Bring to the Classroom, edited by Catherine Compton-Lilly. © 2009 by the International Reading Association.

of the culture of poverty, and therefore, be more effective with their students. Unfortunately, workshops like Dr. Payne's provide educators with five minutes of advice that supposedly helps them recognize that students of Color and students living in poverty actually have cultural capital, as if those two things alone are the means to address the serious disconnect between themselves and their students. It is important to note that scholars in education have critiqued Payne's poverty workshops and her published materials and found that they reinforce negative stereotypes about families who live in poverty and often conflate socioeconomic differences with culture and cultural differences. For a more in-depth critique of Payne's materials, see, for example, Paul Gorski's "The Question of Class" (2007) and Bomer, Dworin, May, and Semingson's (2008), "Miseducating Teachers About the Poor: A Critical Analysis of Ruby Payne's Claims About Poverty."

Foster (2004) and Foster, Lewis, and Onafowora (2005) highlight the limitations of current professional development models in meeting the needs of urban classrooms, asserting that "although professional development is increasingly focusing on supporting teachers in urban schools, too few models effectively link the exemplary practices of experienced urban [educators]" (Foster, 2004, p. 32) to their students and the schooling contexts in which they teach. Thus, what many districts offer by means of professional development is short-term professional development that lacks a collaborative element with other teachers who are, in fact, effective in urban contexts (Foster et al., 2005). The limited engagement of current professional development models have contributed, in part, to what Ladson-Billings (2006) terms the *educational debt*—a debt that she attributes to the often well-intentioned but problematic attempts of educators to use superficial cultural and social connections to engage students, particularly students of Color.

Similarly, educational rhetoric mirrors the U.S. rhetoric that clamors the challenges of living in an increasingly diverse society, as if people of Color have just appeared on U.S. soil. In education, the challenge is therefore not only to prepare students to live in a diverse society, but also to prepare teachers to teach in classrooms that represent this growing diversity. In this chapter, we explore the concept of culturally relevant pedagogy (CRP) as a means of engaging in what it means to live and learn in a global society. It is important to state that CRP is both a pedagogical approach and a political orientation. Thus, part and parcel of subscribing to and espousing CRP is the willingness to acknowledge and redress social inequity. For many educators, politics and pedagogy seem counterintuitive; however, within a CRP framework, politics are always embedded in a teacher's pedagogy. Indeed, we argue that teachers cannot separate out their politics from their pedagogy regardless of their pedagogical orientation. Hence, from our perspective, CRP is admittedly and unashamedly a politically oriented pedagogy.

Understanding CRP: Three Classroom Profiles

To explain CRP, we examine the profiles of three classroom teachers who take three very different pedagogical approaches to classroom instruction. Each profile introduces a fictionalized composite of a teacher in an urban setting synthesized from research projects and professional development opportunities.

The first two profiles are of Ms. Amy Hosford and of Mr. Cody Danielson, composites of teachers who represent the stereotypical practices and beliefs of teachers who work in large urban school districts predominantly with students of Color. Given the contradictory perceptions of the impact and intent of the teachers' pedagogical strategies, it is important for our purposes to highlight the differences in the composites of Ms. Hosford and Mr. Danielson. Each composite represents a differing pedagogical concern. Consequently, to present a single composite would not provide sufficient nuance in terms of the approaches the teachers take. Ms. Hosford, for example, articulates "concern" about the end results of culturally relevant pedagogy through superficial yet seemingly committed discourse. In other words, teachers like Ms. Hosford state that they "love" the diversity in their classrooms; however, the students have very few opportunities to truly share their cultural backgrounds within the context of the curriculum other than during ethnic cultural events like Black History Month, Cinco De Mayo, or Chinese New Year.

Mr. Danielson, on the other hand, focuses on means and processes of his perception of CRP to the detriment of a holistic picture of what it might actually mean to be culturally relevant. In other words, teachers like Mr. Danielson rely on checklists of or tips on "how" to be culturally relevant rather than actually valuing cultural diversity and working toward social change and justice.

The third profile, Ms. Lacy Ellis, is a composite drawn from not only the middle school study that helped to create the Hosford and Danielson composites, but also coauthor Dixson's study of the pedagogical beliefs and practices of African American female teachers, a primary focus of most of her research. Unlike Ms. Hosford and Mr. Danielson, Ms. Ellis provides insight as to what CRP actually looks like in a classroom when it is presented as the embodiment of a teacher's everyday teaching practice and philosophy. Her profile illuminates a focus on both the end results of CRP as well as the means and processes that best support a culturally relevant classroom. Ms. Ellis exemplifies the journey to CRP especially when the path is well paved, and the teacher is not in search of educational "quick fixes."

With each profile, we present "food for thought" boxes to help you analyze the profile at hand. Finally we conclude with some thoughts about culturally relevant pedagogy and attempt to briefly answer the question, "So just what is CRP?" It is our hope that through the presentation of the three cases, you are able to draw the distinctions between what challenges and supports each teacher in becoming more culturally relevant and consequently challenge your own praxis. More importantly, we are cognizant that this chapter alone cannot, and must not, become yet another professional development quick fix. Like Foster (2004), we are aware that teachers working in "low-performing urban schools [have] few opportunities to participate in high-quality professional development" (p. 402) and often have even fewer opportunities to "observe good practice with working-class urban African American students" (p. 402). Thus, as you move forward with the chapter you will notice that we have avoided offering easy "tips," models, checklists, or other means to tell you "how" to be culturally relevant; rather, we invite you to continue on your own journey of becoming culturally relevant.

Teacher Profile 1: Ms. Amy Hosford

Ms. Amy Hosford is a sixth-grade teacher at Addison Middle School. Addison is located in one of the most highly gentrified neighborhoods in Roseland, a medium-sized Midwestern U.S. city with a large "urban" school district. Ms. Hosford has been teaching for 11 years. Addison Middle School is the second school in the district in which she taught. Ms. Hosford was one of three teachers on a sixth-grade team who teach social studies and English language arts. Ms. Hosford is a White female in her mid-30s. Her presence in her classroom can be described as "hovering." In her classes, she requires students to remain seated at all times. When she interacts with her students, sometimes while standing in the front of the classroom on the podium using her wireless microphone or standing near her desk located on the eastside of the classroom, she generally gives directives related to "appropriate behavior" or comments on work that she finds inadequate or incorrect. She is loud and often raises her voice during most, if not all, classroom interactions with students.

Ms. Hosford's classroom is just that: *her* classroom. She believes that sixth graders lack organizational skills and need a highly structured classroom with clearly established routines. Moreover, given what she learned in workshops on cultural diversity and through conversations with other colleagues, she believes that most of her students, many of whom are African American and from low-income families, lack structure at home. Thus, in an attempt to be responsive to her students' needs, she believes is it her responsibility to bring structure to their lives. Consequently, she also believes the time that students spend in her classroom is the only time they will have that structure.

The physical arrangement of the classroom also reflects her belief in her students' need for structure and routine. The classroom is divided into seven round tables that hold 4–6 students each. Each table has a "folder holder" to help students keep track of their papers and folders for each subject. She also has work stations where students can presumably work in groups on special projects, hands-on, or other authentic learning tasks although many, if not most, of the special projects and hands-on tasks are commercially designed activities taken from activity books to help students learn "critical thinking." She rewards students with time at the work stations based on their good behavior. In other words, although she has the work stations with authentic learning and hands-on assignments in her classroom, they are not a part of the larger classroom curriculum and activities that students have access to regularly. Ms. Hosford decorated the walls with commercial teacher materials ranging from posters on the writing process, to values and citizenship rules, to famous Black Americans such as Rosa Parks, Martin Luther King, Jr., Oprah Winfrey, and Thurgood Marshall.

Above and beyond the general organization of the classroom are missing links to a puzzle that represents the historical timeline of significant dates in Black history. She described the puzzle as a way to make her African American students see their culture represented in the classroom. This timeline is a puzzle that Ms. Hosford made herself, but it is missing three pieces that would make it complete. Unfortunately, the missing pieces seem to suggest a different commitment to her African American students: an incompleteness or lack of sincerity about her commitment to and interest in African American history. Ms. Hosford explained that "since moving schools I had misplaced a couple of pieces and then once I found them just haven't really had the time to put them up"; so the puzzle remained incomplete for the entire school year.

When asked to talk about the role of middle school teachers, she believed that their role is to help students adjust to the shifts and changes in their hormones. She attributes their erratic behavior to this hormonal shift. She believed that the middle school teacher serves as both a role model and an advocate for students, particularly urban students who were doubly plagued by "raging hormones" and unstable home lives. Ms. Hosford articulates the need for children to have mentors and advocates while simultaneously positioning children as being victims to both their bodies and environment. Throughout the course of our classroom observations and interviews, she used common educational jargon such as "differentiated" and "student-centered" to suggest that she embraced ideas related to the notion that "every child can learn" and one that supported and valued the uniqueness of each child, yet she also described the students and the knowledge they bring to school as deficient, and that their home lives are in such disrepair that learning was impossible.

Ms. Hosford also articulated a colorblind discourse, a way of talking about racial differences as if one literally does not physically see racial differences, as a means to support her assertion that students needed high expectations. Ms. Hosford did not use overt racial language to talk about the needs of students but instead used euphemisms like "urban" and "rural" to describe "different" students, thereby engaging in what we describe as a colorblind discourse. By not using overt racial language where she talked about the needs of Black, White, Asian, or Latino/a students, she essentially reassigned racial codes for geographic codes as proxies for race. She also gave the stereotypic response that it didn't matter to her if her students were "purple, yellow, or green." She believed that paying attention to racial differences would segregate her students, and that she should give all the students the same thing. Thus, although Ms. Hosford did not want to base her teaching on the race of her students, she also ignores their cultural backgrounds as means to engage them in the learning and classroom environment. In essence, equality is not equity and recognizing the cultural differences of our students is not the same as being racist.

Billy Williams is a composite student in Ms. Hosford's class who has expressed that he is often disenfranchised from the schooling experience, from Ms. Hosford's notions of how he is treated in school, and from what his teacher thinks about him. The following are some of Billy's own words when interviewed about schooling and being a student in Ms. Hosford's class:

Interviewer: Do you think what you're learning at Addison right now is hard? Do you think what you're learning right now in sixth grade, do you think it's hard?

Billy: Some stuff that they try to give us that when they're really mad at us or something, yes, but a lot of stuff is just pay focus—um, focused attention then it won't be hard.

Interviewer: So you're saying that the work—the work gets hard if the teachers are mad at you?

Billy: Yeah. A lot of teachers like Ms. Hosford get mad at you and then they just give you hard work.

Billy also shared his ideas on how he would structure a school in his own culturally relevant vision:

Interviewer: If you could make up your own school, what would you want that school to be? If you had the power to create the kind of teachers you get, the type of school it is, what type of school would that be?

Billy: We'd have like lunch for like an hour and recess for half of an hour. We'll have to go upstairs and do all of our work. No skipping. The teachers, they'd come to the school everyday. No substitutes. No mean teachers. They'd come to the school and be polite to the kids and bring a lot of stuff that can add fun to the school.

As we can see, Billy has a sense of how he is treated as a student that is in direct conflict with much of the discourse that Ms. Hosford articulates with her classroom practice. Billy's interview is demonstrative of what many in Ms. Hosford's classroom reported during interviews. At the same time, Billy has a sense of what schooling could and should look like that is not at odds with how many of the teachers—Ms. Hosford and Mr. Danielson for example—would like to see at the school, too. How can teachers include Billy and his peers in the process of decision making? If Ms. Hosford and other teachers understand CRP, how can the practice in their classrooms match Billy's perceptions of his class and with his vision for a good school?

What a Teacher Struggling to Engage in CRP Might Sound Like

One type of teacher who is struggling to engage in CRP is focused solely on a need for CRP as an end. "CRP" may be a term the teacher has heard of but when asked to talk about the significant meaning of being culturally relevant, the teacher is hard pressed to give details. This teacher may engage in very traditional classroom practices, albeit those practices may have more contemporary names that align themselves with current pedagogical workshop buzzwords—differentiate, student-centered, scaffold—yet the teacher has a limited understanding of and ability to implement the concepts appropriately. This teacher places a lot of focus on what he or she believes the students cannot do and articulates how difficult it is to work with "these children." Because the teacher lacks an understanding of what cultural relevance means or might look like, the teacher defends ineffective practice by labeling everything "culturally relevant."

You may hear this teacher say things like "Well sure, all of my children can learn, but their home lives are just too bad. I can't be expected to do everything for everyone. Of course I am culturally relevant, I even put Tupac on Math worksheet 4.1 for problem 28 to help these kids, but you know, it's just so hard when you come from such a deficient life. What am I supposed to do? I am doing everything I can for these people."

Teacher Profile 2: Mr. Cody Danielson

Mr. Cody Danielson is a veteran teacher at Addison Middle School. Mr. Danielson is a White male in his mid to late 40s. He was born and raised in the Midwestern United States. He has been teaching for more than 20 years and has been teaching in Roseland for 12 years. Prior to coming to Addison, Mr. Danielson taught in a rural school district for 8 years.

Mr. Danielson rarely talks about his students outside of very narrowly defined clinical and classroom senses. When asked to talk about students out of the classroom, he always brought the subject back to the classroom and what he does in terms of professional development. During interviews, Mr. Danielson indicated that he was taking district-sponsored professional development for literacy and had learned that audio books are a strategy to use with struggling readers. Consequently, he asked his principal to purchase audio recording materials and copies of all the texts used in sixth grade on audiotape. When researchers visited his classroom during the literacy block of the school day, he always had the audio books playing while the students listened and followed along. All students, regardless of their actual reading level or ability, listened to all texts on audiotape or CD. When asked about why he had his entire class listen to audiotapes or CDs, Mr. Danielson explained that the workshop presenters identified this as a good strategy and that his goal "was to help his students any way he can." When asked if there were students who could read the texts independently, he said, "I am sure there are. But the professional development trainers said that good teaching for one is good teaching for all. So they will all get the audio books."

As a teacher, Mr. Danielson relies solely upon the expertise of trainers and pedagogical others to direct the learning in his class, overlooking his own understanding of teaching, and more importantly the wealth of knowledge and expertise that students have and bring to the classroom. When asked to talk about the strengths of his students, he talked about the students as a whole, as if the entire class represented one entity, and spoke about the students in vague and abstract language. Often referring to his students as "the class," Mr. Danielson focused conversation on how to best organize the strategies and programs learned in professional development for "the class."

In October, after the traditional 30-day count that establishes the number of students in the entire school, for each grade level and each classroom, Mr. Danielson was uprooted from his sixth-grade classroom and placed in a seventh-grade class. The previous teacher for this seventh-grade class had left on a mental health leave. On the Friday before the transition, Mr. Danielson was frantic, distraught, and in a state of panic. When asked why he was in such a state, he said:

> This is a complete mess. How can I go to this new class? There are no audio books. Apparently, Ms. Gray [the teacher on mental health leave] did not follow through with the audio books or the 6 + 1 writing strategy training. There are no audio books—how in a weekend will I get all of these audio books for the class on Monday? None of the 6 + 1 traits are posted on the board, so I am going to have to make all new ones this weekend. This is no way to leave a classroom. The class cannot be making much progress without the necessary materials in place.

Mr. Danielson placed his entire focus of the transition on making his room compliant with the tips from the professional development workshop, not his new students. Who are they? How will he connect with the students? Rather, he focused on preparing for the strategy audio books. He was preparing to implement this strategy wholesale whether the students would need or respond to that kind of support.

Mr. Danielson could recite, at length, strategies he learned in professional development workshops, programs the school sponsored to encourage student learning and family involvement, and what professionals had told him was the best practice with those students in his class. Despite all of this knowledge, he was hard pressed to give any details about his students as individual learners and people. Furthermore, this focus on "strategies that work" had blinded him to his students' wonderful contributions and talents.

Teacher Profile 3: Ms. Lacy Ellis

Ms. Lacy Ellis has taught grades 5–8 at Dreton Community School for 15 years. Dreton is located in Crescent, a major city in the southern United States. Ms. Ellis was born and raised in Crescent. She and her husband have two daughters who also attend Dreton.

Ms. Ellis became a teacher after working for a few years in another field. She received her undergraduate degree in psychology from a historically Black college and sought her teaching credential through a number of alternative certification venues, finally receiving it from the local university, a predominantly White institution. It is important to note that although she has been a full-time classroom teacher for 15 years, she has been certified for only 4 years. For a number of reasons, Crescent City Schools has a large number of uncredentialed teachers who are pursuing certification while they teach full time. Ms. Ellis has been pursuing certification for 11 of her 15 years. The frequent changes in state licensure requirements in addition to mandates for "highly qualified teachers" as a result of the No Child Left Behind legislation, made it nearly impossible for her to work full time and obtain her credential. Thus, she took classes at night and during the summers. She is fully licensed as a middle school math and language arts teacher.

Ms. Ellis is one of two teachers of Color in her school and the only credentialed African American teacher. Although her school has two other African American women who work in the school, they are paraprofessionals and not licensed classroom teachers. Ms. Ellis makes a concerted effort to be visible in the school community. She participates in events both at school and outside of school where her students and their families might attend. She believes that it is important that students and families see her as an ally and a support if they should need it.

Ms. Ellis is sensitive to the experiences of her students, many of whom lived at home with just their mothers. She believes that mothers, married or unmarried, who are often the primary caregivers for children, are also solely responsible for their moral, social, and ethical development. Given this orientation to child rearing as women's work, she believes that as a teacher, she can share in that responsibility and makes every effort to do so for her students. As an African American woman, she also believes that African American girls have specific needs that African American women teachers can address.

When asked to describe the needs of African American girls, she explained that Black girls are sometimes raised with certain "values, ideas, and expectations," and they may experience conflicts with each other because they are all "strong." As such, she believes her role is to help the young women develop their strengths in a way that benefit them and not get them into trouble with each other and with teachers. She encourages them to be self-assured and confident, to assert themselves, and to be leaders. She also believes that because she is a Black woman and the mother of two Black girls, she can communicate with her students in a style with which many of them are familiar, "'Cause they know, even though I'm their teacher, I can talk to them the way that their parents talk to them at home."

Ms. Ellis is also committed to teaching about difference. Despite this commitment, she was reluctant to describe her curriculum as multicultural, in part because of how most teachers superficially include people of Color under the auspices of "multicultural education." She shared her perspective as a Black woman teacher on multicultural education:

I am constantly trying to bring in different perspectives, and if we want to call that multicultural, then, yes. In terms of materials that I use for instruction, I do supplement with what I already have—where I feel that I can do it and it's not just pulling something out of the woodwork just to do it. I don't do that. But the simple fact that I am who I am means that I'm going to convey what I want them to learn anyway. They're going to get that from me. And even though, I try to have a little diversity [pointing to the pictures of notable people of Color on her wall] . . . just talking about ethnic groups because it's "their" month—that's not multiculturalism to me. I mean, that's just taking a unit and trying to make it multicultural. I mean, if you're a multicultural person, then you teach multiculturally.

Unlike Ms. Hosford who did not "see" color and thought that the specificity of Black history was not important as evidenced by the missing pieces of her Black history puzzle, Ms. Ellis directly addressed issues of White privilege and domination. Specifically, in her social studies curriculum, Ms. Ellis identified the ways in which the Framers of the Constitution essentially disenfranchised African slaves, White women, and White unpropertied citizens of the young nation. Not one to sugarcoat issues of race with her fifth-grade students, Ms. Ellis addressed issues of racial oppression directly and engaged her students in discussions about such issues. In this way, Ms. Ellis created opportunities for students to understand how history is constructed and encouraged her students to be critical of knowledge. She also helped students understand the ways in which oppression worked across aspects of identity—race, class, and gender.

The Composite of a Culturally Relevant Teacher

Culturally relevant teachers

- Know that the children they teach are tied to their own futures and destinies.
- Consistently challenge themselves to learn about their students and their students culture and community.
- See themselves in the eyes of their students.
- Organize learning so that it builds on and maximizes students' strengths.
- Maintain the utmost respect for their students and their students' families.
- Develop meaningful relationships with their students and families.
- Believe that they are teaching for social change and social justice.
- Create an intellectually rich and stimulating classroom environment.

Teachers who are *not* culturally relevant

- Only work in their school's community, but do not live, shop, socialize, or worship in the community.
- Have a superficial understanding of their students' community and culture.
- Refer to or describe their students and their families by names or labels such as "urban," "rural," "suburban," "struggling," "GED," and "needy."
- Refer to the children and the families by their race or ethnicity, such as the "Black/African American," "Puerto Rican," or "Asian" family.

- Engage in conversations with colleagues or others outside of the educational world about the limits and challenges of students and families rather than talk about their strengths.
- Organize learning and the curriculum around Eurocentric knowledge.
- "Chase the fumes" of the school bus into or out of the building on a consistent basis.
- Believe that teaching is neutral and not political.
- Organize the classroom around "control and discipline" practices such as
  a) flickering lights
  b) forcing children to move in military-like fashion during transitions and when in the hallway
  c) isolating children into corners
  d) humiliating children, particularly in front of others
  e) using buzzers and ringers to control the movements of children
  e) having children sit silently or with heads on desks to control behavior
- Hold the view that learning is a one-way endeavor that they cannot and do not learn from their students

So Just What Is CRP?

Now that you have meet three teachers at differing levels of success with delivering CRP, think about what worked (or did not quite work) with each teacher's instructional approach. The reproducible on page 124 provides you with a chart and some reflexive questions to help you begin thinking about what was present and absent in each of the teacher profiles you have read. Take a few minutes to work through the chart and questions before going on to better understand what makes a pedagogy culturally relevant.

In *The Dreamkeepers: Successful Teachers of African American Children*, Ladson-Billings (1997) examines the pedagogy of eight teachers, a sample that included five African American women and three White women, whose practices she describes as culturally relevant. Ladson-Billings describes cultural relevance as being more than just a teacher's awareness of and facility with language (e.g., African American Vernacular English) and suggests that,

> culturally relevant teaching uses student culture in order to maintain it and to transcend the negative effects of the dominant culture . . . for example, by not seeing one's history, culture, or background represented in the textbook or curriculum or by seeing that history, culture, or background distorted. The primary aim of culturally relevant teaching is to assist in the development of a "relevant black personality" that allows African-American students to choose academic excellence yet still identify with African and African American culture. (p. 17)

Ladson-Billings defines CRP as one that empowers students on a variety of levels (socially, politically, intellectually) so that they are equipped and prepared to not just contribute to society, but to change it. She describes culturally relevant teachers as teachers who see their teaching as an art, rather than a skill. Further, she identifies

15 characteristics of CRP and teachers. These characteristics range from descriptions of personality traits such as having high self esteem and a high regard for others, to beliefs about the profession of teaching as an art and public/community service, to the practice of teaching as helping students to make connections between their community and school, to a commitment to student diversity and individual differences and working toward excellence.

Ladson-Billings (1997) suggests two categories of culturally relevant teachers— *conductors* or *coaches*. She describes conductors as teachers who "believe that students are capable of excellence and they assume responsibility for ensuring that their students achieve excellence" (p. 23). These teacher-conductors are deeply invested in the success of their students such that the students' successes are a direct reflection of their guidance and direction.

Similarly, Ladson-Billings (1997) describes teacher-coaches as also believing that their students can achieve excellence; however, they see their work with students as something they share with parents, community members, and the students—as being a part of a team. Here the West African phrase "It takes a village to raise a child" becomes manifested in the lives of teachers and students.

Conclusions

In this chapter, we have examined the pedagogical practices of three fictional—but based on real-life—teachers to illustrate what is and *is not* CRP. The teachers represent composites of typical teachers found in many school districts, many of whom attend professional development that Foster (2004) and Foster et al. (2005) suggest is not effective in meeting the needs of urban school communities. Our particular focus was on teachers who work with students of Color in particular and specifically under-resourced students of Color in urban school districts. Using the "What Not to Wear" cable television show as an analogy, we hope that the teachers Ms. Hosford and Mr. Danielson have effectively illustrated "what not to do" when one decides to practice from a CRP framework. Whereas Ms. Hosford is

Components of CRP

CRP is premised on three basic ideas:

1. *Academic Achievement* includes but is not limited to objective measures of achievement. It is focused on teaching and learning rather than discipline. It assumes that children already know "stuff" and that it is the teachers' job to scaffold their students' knowledge.

2. *Sociopolitical Awareness* presumes that knowledge is constructed and used toward the eradication of injustice. It understands that the role of the teacher and the learner is never neutral but situated socioculturally, sociohistorically, and sociopolitically.

3. *Cultural Competence* suggests that teachers understand that they as well as their students are cultural beings. It appreciates and understands students' cultures and uses them as the basis upon which the teaching and learning process is premised.

more concerned about appearances and having culturally relevant decorations but no substance, Mr. Danielson focuses so tightly on the rules that he overlooks his students. Ms. Ellis ultimately provides an exemplary model of CRP as its three basic tenets—academic achievement, sociopolitical awareness, and cultural competence—are clearly manifested in her practice.

Although well-meaning teachers have tried to be culturally relevant, unfortunately many have missed the mark in part because they do not fully embrace and understand the three significant aspects of culturally relevant pedagogy (academic achievement, cultural competence and sociopolitical awareness). Culturally relevant teachers don't just "do." They are.

Recommendations for Educators and Classroom Applications

No professional development offering, academic text, or coaching can make a teacher "be culturally relevant." As authors of this chapter, we struggled with creating a list of "recommendations" for teachers because it is our belief that it presents CRP as a simple task, implying that a teacher can be given a strategy to "become" culturally relevant. This is the approach that we saw with Mr. Danielson that ultimately prevented him from being the culturally relevant teacher that Ms. Ellis is. We propose that CRP is not something that one can be taught to possess through orchestrated strategies; it is not something that one can be "given"—rather it is dispositional, attitudinal, and political. In other words, culturally relevant teachers are not "made," they just "are." That is, culturally relevant teachers hold an unshakable belief in the full humanity of those students described as "the least of these." Similarly, culturally relevant teachers believe that all children, regardless of socioeconomic background, marital status of their parents, linguistic background, race, and physical and mental ability have innate talents that teachers must nurture. Moreover, culturally relevant teachers believe that they must connect all learning to the real life experiences of children as a way to address social inequity and work toward social change.

Can we teach teachers to believe in the humanity of all children? Perhaps. Should we? By all means. Can we teach teachers that teaching is an inherently political and highly politicized endeavor? Yes. The challenge is not in providing the information to teachers or even providing experiences in which they see these ideals manifest in someone else's pedagogy. The challenge is in having teachers internalize these ideals and then act on those internalized beliefs to the extent that it manifests in the emotional, psychological, educational, and even material benefit of children who deserve it the most. To provide some concrete recommendations for teachers while still holding true to what we know and believe about CRP, we suggest not what teachers can *do* to become culturally relevant, but rather the conditions that prevent, or make it difficult for teachers to *be* culturally relevant.

As mentioned previously during the discussion of Ms. Ellis, teachers who are *not* culturally relevant work in a community and collect a paycheck from the taxpayers of that community, yet do not live, shop, socialize, or worship in the community. These teachers do not develop the in-depth understanding of their students' community and culture. Teachers who are not culturally relevant often refer to or describe their students and their families by names or labels such as "urban," "rural," "suburban," "struggling," "GED," and "needy." They also refer to the children and the families by their race or ethnicity, such as "the Black/African American," "the Puerto Rican," or "the Asian" family.

In addition, teachers who are not culturally relevant may engage in conversations with colleagues or others outside of the educational world about the limits and challenges of students and families. These teachers organize learning around Eurocentric histories and curriculum, and "chase the fumes" of the school bus into or out of the building on a consistent basis. Teachers who lack cultural relevance believe that teaching is neutral and not political. They organize classroom management around "control and discipline" practices such as (a) flickering lights; (b) forcing children to move in military-like fashion during transitions and when in the hallway; (c) isolating children into corners; (d) humiliating children, particularly in front of others; (e) using buzzers and ringers to control the movements of children; and (f) having children sit silently or with heads on desks to control behavior. These teachers hold the view that learning is a one-way endeavor—that they cannot and do not learn from their students.

However, we also provide a list of characteristics of culturally relevant teachers to help teachers think through their practice and ways they can incorporate CRP ideas into their teaching. Culturally relevant teachers know that the children they teach are tied to their own futures and destinies. These teachers see their reflection in the eyes of their students and maintain the utmost respect for their students and their students' families. Culturally relevant teachers develop meaningful relationships with their students and believe that they are teaching for social change and social justice. Finally, culturally relevant teachers create an intellectually rich and stimulating classroom environment.

Certainly, a teacher will not "become" culturally relevant overnight. This orientation toward cultural relevance is, again, dispositional. In this way, teachers are either inclined to believe that children of Color and children who live in poverty have a valuable and respectable knowledge and experience base or they do not. A wavering belief in students of Color is simply not enough. The kind of professional development that must humanize children and their communities is very different from one that helps teachers understand CRP. Thus, what we have tried to demonstrate in this chapter are the ways that teachers, because of their fundamental beliefs about the innate humanity and talents of *all* children and especially children of Color, either are or are not culturally relevant.

REFERENCES

Baudrillard, J. (1983). *Simulations*. New York: Semiotext(e).

Bomer, R., Dworin, J.E., May, L., & Semingson, P. (2008). Miseducating teachers about the poor: A critical analysis of Ruby Paynes' claims about poverty. *Teachers College Record, 110*(12).

Foster, M. (2004). An innovative professional development program for urban teachers. *Phi Delta Kappan, 85*(5), 401–406.

Foster, M., Lewis, J., & Onafowora, L. (2005). Grooming great urban teachers. *Educational Leadership, 62*(6), 28–32.

Gorski, P.C. (2007, Spring). The question of class. *Teaching Tolerance, 31.* Retrieved October 22, 2007, from www.tolerance.org/teach/magazine/features.jsp?p=0&is=40&ar=777

Ladson-Billings, G.J. (1997). *The dreamkeepers: Successful teachers of African American children* (2nd ed.). San Francisco: Jossey-Bass.

Ladson-Billings, G.J. (2006). *From the achievement gap to the education debt: Understanding achievement in U.S. schools.* [Keynote Address/Motion picture]. (Available from American Educational Research Association, 1430 K Street, NW, Suite 1200, Washington, DC 20005).

SUGGESTIONS FOR FURTHER READING

Gay, G. (2000). *Culturally responsive teaching: Theory, research, and practice.* New York: Teachers College Press.

Howard, G. (2006). *We can't teach what we don't know: White teachers, multiracial schools* (2nd ed.). New York: Teachers College Press.

Ladson-Billings, G.J. (2001). *Crossing over to Canaan: The journey of new teachers in diverse classrooms.* San Francisco: Jossey-Bass.

Tatum, B.D. (2003). *Why are all the black kids sitting together in the cafeteria?: And other conversations about race.* New York: Basic Books.

Comparing the Teacher Profiles: What Works?

What makes a culturally relevant teacher? Examine the three cases presented and begin to define CRP.

Use this space to think about what was working, not working, present, or absent in each case.

Ms. Hosford	Mr. Danielson	Ms. Ellis

Given the three cases, who would you identify as the teacher you think is most culturally relevant?

Why?

What does your choice reveal about your evolving understandings of CRP?

CHAPTER 9

Diverse Families, Welcoming Schools: Creating Partnerships That Support Learning

JoBeth Allen

The "local Barbie doll" chain e-mail, frequently forwarded and radically excerpted below, is making the rounds—perhaps you've seen a version for your area. The e-mail proclaims, "Mattel recently announced the release of Limited Edition Barbie Dolls for the [local] Market" and provides a description of "local" Barbie similar to what follows:

> **[White, wealthy neighborhood] Barbie**: This princess Barbie comes with an assortment of Kate Spade handbags, a Lexus SUV, and a longhaired foreign dog named Honey and a cookie-cutter house. Optional Percocet prescription available.
>
> **[Rural county] Barbie**: This model, with tangled hair and missing teeth, comes dressed in her own Wrangler jeans two sizes too small, a NASCAR shirt, and Tweety Bird tattoo on her shoulder. She can spit over 5 feet and kick Ken's butt when she's drunk . . . . Also available with a mobile home and mullet-haired Ken who serves as her cousin/boyfriend.
>
> **[Artists' neighborhood] Barbie**: She has long straight brown hair, arch-less feet, hairy armpits, no makeup and Birkenstocks with white socks. She does not want or need a Ken doll, but if you purchase the optional Subaru wagon, you get a rainbow flag sticker for free.
>
> **[Black, poor neighborhood] Barbie**: This Barbie is only 14 and comes with a stroller and infant doll. Optional accessories include a GED and a bus pass. Gangsta Ken and his 1979 Caddy were available, but are now very difficult to find since the addition of the infant.

As Freire (1970) observes, to the oppressors, the oppressed are "other"—those [trailer park, housing project, ghetto, redneck] people who are labeled subversive, violent, pathological, "incompetent and lazy" (p. 60) in a process of dehumanizing and marginalizing. What takes the Barbie stereotypes e-mail beyond disgusting to deeply damaging is that it was sent by a teacher to a network of highly committed educators who teach children from these neighborhoods. She thought they would find it "funny" and "pretty true." They did not.

It is my fervent hope that teachers who do find these racist, classist, and sexist stereotypes "funny" and "pretty true" will high-tail it out of education. However, all of us have unexamined assumptions about "good parents," "healthy home lives," and our Goldilocks ideal of parental involvement—not too little, not too much, just right (as we define it, of course). We all have unexamined stereotypes, both positive and negative, related to race, social class, gender, sexual orientation, language, religion, immigration status, and other aspects of circumstance and identity on the rich sociocultural playgrounds of our schools and communities. These stereotypes can—and do—impede relationships between families and educators unless we actively work to replace such limited and limiting views of "those children" and "families in that neighborhood" with deep and respectful knowledge of specific students and their families. These relationships are the foundation of partnerships that support student growth and development as learners.

In this chapter, we'll learn what kind of family–school partnerships make a difference for students' learning, examine our assumptions about ourselves and others as cultural beings, and investigate strategies teachers across the country have developed to create dynamic, respectful, and reciprocal partnerships with families. In each section, we'll examine ways that teachers have created invitations to families to become a part of their children's education, sometimes at home, sometimes at school. We'll explore, for example, how teachers and families across the United States have used the tools of literature and discussion to explore complex cultural intersections and divergences, dialogue journals to support emerging readers, and cameras to bring students' out of schools lives into the classroom.

Why It's Essential to Nurture Successful Family–School Partnerships

Contrary to the prevailing mythology, when parents walk into their children's schools, it does not automatically increase their children's learning. Mattingly, Radmila, McKenzie, Rodriguez, and Kayzar (2002) analyzed 41 parental involvement programs; they concluded that what the programs counted as parental involvement didn't *necessarily* improve student achievement. Think of the ways we often "count" parental involvement—being room parents, helping the teacher, signing behavior reports, attending PTA meetings. Although all of these things might be appreciated, there is little if any connection to student learning.

We need to focus our efforts differently. Our well-intentioned plans to increase parental involvement in traditional "get them to the school" events are missing the critical connection among educators, families, and students. Henderson and Mapp (2002) examined 80 studies on parental involvement, preschool through high school, throughout the United States. They concluded that "The evidence is consistent, positive, and convincing: many forms of family and community involvement influence student achievement at all ages" (p. 7) and across cultural groups. The critical factor was that parental involvement had to be related to their children's academic learning. A second important conclusion Henderson and Mapp (2002) reached was that "When programs and initiatives focus on *building respectful and trusting relationships* among school staff, families, and community members, they are more effective in creating and sustaining connections that *support student achievement*" (p. 43; emphasis added). Henderson and Mapp (2002) offer the following additional key findings as support for the positive effects of successful home–school partnerships:

- Programs and interventions that engage families in supporting their children's learning at home are linked to improved student achievement. (p. 25)

- The more families support their children's learning and educational progress, both in quantity and over time, the more their children tend to do well in school and continue their education. (p. 30)

- Families of all cultural backgrounds, education, and income levels can, and often do, have a positive influence on their children's learning. (p. 34)

- Family and community involvement that is linked to student learning has a greater effect on achievement than more general forms of involvement. (p. 38)

- Programs that successfully connect with families and community invite involvement, are welcoming, and address specific parental and community needs. (p. 43)

- Parent involvement programs that are effective in engaging diverse families recognize cultural and class differences, address needs, and build on strengths. (p. 48)

- Effective programs to engage families and community embrace a philosophy of partnership. The responsibility for children's educational development is a collaborative enterprise among parents, school staff, and community members (p. 51) where power and responsibility are shared. (p. 67)

Creating Family–School Partnerships That Make a Difference

Psychologist and cofounder of Head Start, Urie Bronfenbrenner (2004), developed a model of human learning and development that emphasizes that humans do not develop in isolation, but in relation to their environments of family and home, school, community, and society. Bronfenbrenner (2004) theorized that it was the unique interaction of these systems—the specific, constantly evolving, nested contexts—that had an impact on each child. He argued that growth is facilitated when there are strong, positive, consistent links between settings (e.g., home and school). Children need links created by their families and their teachers that are positive, that develop mutual trust, that create shared goals, and that share power and responsibility on behalf of the child.

The key to building these trusting, positive relationships between people in different settings (i.e., family members and educators) is two-way communication. Specifically, Bronfenbrenner (2004) argues that children show the most growth in the transition between primary settings when "valid information, advice, and experience relevant to one setting are made available, on a continuing basis, to the other" (p. 217). Families share information and advice with teachers. Teachers share with parents. Children benefit.

At school, we work hard to provide parents with information, advice, and commentary on our students through newsletters, parent–teacher conferences, report cards, and school-based programs. It has been harder to learn from families their information, advice, and experiences that will help us be more effective teachers. In this chapter, we'll examine how committed teachers and families spin strands of communication and weave the web of caring that supports each child, each teacher, and each family so that all children learn to their full potential.

Starting With Ourselves: Exploring Cultural Memoirs

Who am I as a cultural being and what are the influences in my life that have made (and are making) me who I am? I ask this of myself and teachers in my classes as we embark on journeys of self-discovery (Allen & Labbo, 2001). Writing cultural memoirs is a way of reflecting on not only our own cultures, but also on the cultures of our students and their families and how our different as well as shared cultural backgrounds influence our classroom relationships. The writing and sharing of cultural memoirs leads to important questions about home–school relationships: How could exploring my cultural influences help me think about the cultural influences of my students and their families? How could that new understanding of myself and of my students and their families help me form stronger relationships that build on cultural resources?

Reading Cultural Memoirs. A great place for teachers and parents to start is by reading and sharing memoirs that are deeply contextualized in time and place as well as in social and political issues (see Flood & Lapp, 1994, on teacher book clubs). Rick Bragg's (1997) *All Over But the Shoutin'* tells the story of how he became an award-winning journalist, but the lens is on growing up in poverty that could have easily buried him. James McBride (1996) focuses on race as he tells two tales in *The Color of Water: A Black Man's Tribute to His White Mother.* His own memoir alternates with his mother's as she recounts leaving her conservative, White, Jewish family to live a Black, Christian community. Who could be unmoved by Richard Rodriguez (1982) when he describes his Mexican father trying to say the familiar blessing over dinner in the unfamiliar English tongue and his children laughing at him in *Hunger of Memory: The Education of Richard Rodriguez?*

Teachers and parents may not have the time or inclination to read book-length memoirs, so other ways of exploring culture include shorter memoirs from popular magazines, children's picture books, a taped TV bio-pic, a poem, even a YouTube clip. You might start with excerpts from a longer book; for example, Concha Delgado-Gaitan (2001) includes a short cultural memoir in the final chapter of *The Power of Community: Mobilizing for Family and Schooling.* Reading and discussing multiple texts is important to avoid stereotyping, and to provide more points of

Recommended Cultural Memoirs

Cisneros, S. (1991). *The House on Mango Street.* New York: Vintage.

Hansberry, L. (1996). *To Be Young, Gifted and Black.* New York: Vintage.

Lamott, A. (1999). *Traveling Mercies: Some Thoughts on Faith.* New York: Anchor.

Min, A. (1994). *Red Azalea.* New York: Berkley.

Neale Hurston, Z. (1991). *Dust Tracks on a Road.* New York: Harper Perennial.

Ortiz Cofer, J. (1990). *Silent Dancing: A Partial Remembrance of a Puerto Rican Childhood.* Houston, TX: Arte Público.

Pattillo Beals, M. (1995). *Warriors Don't Cry: Searing Memoir of Battle to Integrate Little Rock.* New York: Archway.

connection for teachers and family members to share their own cultural experiences and influences.

Gathering Photographs and Other Cultural Artifacts. As you read other people's cultural memoirs, begin gathering pictures and other important objects from different periods in your life. Go through those boxes, albums, and digital picture files while asking yourself, What were my cultural influences? It may help to think in terms of common as well as more invisible cultural categories: race, social class, gender, ethnicity, geographic region, religion, nationality, language and dialect, sexual orientation, schooling, physical or mental health or ability, and family structure. Within these categories, what has shaped your values, beliefs, and sense of yourself? For example, my students sometimes say they don't have a culture—"I'm just a plain girl who was born in America and basically that's it!" one told me. As she thought and wrote more about it, she realized that by being a White, middle class, Baptist, heterosexual, Southern female she had many powerful influences from home, church, and school. We all have practices, beliefs, and attitudes about each of the categories above, whether we are in the majority or minority or some more hybrid place.

As you think about your cultural influences, return to places where you lived and take new pictures, collect new artifacts. Photograph the places you played, worshipped, sneaked cigarettes, went to school, met your first love, and rode bikes with your best friend. Photograph parts of town that were not a part of your life; examine who you are in relation to people who had different schools, places of worship, social groups, and neighborhoods. One teacher wrote a poetic cultural memoir, shaping it as a conversation with a tree. That tree had been her only friend and confidante in a childhood marked by dissent and desertion. She had never written about those years, finding it too painful, too personal, and something of a betrayal of her mother. But she took a picture of that tree, and it all began spilling out. Where might you go?

Talking About Cultural Influences. This is such a crucial step—this is where you have the opportunity to reflect on your cultural influences, to have others ask you questions, and to make connections you've never explored. You might start with someone in your family who lived some of these memories with you and then talk with someone who doesn't know your whole life history, someone who might ask different kinds of questions. Here are some questions to prompt cultural reflections:

- What were your family's attitudes about (religion, race, Northerners, people living in this part of town)? Were there differences in your family? How did you come to your current beliefs?

- Tell me more about your high school years—what was the culture of your school?

- Who or what is missing from these photographs?

- If you stepped into this photograph now, at your age, how would things be different? What would you say or think or do?

- Your family seems very close. How do you think your (mom, aunt, grandpa) shaped you? Was it by example, stories, lectures, or something else?

- What was going on in the country that influenced you during these (high school, military service, college) years?

Writing and Sharing Cultural Memoirs. Have fun with this. Create a form that fits how you want to represent your multicultural self. You might create a photo essay, iMovie, or PowerPoint with lots of energy and action. Your reflections could take poetic form, or become a children's picture book, or an all-about-me alphabet book. If you feel adventurous—or just can't choose—create a multigenre or multimedia piece.

Finally, share your cultural memoir. Share it with your family, your teaching team, and your students. The greatest impact, however, will be sharing cultural memoirs in small groups of teachers and parents. It is such a powerful way to get to know each other and to build a foundation of respectful and trusting relationships. When we make culture central to creating family–school partnerships, we acknowledge differences with respect, marvel at similarities across differences, and open up dialogue about how to support each student as a unique learner with his or her own cultural influences.

Cultivating Homegrown Partnerships: Engaging Families

I learned about genuine family–school partnerships from Betty Shockley and Barbara Michalove, first- and second-grade teachers (respectively) who invited parents and other family members to join them in teaching their children to read and write. Through our two-year collaboration (Shockley, Michalove, & Allen, 1995), we learned that

> Programs are implemented; partnerships are developed. Programs are adopted; partnerships are constructed. . . . By their very nature, most programs have steps, elements, or procedures that become static. A program cannot constantly reinvent itself, change with each year, be different in every classroom, and for every teacher-family-child relationship. (p. 91)

That reinvention is what makes each partnership homegrown. In this section, we'll look at how these two teachers invited families to create partnerships with them that supported their children's literacy development.

Betty, Barbara, and I are European American, middle class, experienced educators who joined in partnership with families in a high-poverty, predominantly African American school in Georgia. As mothers, we wished we had received more meaningful invitations to collaborate with our children's teachers; this desire along with our shared commitment to learning with the families Betty and Barbara taught led to our research (Shockley et al., 1995). To connect home and school literacy learning Betty and Barbara created partnerships with families from first through second grades (they got permission for the children to stay together; unfortunately, this is a rarity). With parents, Betty designed and Barbara modified "parallel practices"; these included a letter from parents/caregivers about their child, home reading journals, oral and written family stories, learning albums, and adult literacy conversations.

"Tell Me About Your Child." Betty and Barbara began with the parents' perspectives of their own children, inviting them to "Tell me about your child."

Betty's invitation was a lined piece of paper with this invitation at the top: "Hello! Welcome to first grade! Parents have homework first! Please write and tell me about your child." Every family wrote back. Who could resist such an invitation? One parent confided, "Torry's confidence in himself is not the greatest. However, he will overcome this with love and attention." (All names are pseudonyms.) Another bragged, "Ashley can find anything around the house and make it into something beautiful and interesting" (Shockley et al., 1995, p. 19). Another parent wrote, "Lakendra like to be my big girl; she's very out-spoken about what's she feel. Me and Lakendra have no secrets from each other. I can trust my big girl and she can count on me. She's my little star" (p. 41). And this was in a school where some people said, "These parents just don't care."

Home Reading Journals. Teachers and families kept a dialogue going all year in spiral-bound or sewn lab books that the children took home two to three times a week along with books from the classroom libraries. Parents or others in the family sustained a remarkable commitment to read with their children, talk about the books, and write together in the journals. One child told Betty, "My mom read . . . while I was taking a bath. Yeah, I was in the tub and she was sitting on the toilet— the lid was down—and reading to me" (Shockley et al., 1995, p. 20).

Betty and Barbara honored the families' investment of time by responding to every entry in these dialogic journals. For example, Lakendra and her mother, Janice, read together every night, and Betty supported these home-reading events, as we see from these excerpts from their journal (Shockley et al., 1995, pp. 42–43).

Janice: In the story "I Can Fly," Lakendra did very good. Her reading was very good. And maybe she's ready to move on to a few more words. I mean a book with a few more words. If you think so also. (9/30)

Betty: I agree. She can read more difficult books but like everybody, young readers enjoy reading things that are easy for them too. (10/1)

Janice: Ms. Shockley, In the story of the Halloween Performance, Lakendra seem to have some problems with many of the words. Maybe she get a story with too many difficult words for her right now. But still I enjoyed her reading. Thank You. Janice Barnett (10/2)

Betty: . . . When you get ready to read together each night, you might begin by asking Lakendra—Do you want to read your book to me or do you want me to read to you? Sometimes after you read even a more difficult book she may ask to read it after you. Let her be the leader. One of the most important things about sharing books together is talking about them together. Thanks. (10/3)

Janice: Lakendra was very excited about the books she chose to read to me. So excited she read them over and over again. And I was so pleased. Maybe last night she did want me to read the story to her I don't know but I will ask her from now on. Because she was a little upset that she didn't know a lot of the words. And I don't ever want her to feel pressured. Thanks. Janice Barnett (10/3)

The journals also became places for expressing family values, beliefs, and practices. When Debbie and her son Adrian read *Galimoto* (Williams, 1991) in second grade, Debbie wrote in the journal, "This book shows what hard work and determination can do for you. I asked Adrian what he thought the moral of the

story was and his response was 'don't let someone tell you what you can't do.'"
Barbara responded the next day,

> Good for you, Adrian. I think you're right, and be sure not to let anybody tell you that you
> can't do something that you know you can! I also like the setting of this story. Last year we
> had a visitor from Somalia . . . . He told us all the children make galimotos [cars] out of odds
> and ends . . . (Shockley et al., 1995, p. 35)

Betty and Barbara wanted reciprocal relationships with families, so their invitations were open rather than prescriptive, encouraging families to establish their own styles and uses of the journal. Parents, big brothers, and other family members talked about stories, illustrations, information they learned, insights about their children's literacy development, and concerns that fill every family's life (Shockley, 1993). This extended written communication, not about enlisting parents to solve discipline problems or to sign reading logs, established deep relationships. It also supported emerging readers and writers at home as well as at school in ways neither teacher nor parent could have accomplished alone, as Dennis's mother attested.

Dennis, a child with many early indicators that he would fail, did not. He had a powerful team in his corner—a teacher who believed in him and parents who accepted that teacher's invitation to read and write together all year. In May, his mother wrote,

> Dennis read really good I only told him about 4 or 5 words when he finished reading I
> clapped my hands and gave him a big kiss on the cheek and told him he did great. He's
> really becoming a smart child. I was just thinking to myself. If a child has wonderful teacher
> and wonderful parents that takes up time with him and helps him to read and learn new
> things he turns out to be a genius. What I think my little Dennis will be someday. (Shockley
> et al., 1995, p. 144)

Oral and Written Family Stories. Betty and Barbara respected both the content and form of whatever family members wrote in the journals. Consequently, many who might not have viewed themselves as writers took great risks not only to write several times a week, but also to contribute to family story books, another way of bringing home cultures to the center of the classroom curriculum.

"The invitation was open-ended," Betty emphasized, "and each family wrote something different, from narratives about marriage, birth, death, and religion to poetry and family sayings" (Shockley et al., 1995, p. 22). Not all stories came in right away; this was an even more public risk, writing stories. But as several of the children brought their stories to school and read them to the class, more children urged their parents, "Let's write a story about our family!" Eventually, every family contributed to the class book. One family story began, "What me and my family believes. We believe that Jesus is our lord and savior." What an invitation—to share at school deeply held family beliefs. Janice and Lakendra contributed family sayings that quickly became class favorites such as, "If you kill a frog, you will stump your toe."

In a second-grade class meeting, the children were eager to publish another family storybook. They asked their parents or grandparents to write about "when you were little." Barbara loved these "Stories of Our Lives." Ashley's story was about being attacked by a bulldog, while her mother reminisced about a tire swing in the family oak tree. Greg recalled a ride at Disneyland; his aunt wrote about moving from California to Georgia. Frances Ward, the teaching assistant, recounted swallowing a marble as her mother quilted. Barbara wrote a Hanukkah memory (Shockley et al., 1995).

These books became well-read classroom treasures and public celebrations of families and their stories at a book reading and signing party. The children saw their parents and teachers as readers and authors, enjoying each others' stories and encouraging the next generation of storytellers to continue the tradition.

Connecting Through Family Funds of Knowledge

The concept of family "funds of knowledge" began in Tucson, Arizona, USA, with a group of teachers and anthropology and education professors (González, Moll, & Amanti, 2005). They successfully challenged the deficit model of families and children and provided a powerful alternative. For nearly two decades, the goal of this way of learning from families has been "to alter perceptions of working-class or poor communities and to view these households primarily in terms of their strengths and resources (or funds of knowledge)" (González et al., 2005, p. x).

Teachers in the original funds of knowledge study group served working class Mexican and Yaqui Indian families. The teachers and professors worked in teams to learn about the home lives of the children and families by spending time there. They created meaningful relationships with families by visiting homes, usually of three children each year, and entering into conversations—*not* scripted interviews. The conversations centered on three main areas of information, usually gathered in three visits:

1. Family history and work history (often through family stories about crossing the border, other moves, extended families, religious rituals and traditions, and informal as well as "hired" work experiences)

2. Routine household activities (e.g., gardening, home and car repair, caring for children, and recreational activities)

3. Parents' views of their roles vis-à-vis their children (e.g., raising children, languages used at home, and schooling—both their own and their children's, in their home country as well as the U.S. if they were immigrants)

Teachers did their homework; they studied both the history of that border-region community and the labor histories of the families (especially related to mining and agriculture). The authors stressed that the primary purpose of their home visits was "to foster a relationship of trust with the families" (González et al., 2005, p. xi). As teacher researchers, they also wrote about their home visits from their notes about what they observed in the neighborhood, the home, and their conversations.

Throughout the year teachers met in study groups to discuss what they learned and to create thematic units of study based on the funds of knowledge they learned about in these home and community visits. They learned that families had a wealth of knowledge about ranching, farming, mining, construction, and repair. Their business knowledge included appraising, renting and selling, labor laws, and building codes. Household management acumen included budgeting, childcare, cooking, and repair. Many had knowledge of both contemporary and folk medicine for people as well as animals. Religious knowledge included rituals, texts (especially the Bible), and moral and ethical understandings.

Let's look at what kind of relationships can develop from getting to know students' parents and their funds of knowledge. Kindergarten teacher Marla Hensley (2005) found a wealth of talent on home visits with Alicia, one of her African American students. Alicia's father Jacob was a groundskeeper and had helped the class plant a garden. Jacob also played guitar and keyboard and wrote poetry and songs. At Marla's invitation, Jacob and the kindergartners wrote a musical version of "The Little Red Hen" that combined gardening, music, and the study of bread making in various cultures. Another home visit revealed an African American foster parent skilled in dance; she choreographed the musical on her days off. From home visits as well as listening and talking with children, Marla enlisted family members as costume makers, stagehands, makeup experts, and bread makers— including Navajo fry bread and tortillas. The students performed the musical five times, each time gaining more confidence in themselves and pride in their parents' contributions.

Alicia's father had not previously been "involved" in traditional school terms. He rarely went to PTA meetings, finding the tone quite negative. However after his experience with Marla's class, Jacob wrote a musical for his fifth-grade son's class about social issues. He decided to run for PTA president and won. His more positive approach "inspired much greater attendance and a more balanced ethnic representation" (Hensley, 2005, p. 145). The PTA became more politically active, and Jacob was featured on the evening news. Because one teacher formed a relationship with him and valued his talents, Jacob became a valued member of the school family and one of its most eloquent advocates.

Forming Relationships With Families That Support Children's Learning. Many educators have been inspired by the work of González et al. (2005), who outline the key tenets of forming relationships with families that support children's learning. They found that all families have important experiences, skills, and bodies of knowledge—funds of knowledge. These funds are essential to the ways the families function in the home as well as in work and community settings. They are also resources for their children that the teacher can tap into.

González et al. (2005) also found that families use these funds of knowledge through social networks and relationships. Networks of family and friends were "flexible, adaptive, and active" (p. x) and included multiple people outside the home. This told them that their students often had many "teachers" who knew them well in multiple contexts.

Another important tenet identified by González et al. (2005) is that teachers learn about how children learn. In most of the Mexican and Yaqui families, children were active participants and asked questions that guided their own learning. In contrast, Yup'ik children primarily observe, often silently, until they are ready to try the skill themselves, and many European American middle class children learn primarily from verbal instruction.

Finally, they also reveal that "confianza"—mutual trust—is essential in establishing a relationship between educators and family members. The home visits allowed teachers and parents/caregivers to not only learn about each other, but also to trust each other—to trust that each adult was working in the child's best interest. Creating reciprocity (a healthy interdependency) is critical for the relationships to be enduring; in other words, although roles may not be the same, both teachers and parents "give" in ways that support each other and that support the child.

For example, teachers in rural Kentucky (McIntyre, Kyle, Moore, Sweazy, & Greer, 2001) visited some of their students' homes—some as many as 10 times a year—to learn from families their interests and how children learned outside of school to incorporate what they learned into their teaching. This information influenced teaching decisions, from determining what kind of homework went home with certain children (e.g., those who had help at home and those who worked independently), to developing a unit on Animals at Home, to creating an Agricultural Field Day involving community members. The learning was reciprocal. Family members asked teachers about many aspects of their child's schooling, and teachers provided child-specific information about school assignments, programs, and opportunities. In the Houston Funds of Knowledge Project (Patterson et al., 1999), elementary teacher Rubén Gonzales found the home visits so valuable to his teaching that when he became a principal, learning about and incorporating family funds of knowledge was the primary professional development in his school.

Home visits are at the heart of forming the kind of relationships that generate a deep understanding of family knowledge. Although there is no substitute for the kind of personal relationships developed in home visits, it is not always possible for teachers to visit every student's home on a regular basis. So try cameras!

Photographs of Local Knowledge Sources (PhOLKS). A teacher study group in Athens, Georgia, USA, used photography to learn family funds of knowledge (Allen et al., 2002). The PhOLKS group served a diverse student population (in local terms, Black, Hispanic, White, and international students) primarily in low-income urban and rural schools. Our group represented a range of life and teaching experiences: women and men teaching prekindergarten to fifth grade, a media specialist, a teacher of English-language learners, and two teacher educators. We were African American, Colombian, and European American; Christian and Jewish; originally from the Northeast, Midwest, and deep South; with childhoods from poor to privileged economically and educationally. This diversity was essential in mediating our understanding of cultural differences as we shared our students' pictures and the dictation or writing about the photos from the children and their family members.

With a small grant from the Spencer Foundation, we purchased three 35mm cameras, film, and processing for each classroom. We invited students to take the cameras home and to photograph what was important to them in their homes and neighborhoods. It's important that each teacher, each school, create a process that is respectful of local cultures; for example, families may not want to be photographed, schools may not have funds for film processing, students may want to use video techniques or sketch rather than photograph important places. Still, it may help to have a starting point; here is the process, with variations, that we developed.

We shared photographic essays with our students such as *My Painted House, My Friendly Chicken, and Me* (Angelou, 1994) and *Daddy and Me: A Photo Story of Arthur Ashe and His Daughter, Camera* (Moutoussamy-Ashe, 1993). Some teachers read and discussed books that taught about photography; others invited parents who enjoyed photography to help children learn how to "see" through the camera's eye. Some teachers brought in their own photographs and invited the children to share some of theirs. ESL teacher Carmen Urdanivia-English read from her memoir about growing up in Colombia and invited a reporter from a Spanish-language newspaper to show her students ways to document their family and community histories.

In addition, three children took the cameras home every three days. Teachers had the film developed quickly, and then asked children to write or dictate stories about their photos. Teachers invited family members to write about the pictures; they contributed detailed descriptions, memories, poetry, letters, and intimate personal stories. Cyndy Piha expressed what many of us felt. She wrote that it was an "incredibly moving experience" to see her students' home lives. "It was like going from house to house . . . . I have a very wide range of children— economically, educationally, ethnically—and every single one of them has a very rich life outside of my classroom, and I forget that" (Allen et al., 2002, p. 315).

We met monthly to learn from, connect with, and reenvision children and family members. We documented how children explored personal, social, and cultural connections, as when Najma taught his classmates about his Muslim religion through pictures of his mosque.

Understanding the Power of Dialogue

Power is not a dirty word. It is, however, a word that demands constant interrogation. In any situation, institution, interaction, or relationship, we have to ask Who has power, who is powerless? Is power used to oppress or liberate? Is power patronizing or partnering? Is power in the individual or the alliance? Is power used selflessly or greedily? Is power used to maintain or dismantle unjust social structures? Is power on the table or under the table?

We put power on the table as teachers and family members when we engage in dialogue—not just any conversation but genuine dialogue. According to Freire (1970), dialogue is very different from a conversation. In genuine dialogue, people come to understand another person's perspective. They may even change their own perspective. Freire's (1970) definition of dialogue is the encounter between people, mediated by the world in which they live (e.g., the multiple worlds of classroom, school, district, home, and community), "in order to name the world" (p. 76). This naming is important. It puts power on the table. We have to name structures that harm our children and confront acts of oppression perpetrated by social and educational systems. We have to name school practices we know are complex at best and damaging at worst. In honest dialogue, we cannot pretend to parents that retaining their child will enhance rather than diminish his or her chances of graduating from high school, nor can we urge compliance with taking Ritalin without thoroughly exploring the pros and cons for this particular child.

Dialogue is not easily achieved; people more often debate, talk past each other, or otherwise fail to meet Freire's (1970) conditions of genuine dialogue: a profound love for people, the humility to perceive our own ignorance, an intense faith in humanity, the hope that through dialogue the world will become better, and critical thinking and problem solving that leads to actions.

Along with these exacting conditions, we have the opportunity as teachers to issue as well as respond to invitations to dialogue. One opportunity for dialogue that parents often implicitly offer is the "hand-off chat." Delgado-Gaitan (2004) notes, "In communities where children walk to school, many Latino parents make it a point to walk with them. They take that opportunity to talk with the teacher and check in about their child's progress" (p. 28). They may ask for clarification about an assignment, share something that is going on in the family, make a connection to the curriculum, or discuss a family issue. "Hand-off" times can also be a prime time for teachers to share a positive learning example or suggestions for working together at home.

Molly Rose, a first-grade teacher in an urban school, created multiple opportunities to have a dialogue with parents (Lawrence-Lightfoot, 2003). Molly expected every parent to be involved, and they were, likely because the invitations were plentiful, varied, and genuine. "Almost everything I do with parents is with the child at the center," Molly explained (p. 61). For instance, Molly sent a letter to the child before school started, telling what Molly did during the summer; for example, "I read a lot of good books, I went swimming, and I went hiking" (p. 62). She drew a picture of herself, and asked the children to draw pictures of themselves and have an adult help them write back to her. When families came to school, these letters decorated the classroom.

She also held "getting to know you" conferences with each parent or guardian during the first month. "I try very hard not to talk at all. This is purely a listening conference. . . . The parents are the experts, and I'm seeking their wisdom and their guidance. . . . I'm saying come and tell me all about your child," Molly said (p. 62).

Molly sent home weekly communications including student work from the previous week. There was a note from Molly about the child as a learner on one side and a space for parents to write a response on the other side. There was also the Rose Room Letter that included 10–12 questions parents could ask their children about what went on in their school lives that week.

In addition, she held student-led parent, teacher, and student conferences. Molly involved her students in every aspect of the three-way conferences because "in learning how to gather the evidence, make informed judgments, and report their self-evaluations to their parents and teacher, they develop the skills of documentation and discernment" (Lawrence-Lightfoot, 2003, p. 91). Although Molly shared a few "disastrous" conferences, the overwhelming majority were highly successful in informing parents and empowering students. Parents told her they had never heard their child speak with such authority.

Beware of ghosts. All our best intentions, and all parents' best intentions, may be overpowered by what Lawrence-Lightfoot (2003) calls "ghosts in the classroom." She told about a father who, as he was leaving an otherwise unremarkable conference, blurted out, "That same thing happened to me in fifth grade, and I swear it is not going to happen to my child!" Lawrence-Lightfoot comments, "His passion exploded in defense of his child and in self-defense of the child he was" (p. 3).

Conclusions

If we focus on family–school partnerships that support student learning, if we acknowledge and explore the crucial ways cultural histories and (mis)understandings color our relationships with students and their families, if we experience the joy and insights of learning with and from families and entering into dialogue, the border lands between kitchens and classrooms can become what hooks (1994) calls "a location of possibility." She explains,

> In that field of possibility we have the opportunity to labor for freedom, to demand of ourselves [as teachers] and our comrades [students and their families] an openness of mind and heart that allows us to face reality even as we collectively imagine ways to move beyond boundaries, to transgress. This is education as the practice of freedom. (p. 207)

When we as teachers get to know the families of our students beyond the official data sheet and a harried open house or conference encounter, we are much less likely to fall into "Barbie" classifications of families. When we learn where families came from, what they value, what they do on the weekend, how they use math on their job at the factory or hospital, what they read and write, and how they are helping their children learn at home, families become people and not amorphous members of racial, economic, or linguistic groups. Developing respectful relationships and partnerships focused on student learning gives us as teachers the insight and strength to counter vicious e-mails like the forwarded "Barbie" chain e-mail and to challenge those who see cultural differences as deficits to be stereotyped and ridiculed.

Maybe the next time we get an e-mail like that we will come back with a reply like the following:

> "You know the Johnson's live in the Garden Springs Mobile Home Park in [rural county]— I have David this year, didn't you have Cloe two years ago? I've gotten to know their mom, and she is pretty amazing—working two jobs to support the family. She can't get here for conferences, so we met at the cafeteria at the poultry plant where she works. She isn't home to read with David every night like most of my students do with their families, so she suggested that she and the kids have 'book parties' every Sunday after church. They read together and write in their journal. David is always beaming on Mondays, eager to tell us about what they read and to give me the journal to respond to. I've maybe had similar thoughts in the past, but now the kind of stereotype in your e-mail about families from [rural county] really offends me."

I hope I have the courage to do that the next time.

Recommendations for Educators and Classroom Applications

You've started by reading this chapter alone—now find colleagues to share it with. You've started by thinking about yourself as an educator—now issue an invitation to explore these issues and opportunities with families of the students you teach. Start someplace comfortable—move to the less comfortable. Start by taking stock of the ways you are already building relationships with families—move to strengthening relationships that directly support student learning. One way of doing this is for teachers and parents to make a list of everything the school is currently doing, or parents are currently doing, that you see as "parent involvement." Make a 3-column chart and include the following three headings: Builds Deep Relationships, Supports Student Learning, Does Neither (But We Keep Doing It Anyway). Finally, examine the activities and invitations in the first two columns and ask, Which families are benefiting? Which families are not? How can we change this activity/invitation so that it supports student learning and builds reciprocal relationships? What should we eliminate so we have time to create more meaningful and beneficial partnerships?

Maybe you'll start with your parent–teacher conferences and make them student-led conferences like Molly Rose held. Maybe you'll start a book club focusing on cultural memoir and invite parents to gather in a convenient neighborhood restaurant, recreation center, or library—someplace everyone feels comfortable and can get to conveniently. Maybe you will add home–school reading journals to your literacy instruction—just that one change could have far reaching effects.

It isn't so important where you start. The important thing is to start.

REFERENCES

Allen, J., Fabregas, V., Hankins, K., Hull, G., Labbo, L., Lawson, H., et al. (2002). PhOLKS lore: Learning from photographs, families, and children. *Language Arts*, 79(4), 312–322.

Allen, J., & Labbo, L. (2001). Giving it a second thought: Making culturally engaged teaching culturally engaging. *Language Arts*, 79(1), 40–52.

Bronfenbrenner, U. (2004). *Making human beings human: Bioecological perspectives on human development*. Thousand Oaks, CA: Sage.

Delgado-Gaitan, C. (2004). *Involving Latino families in schools: Raising student achievement through home-school partnerships*. Thousand Oaks, CA: Corwin.

Flood, J., & Lapp, D. (1994). Teacher book clubs: Establishing literature discussion groups for teachers. *The Reading Teacher*, 47(5), 74–76.

Freire, P. (1970). *Pedagogy of the oppressed*. New York: Continuum.

González, N., Moll, L., & Amanti, C. (Eds.). (2005). *Funds of knowledge: Theorizing practice in households, communities, and classrooms*. Mahwah, NJ: Erlbaum.

Henderson, A., & Mapp, K. (2002). *A new wave of evidence: The impact of school, family, and community connections on student achievement*. Austin, TX: Southwest Educational Development Laboratory.

Hensley, M. (2005). Empowering parents of multicultural backgrounds. In N. Gonzáles, L. Moll, & C. Amanti (Eds.), *Funds of knowledge: Theorizing practices in households, communities, and classrooms* (pp. 143–152). Mahwah, NJ: Erlbaum.

hooks, B. (1994). *Teaching to transgress: Education as the practice of freedom*. New York: Routledge.

Lawrence-Lightfoot, S. (2003). *The essential conversation: What parents and teachers can learn from each other*. New York: Random House.

Mattingly, D.J., Radmila, P., McKenzie, T.L., Rodriguez, J.L., & Kayzar, B. (2002). Evaluating evaluations: The case of parent involvement programs. *Review of Educational Research*, 72(4), 549–576. doi:10.3102/00346543072004549

McIntyre, E., Kyle, D., Moore, G., Sweazy, R.A., & Greer, S. (2001). Linking home and school through family visits. *Language Arts*, 78(3), 264–272.

Patterson, L., Guadarrama, I., Baldwin, S., Gonzales, R., Keith, L., & McArthur, K. (1999). To claim our ignorance and make new friends: Collaborative family inquiry and culturally responsive literacy teaching. *Networks: An On-line Journal for Teacher Research*. Retrieved June 3, 2008, from journals.library.wisc.edu/networks

Rodriguez, R. (1982). *Hunger of memory: The education of Richard Rodriguez*. New York: Bantam.

Shockley, B. (1993). Extending the literate community: Reading and writing with families. *The New Advocate, 6*(1), 11–23.

Shockley, B., Michalove, B., & Allen, J. (1995). *Engaging families: Connecting home and school literacy communities*. Portsmouth, NH: Heinemann.

LITERATURE CITED

Angelou, M. (1994). *My painted house, my friendly chicken, and me*. New York: Clarkson Potter.

Bragg, R. (1997). *All over but the shoutin'*. New York: Pantheon.

Delgado-Gaitan, C. (2001). *The power of community: Mobilizing for family and schooling*. Lanham, MD: Rowman & Littlefield.

McBride, J. (1996). *The color of water: A black man's tribute to his white mother*. New York: Riverhead.

Moutoussamy-Ashe, J. (1993). *Daddy and me: A photo story of Arthur Ashe and his daughter, Camera*. New York: Knopf.

Williams, K. (1991). *Galimoto*. New York: HarperTrophy.

SUGGESTIONS FOR FURTHER READING

Allen, J. (2007). *Creating welcoming schools: A practical guide to home-school partnerships with diverse families*. New York: Teachers College Press; Newark, DE: International Reading Association.

Boethel, M. (2003). *Diversity: School, family, and community connections. Annual report of the National Center for Family and Community Connections with Schools*. Austin, TX: Southwest Educational Development Laboratory.

Casper, V., & Schultz, S. (1999). *Gay parents/ straight schools: Building communication and trust*. New York: Teachers College Press.

Comer, J.P., Haynes, N.M., & Joyner, E.T. (1996). The school development program. In J.P. Comer, N.M. Haynes, E.T. Joyner, & M. Ben-Avie (Eds.), *Rallying the whole village: The Comer process for reforming education* (pp. 1–26). New York: Teachers College Press.

Compton-Lilly, C. (2003). *Reading families: The literate lives of urban children*. New York: Teachers College Press.

Hankins, K. (2004). *Teaching through the storm: A journal of hope*. New York: Teachers College Press.

Igoa, C. (1995). *The inner world of the immigrant child*. New York: St. Martin's.

King, S.H., & Goodwin, A.L. (2002). *Culturally responsive parental involvement: Concrete understandings and basic strategies*. New York: American Association of Colleges for Teacher Education.

Ladson-Billings, G. (1994). *The dreamkeepers: Successful teachers of African American children*. San Francisco: Jossey-Bass.

Paratore, J. (2001). *Opening doors, opening opportunities: Family literacy in an urban community*. Boston: Allyn & Bacon.

Perez, D. (2005). Voces del corazón: Voices from the heart. *The Quarterly of the National Writing Project, 27*(2), 24–28.

Swap, S. (1993). *Developing home-school partnerships: From concepts to practice*. New York: Teachers College Press.

Valdés, G. (1996). *Con respeto: Bridging the distances between culturally diverse families and schools: An ethnographic portrait*. New York: Teachers College Press.

Weiss, H.B., Kreider, H., Lopez, M.E., & Chatman, C.M. (Eds.). (2005). *Preparing educators to involve families: From theory to practice*. Thousand Oaks, CA: Sage.

CHAPTER 10

Basketball, Rap, and SmackDown: Popular Culture and Literacy Learning

Catherine Compton-Lilly

Kenny (pseudonym) flat-out refused to attend his lessons. After three months of Reading Recovery, he made it perfectly clear that he was no longer going. I was a university professor and Reading Recovery trainer who was teaching children at Kenny's school. After talking with his Reading Recovery teacher, we agreed to at least temporarily exchange students. What did we have to lose?

Despite my 14 years of teaching 6-year-olds in high-poverty urban schools, I felt a strong sense of trepidation as I went to get Kenny for his first lesson. I knew that his teacher was an extremely capable teacher with a strong commitment to students, and I feared that I, too, might be unsuccessful. I worried that he might refuse to come with me. If that happened, what would I do?

Kenny's teacher had sent me his writing journal and his familiar reading books. As I laid them out on the table prior to starting the lesson, I noticed that all six books were published by the same company and all but one of them were about quintessentially suburban families engaged in scenarios that are roughly analogous to those encountered in the Dick and Jane series. The remaining book was an animal story. When Kenny arrived, he groaned when I took out his books. I realized immediately that those books were not the answer. Instead, I pushed the books aside and asked Kenny about his interests, and I suspect that listening to his answers made all the difference.

Popular culture and media literacy have been presented as a means of engaging student with literacy in a range of educational settings by numerous researchers. Evans (2005) and her colleagues examine the potential use of popular culture in classrooms by exploring a variety of popular texts including computerized texts and games, video games, text messaging, digital writing and editing, and digitized film. The book is full of examples of how teachers in elementary classrooms have draw upon the popular interests of children to design engaging and effective learning experiences. Similarly, in their work with young "marginalized and disadvantaged students" (p. 77) in Australia, Pickering and Painter (2005) describe how they drew upon their students' media knowledge of Shrek and Bart Simpson to engage their students in the creation of a respectful learning community. They describe the importance of using visual literacies including computers, televisions,

Breaking the Silence: Recognizing the Social and Cultural Resources Students Bring to the Classroom, edited by Catherine Compton-Lilly. © 2009 by the International Reading Association.

videos, and multimodal texts to "facilitate our students' exploration of the social aspects of learning, using their existing funds of knowledge to experience successful outcomes—social and academic" (p. 91).

Mahiri (2000/2001) refers to "pop culture pedagogy" (p. 382) and tells us that this type of pedagogy involves multiple media, including television, Internet, video games, and movies. He suggests that

> teachers continue to become more aware of the motives and methods of youth engagement in pop culture in terms of why and how such engagement connects to students' personal identifications, their need to construct meanings, and their pursuit of pleasures and personal power. (p. 385)

Alvermann and Hagood (2000) describe how teachers can tap the musical interests of high school students to elicit multiple interpretations of popular songs. They encourage teachers to invite students to imitate and parody popular music as well as write and share original songs. As described in Chapter 8, one aspect of culturally relevant pedagogy involves identifying the experiences and interests of children to support school learning.

Morrell (2002) describes how hip-hop music and culture can be incorporated into the study of poetry in English classrooms. The hip-hop movement can be conceptualized as a historical and literary period and can be studied alongside other literary eras such as the Elizabethan Age or the Post-Industrial Revolution. Analysis of traditional poems is enhanced when students use hip-hop music, a familiar genre of poetry, "as a lens to examine the other literary works" (Morrell, 2002, p. 74). Morrell (2002) also suggests that students can compare popular films with classic literature to develop their critical analysis skills and to recognize the intersections that exist among literature, popular culture, and their lives.

Fisher (2007) demonstrates how spoken word poetry, a medium that draws on the music and video resources that students bring to high school classrooms, can engage students with oral and written literacy in complex and sophisticated ways. She describes a group of high school students and graduates who meet in school and outside of school to write, perform, and publish spoken word poetry. She describes how encouraging students to use the media resources and the life experiences they bring engages students in "building literate identities" (p. 92) and ultimately refining and extending their literacy practices.

Other researchers have extended this work to the teaching of young students. Dyson (2003) illustrates that young students bring many different interests and knowledges to literacy classrooms. Their media resources include television shows (i.e., *SpongeBob SquarePants, Disney Princesses, Kim Possible, Jimmy Neutron*), music (i.e., children's songs, gospel music, rap), sports (i.e., football, basketball, and baseball), superheroes (i.e., Spider-Man, Batman), and video games (i.e., Mario, Pokémon).

In a similar vein, Vasquez and Smith (2003) explore how students' participation with Pokémon characters can be appropriated in ways that support students as literacy learners in classrooms. They describe the complicated learning and processing involved in students' interactions with Pokémon cards. Not only did the students in this study display their ability to work with large amounts of information

Examples of Cultural and Media Resources Possessed by Students

Television Shows and Movies—Students might produce writing about characters from television programs and videos. Although younger students may find Disney movies to be helpful writing stimuli, older students may gravitate toward teenage comedies and reality shows.

Music—As Dyson (2003) reports, popular music can be a stimulus for writing as students write about their favorite music artists. As Morrell (2002) explains, hip-hop lyrics can be analyzed for some of the same literacy devices as the books that are assigned in classrooms.

Sports—Students' interests in sports can be the basis for writing and reading activities. Texts such as *Sports Illustrated for Kids* can provide students with interesting nonfiction texts that they can use as models for their own writing.

Comic Books—Comic books have long been a student favorite. Illustrations can provide valuable context clues for struggling readers. Many students with artistic abilities may find writing and drawing comic strips to be enjoyable and productive.

Video Games—Some video games engage students in story-like worlds and provide them with settings and contexts that can be used in their own writing.

Toys—From stuffed animals to matchbox cars, the toys children play with can be personified in both their play and their writing. As children play together, they create stories that can become the basis for writing.

Online Activities—Instant messaging, e-mailing, blogging, and creating webpages are all online activities that involve writing and can be integrated into classroom assignments.

(i.e., character names, traits, types, and abilities) but they also used that information to design their own Pokémon characters and the accompanying Pokémon cards.

In this chapter, I explore popular culture as a valuable tool for helping children to become literate. Specifically, I present the story of Kenny to explore possibilities for using popular culture in classrooms and to describe how popular culture can draw children into literacy and help them to recognize the many purposes literacy can play in their lives.

Kenny and Popular Culture

Kenny is a Black 6-year-old who stands at least six inches taller than his first-grade peers. He is among a small handful of Black students in his class. Kenny has a strongly supportive mother; she explains that when Kenny gets frustrated he acts like a "class clown" and tries to distract other children. When he gets home from school, he complains to his mother that the other children tease him and call him bad names; his mother reports that he often breaks down and cries at home although I would not have guessed this based on his school persona. In kindergarten, he was suspended for hitting his teacher.

Kenny's less-than-enthusiastic response to his Reading Recovery books, combined with my awareness of the successes other teachers had with accessing popular culture in classrooms, led me to suspect that popular culture might offer a means of helping Kenny to engage with literacy tasks and become a capable reader and writer.

At Kenny's first lesson, I told Kenny that I wanted to know about him and asked him what he liked.

Kenny:	I like going places.
Catherine:	Oh, where do you like to go?
Kenny:	To the park.
Catherine:	Good, where else?
Kenny:	Chuck E. Cheese.

Although I had no doubt that Kenny liked to visit both the park and Chuck E. Cheese, I also realized that these were answers I had heard a million times from 6-year-old children. They are generic answers, safe answers, school-sanctioned answers—"Teacher, leave me alone" answers. These were not answers that told me anything about Kenny. They were the answers that in his short history of schooling Kenny had learned to give to teachers.

Therefore, I changed the subject:

Catherine:	Hey Kenny, what kind of music do you like to listen to?
Kenny:	Um, um, instruments.
Catherine:	Is that what you listen to at home?
	[Kenny looks down at his shoes but smiles as he shakes his head]
Catherine:	No, you don't? Tell me what kind of music you really listen to.
Kenny:	[Kenny looks up and speaks in a tentative voice] Rap.
Catherine:	Oh, you like rap? Do you like Bow Wow?
Kenny:	[Kenny's eyes widen] You know about Bow Wow?

I explained that I had taught for many years and that my students had taught me about Bow Wow and other rap artists. Now Kenny was interested. He looked me in the eye as I asked him if he knew how to rap. He answered "yes" and promised to perform a rap at the end of his lesson. I then asked if he played any video games. He talked about playing *SmackDown*, a video wrestling game and explained that he watched wrestling on television. As he spoke, I listed the different topics that he mentioned. Alongside rap music and wrestling were basketball and race cars. He then surprised me by saying that he wanted to be a teacher when he grew up.

As the conversation ended, we turned to our lesson for the day. Although he was well into his lesson series, his Reading Recovery teacher and I had agreed that less-structured and unconventional lessons might be best. We envisioned lessons that involved engaging books and personally selected writing topics. Not only would this provide Kenny with engaging literacy experiences, it would provide me with additional opportunities to learn about Kenny and his interests.

I asked Kenny to choose a familiar book. He chose the animal story, the one book that did not feature quintessential suburban families. He read the book fluently but with little expression or signs of interest. It was apparent that he had learned many of the sight words that appear and reappear in the book series, but I noted that he had few strategies when confronted with an unknown word. I quickly realized that text selection was going to be critical and rapidly searched through the pile of books that I had at the school. Kenny's interests were decidedly masculine. They reflected aspects of popular culture, and in some cases, they reflected topics that are popular with male family members, particularly his father. Masculinity is an important part of Kenny's story.

Initially, the books I chose for Kenny had to be consistent with his developing identity as a boy. I found a book about a dog whose master placed a bow on top of his head (Wilhelm, 1996) leading the other dogs to make fun of him and refuse to play with him. Kenny laughed at the "sissy" dog in the story and relished the story, especially the part when the dog pulled the sissy bow off his head. Later in his lessons, we returned to this story to talk about what it meant to be a "sissy" and how people should be treated.

Later in the lesson, Kenny illustrated and wrote a short story about playing basketball. He spoke about his greatest shots, friends in his neighborhood, and his dad as he glued orange basketballs cut from construction paper onto blank white pages. He then drew the players and with my help crafted a sentence or two about each drawing. On the last page of the book, Kenny was the hero who shot a perfect basket as his friends watched and cheered.

Reaching Kenny Through Popular Culture

When Kenny was no longer reading familiar books with large numbers of known words and when he was writing, it became painfully apparent that Kenny did not know all the letters of the alphabet. I did an informal assessment of his letter knowledge and found that for many letters he knew neither the names nor sounds associated with those letters. When I asked his Reading Recovery teacher about this, she explained that she had been so busy trying to get Kenny to attend his lessons and behave once he came to his lessons that she had not been able to accurately assess his ability. Of course not knowing letter sounds contributed to the frustration Kenny experienced with reading. His frustration with reading did not reside solely on Kenny's apparent incompatibility with the reading and writing tasks he was asked to do but was complicated by gaps in the knowledge he needed for successful reading.

With this information, I could begin to design an instructional program for Kenny that featured attention to the letters and sounds he was lacking as well as books and materials that recognized and respected his interests and developing identities. I searched for books that were funny and sometimes a bit irreverent. For example, we read *What Would You Like?* (Cowley, 1987), which is about animals that make rather disgusting sandwiches out of other animals. *The Monsters' Party*

(Cowley, 1983) features a monster that jumps in the gelatin like a kangaroo. He enjoyed *The Big Toe* (Melser & Cowley, 1980) in which an old woman is haunted by a spirit when she finds a dismembered big toe in a graveyard. Humor and a bit of irreverence served Kenny well and engaged him in reading tasks that he valued and enjoyed. I sought books that depicted Black characters who behaved in ways that Kenny related to rather than Black characters that acted like White people; the Visions series published by the Wright Group was a helpful resource. In particular, a book entitled *Dad* (Mitchell, Porter, & Cousin, 1997) was of great interest to Kenny.

I transcribed the rap that Kenny performed for me and typed it onto sheets of paper in a book format for him to read. Several of the texts I chose incorporated oral language patterns and rhyme. As Ladson-Billings (1997) reminds us, for many African American children rhythmic texts can be a powerful means of tapping into the linguistic strengths that African American students bring to classrooms.

In addition to writing a book about basketball, we sought other topics that captured Kenny's interests. I conducted an Internet search of the term *SmackDown* and easily located a myriad of websites. These websites provided me with numerous pictures of wrestling stars that I downloaded and that we used for making another book. I was careful to avoid faces covered in blood or depictions of ongoing violence. I also contacted Kenny's mother and made sure she was comfortable with our unconventional subject matter. Kenny taught me much about my own limited perspective, and although I do not share Kenny's enthusiasm for wrestling, I respected his interest and enthusiasm.

Later in his lesson series, Kenny told me that his favorite television show was *That's So Raven*. Once again, I went back to the Internet and was able to find numerous pictures for the television series that again became the basis for Kenny's writing.

The positive trend continued with Kenny never again refusing to come to his tutoring lessons, and Kenny continued to read and write about his interests. The most poignant event occurred weeks later when I picked Kenny up for his reading lesson and Kenny seemed upset. Instead of my usual struggle to keep pace with him in the hallway and his predictable antic of hiding behind a bookcase as we entered the library, Kenny walked slowly and quietly to the library. When we got upstairs, I asked Kenny if something was bothering him. He mumbled, "He turned himself in." Kenny's father was back in jail. That day, Reading Recovery lessons became a letter-writing time as Kenny crafted a simple letter that we mailed to his father:

Dear Dad,

I want you to come home.

From, Kenny.

Writing this letter was an authentic writing experience that enabled Kenny to use writing for a personally important purpose. Popular culture was the hook but helping Kenny to find purpose and meaning in reading and writing was the goal. Over time, Kenny was learning that literacy is a tool that he can use to achieve his own goals and serve his own purposes. The more he engaged in literacy activities that had value to him, the more he recognized the potential of literacy in his own life. Before Kenny was going to invest himself in learning to read and write and risk the vulnerabilities that accompany that journey, Kenny needed to recognize literacy as a tool that would help him to fulfill his own goals and purposes.

Kenny is still attending daily Reading Recovery lessons, but the path has not always been smooth. Kenny remains a cautious reader; he shies away from challenging texts and prefers to copy the words that he wants to write. With his patience and my persistence, things have gotten much better. Kenny is now reading simple chapter books and has proudly announced this accomplishment to his other teachers. Progress has been slow and the setbacks have been common, but I am very certain that without opportunities to read and write relevant texts that related to Kenny's out-of-school interests he would not be the emerging reader that he is today.

Conclusions

Although many people, including teachers, complain about problems associated with television, video games, and the Internet, we must remember that these resources play significant roles in the lives of some children and can be useful tools as children learn to read. These media experiences involve text, often incorporate narrative structures that involve problems and solutions and require problem-solving strategies—skills and experiences that could resonate well with literacy learning. It is up to us whether we want to dismiss these experiences or build on these experiences as we work with children in literacy classrooms.

Although the emphasis in this chapter is on media culture and learning, we cannot and should not dismiss the fact that Kenny is a young Black man. Much work has been done to help us address issues that are relevant to many of our Black students. To teach any student, we need to be willing to learn and extend our teaching practices. The early work of Heath (1983) helps us understand that different ways of talking are relevant. Issues around the language variations that children bring to classrooms and how well these patterns map onto school texts may also be important (LeMoine, 2001). In particular, teachers' attitudes about the language patterns their students bring to classrooms are readily conveyed to students, and this can affect the relationships that are formed between teachers and their students. The ways that teachers speak and interact may be more helpful to some students than to others.

Stories that feature rhythmic patterns can also be helpful. Ladson-Billings (1997) reminds us that

> Part of the deep structure of African American culture is an affinity for rhythm and African American artistic and physical expressions demonstrate these features in sophisticated ways. Jazz, gospel music, rap, poetry, basketball, sermonizing, dance, fashion,—all reflect African American influences of rhythm and pattern. (p. 700)

She explains that teachers need an in-depth knowledge of their students as well as the subject matter they are teaching.

Gender is also salient. Kenny is a child who has media interests and is Black and is male. As with all students, these multiple dimensions come together in unique and complex ways for Kenny. As teachers, we need to be mindful of the multiple ways of being that students bring to invite them into literacy learning in ways that are consonant with their emerging identities and ways of interacting with the world.

As Evans (2005) and her colleagues explain, popular culture can provide more than comfortable and familiar material for using and developing reading and writing abilities. Popular culture can also be the target of analysis as students examine the ways popular culture positions groups of people. Dyson (2003) examines how boys and girls are positioned in elementary classrooms and how the role of popular writing topics, such as sports, play in this positioning. Dyson (2003) describes the role a teacher played when a student commented that only boys like football; these tensions are raised publicly, discussed, and "this process of naming and discussing diffused power struggles and promoted social and intellectual discussions" (p. 103). Likewise, Morrell (2002) argues that students must move beyond using popular culture motifs to "become cultural producers themselves, creating and presenting poems that provide critical social commentary and encourage action for social justice" (p. 74).

However, it is essential to mention a few cautions raised by Kenny's story—it does not offer us a simple formula for working with African American children. It is not a formula for working with little boys. All African American boys do not enjoy basketball, love wrestling, know rap music, or watch particular television shows. The secret is not knowing what African American boys enjoy but in working with every student to identify his or her passions. Sometimes these passions will entail knowledge and experiences that appear to resonate with students' cultural and ethnic backgrounds; at other times these passions will not. As educators, we need to be ready and willing to follow up on students' passions even if it means that we need to expand our own worlds. The key is knowing what each student understands in terms of reading and writing, knowing each student, and using this information to craft instructional program that help students see that school literacy learning can be important to them. This is especially important for students who struggle with literacy and may have learned early on that they are not particularly successful with school literacy or for students who have not learned how school literacy can apply to their own lives.

Educators sometimes worry that allowing students to focus on their interests may not serve them well as they progress through school. I argue that Kenny's attention to media knowledges provides a means of engaging with school literacy and creating a bridge between home and school. I have faith that Kenny's repertoire of literacy abilities will increase with time and he will not remain focused on *SmackDown*. With his natural curiosity and strong school experiences, Kenny will want to engage with many types of text. I maintain that connecting Kenny's literacy learning to his interests and passions as he starts to read will engage Kenny with literacy in a way that the best crafted technical instruction could not. Connections between Kenny's interests and literacy have provided him with a purpose for reading. And that's critical.

Not only did Kenny teach me many lessons about working with students who are struggling with reading and struggling with the relevance of being a reader, Kenny also has lessons to offer other teachers. His case study reveals how opening our classroom doors to popular culture offers promising possibilities for connecting students with reading and writing in ways that value the students and their ways of being.

Recommendations for Educators and Classroom Applications

Using popular culture in literacy classrooms promises to provide students with spaces where they are honored and respected and where the knowledges they bring can be developed. Therefore, take the time to learn about your students and their interests; parents can be a valuable resource for information about their children. All children bring a diverse set of experiences and interests to our classroom. I have worked with children who love puppies, skateboards, monster trucks, Teenage Mutant Ninja Turtles, Big Bird, and Transformers. Any and all of these topics can provide rich materials for reading and writing; pictures and texts can easily be downloaded from the internet.

Value the diverse knowledge that students bring and consider the complex thinking processes that accompany this knowledge. What academic ways of thinking and knowing are similar to the thinking and knowing that students demonstrate with popular culture? How can students' ways of thinking and knowing support classroom learning? Wrestlers featured on *SmackDown* or Pokémon creatures could be the basis for rich discussions about characterization. Jump-rope rhymes and rap music can be used to explore rhyming, and sports teams can be provide a rich material for geography lessons as student identify the cities associated with their favorite teams on a classroom map.

Consider the literate activities inherent in students' use of popular culture. Video games, labels, music lyrics, text messaging, and scoreboards all involve written texts. What have students learned by using these texts that can be used to support classroom literacy learning? When children engage with print, they may not read texts conventionally, but they are learning about how print looks and how letters and words work. They may be learning a few letters or words and gaining a sense of the uses and purpose of written texts. Careful observation of what children are able to do with print will suggest possibilities for helping children build on the knowledge they bring.

Consider what the students' interests tell us about them. How do students position themselves relative to the popular culture images that they encounter? When might cultural knowledge need to be critiqued or extended? How do we help students to hear the perspectives of others and to recognize that not everyone is comfortable with the portrayals of people presented in popular culture? Kenny was a child whose ways of being and knowing were deeply rooted in his identity as a Black male. For other children, being female, clever, active, inquisitive, Spanish-speaking, Jewish, well-behaved, or wealthy may be salient; the ways of being every child brings must be recognized, honored, and sometimes challenged as children are invited to use literacy to achieve their own goals and purposes.

When students are not able to use the rich resources they bring to classrooms, difficulties arise as they did for Kenny. Nichols (2004) warns us that "children must either use the pedagogic routines themselves to display social identities (not just academic identities) or find other spaces within or between pedagogic activities" (p. 103). As teachers we must strive to create spaces that welcome all our students, ushering them into an understanding of the role literacy can play in their own dreams and interests. Using popular culture can help us create those spaces.

REFERENCES

Alvermann, D., & Hagood, M. (2000). Fandom and critical media literacy. *Journal of Adolescent & Adult Literacy, 46*(1), 436–446.

Dyson, A.H. (2003). *The brothers and sisters learn to write: Popular literacies in childhood and school cultures.* New York: Teachers College Press.

Evans, J. (Ed.). (2005). *Literacy moves on: Popular culture, new technologies, and critical literacy in the education classroom.* Portsmouth, NH: Heinemann.

Fisher, M.T. (2007). *Writing in rhythm: Spoken word poetry in urban classrooms.* New York: Teachers College Press.

Heath, S.B. (1983). *Ways with words: Language, life, and work in communities and classrooms.* Cambridge, MA: Cambridge University Press.

Ladson-Billings, G. (1997). It doesn't add up: African American students' mathematics achievement. *Journal for Research in Mathematics Education, 28*(6), 697–708. doi:10.2307/749638

LeMoine, N. (2001). Language variation and literacy acquisition in African American students. In J.L. Harris, A.G. Kamhi, & K.E. Pollock (Eds.), *Literacy in African American communities* (pp. 169–194). Mahwah, NJ: Erlbaum.

Mahiri, J. (2000/2001). Pop culture pedagogy and the end(s) of school. *Journal of Adolescent & Adult Literacy, 44*(4), 382–385.

Morrell, E. (2002). Toward a critical pedagogy of popular culture: Literacy development among urban youth. *Journal of Adolescent & Adult Literacy, 46*(1), 72–77.

Nichols, S. (2004). Literacy learning and children's social agendas in the school entry classroom. *Australian Journal of Language and Literacy, 27*(2), 101–113.

Pickering, C., & Painter, J. (2005). Using Shrek and Bart Simpson to build respectful learning communities. In B. Comber & B. Kamler (Eds.), *Turn-around pedagogies: Literacy interventions for at-risk students* (pp. 77–92). Newtown, NSW, Australia: Primary English Teaching Association.

Vasquez, V.M., & Smith, K. (2003). What Pokémon can tell us about learning and literacy. *Language Arts, 81*(2), 118–125.

LITERATURE CITED

Cowley, J. (1983). *The monsters' party.* San Diego, CA: Wright Group.

Cowley, J. (1987). *What would you like?* San Diego, CA: Wright Group.

Melser, J., & Cowley, J. (1980). *The big toe.* San Diego, CA: Wright Group.

Mitchell, C., Porter, G., & Cousin, T. (1997). *Dad.* Bothell, WA: Wright Group.

Wilhelm, H. (1996). *I hate my bow!* New York: Scholastic.

SUGGESTION FOR FURTHER READING

Dyson, A.H. (1997). *Writing superheroes: Contemporary childhood, popular culture, and classroom literacy.* New York: Teachers College Press.

CONCLUSION

Catherine Compton-Lilly

I n the Introduction to this book, I worried about our current fascination with literacy as sets of skills that students must acquire. I expressed my fear that, in many schools, literacy was being treated as an autonomous skill (Street, 1995) assumed to be learned in the same way by all students. I was concerned that teaching literacy was viewed as the transference of skills rather than learning that is connected to real-life purposes and ways of being in the world. Most of all, I worried that the unique, compelling, and fundamental differences that all students bring were being ignored and denied in the literacy learning experiences of too many students.

I invited each of the chapter authors to contribute to this book because I truly believe that each one of them brings a part of the solution. This book is filled with strategies for addressing problems, but they are not solutions that are easy to implement, and they are not the kinds of solutions that once implemented solve problems forever. They are not activities to be implemented in one day or over the course of a week, and they are not solely about content or pedagogy. The solutions presented in this book are only a starting point for change. Real solutions require long-term and thoughtful commitment to students. In some cases, change will be painful as we each strive to examine our own assumptions and challenge ourselves to seek new ways to know our students and ourselves. In other cases, implementing these solutions will require talking back to administrators and challenging the status quo in terms of how schools operate. They will mean changes in curriculum, assessment, and policy. These solutions are not for the weak hearted and they may not all be for the untenured.

As I read and reread these chapters, I cannot help but wonder how being in classrooms that recognize sociocultural ways of being might have changed the ways Alicia—the student whose experiences I shared in the Introduction to this book—grew to view school and literacy. Recently, I returned to interview Alicia and her former first-grade classmates one last time. The children are now in grades 10 and 11. Of the eight children I remain in contact with, five are still in school. Two of them have had serious run-ins with the law. Three are planning to attend college.

Although these outcomes concern me, I do not believe that they were inevitable or predestined for children of Color growing up in a low-income neighborhood. The children have parents who love them and support them. As a former teacher in Alicia's district, I know there are many teachers who passionately care about their students. Yet too many students are not well served by schools.

What would have happened if Alicia had been involved in projects like the ones described in this book throughout her school career? What if her fourth-grade teacher had involved her in using literacy to address issues in her community like

Breaking the Silence: Recognizing the Social and Cultural Resources Students Bring to the Classroom, edited by Catherine Compton-Lilly. © 2009 by the International Reading Association.

Table C.1. Possibilities for Using the Sociocultural Teaching Strategies in This Book According to Category

Chapters	Language	Self-Reflection	Observation	Instructional Practices
1 New Literacy Studies: Literacy Learning Through a Sociocultural Lens		X	X	X
2 "Decontextualized Language" and the Problem of School Failure	X			
3 "O Say, Do You See?": Using Critical Race Theory to Inform English Language Arts Instruction	X		X	X
4 "First, Do No Harm": A Cautionary Consideration of Classroom Research From a Sociocultural Perspective		X		
5 Cultural-Historical Approaches to Literacy Teaching and Learning		X		X
6 Unpacking the Science Fair: Sociocultural Approaches to Teaching English-Language Learners	X	X		X
7 Posing, Enacting, and Solving Local Problems in a Second-Grade Classroom: Critical Literacy and Multimodality in Action	X	X	X	X
8 This Is How We Do It: Helping Teachers Understand Culturally Relevant Pedagogy in Diverse Classrooms		X		X
9 Diverse Families, Welcoming Schools: Creating Partnerships That Support Learning		X		X
10 Basketball, Rap, and *Smackdown*: Popular Culture and Literacy Learning		X	X	X

Ms. Gatto (see Chapter 1)? Would things be different if in sixth grade she had been taught by a teacher like Ms. Ellis, who was active in the school community and who crafted a culturally relevant classroom where issues related to being Black and female were explicitly examined (see Chapter 8)? What if her second-grade teacher, like Betty or Barbara, had exchanged home literacy journals with Alicia's mother and other family members (see Chapter 9)? What would have changed if her teachers had reflected carefully on their attitudes toward race, class, and gender giving close attention to the ways these dimensions of being have been socially and historically constructed? What would be different?

I suggest that it is possible that Alicia would not feel so distanced from school. She might share stronger relationships with her teachers, and she might view herself as a reader at school and not just in the privacy of her own home. Alicia might feel that she had different options for her future, and she might have found something in the school curriculum to entice her and inspire her in a quest for lifelong learning. These are the sociocultural possibilities that can break the current silence about the importance of children's cultures and the ways of being that they bring to classrooms.

As you have read this book, you might have found yourself wondering, "How can I do all do that? There are so many possibilities and options. I already have a full schedule and endless list of expectations. There just is not enough time." I suggest that each reader find his or her own place to start. Choose the strategy that works best for you, your situation, and your students.

In an attempt to simplify the process, I have categorized the various options into four categories: language, self-reflection, observation, and instructional practices (see Table C.1). These categories are only approximate; they are neither self-exclusive nor comprehensive, but they do offer a beginning for change. I challenge readers to consider the various options that were presented and choose a place to start. You might start with one or two options seeking a balance of strategies that draw upon the four categories. You may choose to focus on one category—choosing a sampling of activities that focus on language or self-reflection. You may already be implementing some of the activities described or similar activities that you have crafted from your own work with students. Certainly, no one will be able to do everything, but finding a place to start is the beginning. Schools can be healthy places for children and all children can be successful students. However, we must find ways to break the silence and invite all children into the world of school to help them find and create spaces that respect and nurture their many talents. This is the quintessential challenge for schools and we are the people who must make it happen for children.

REFERENCES

Street, B. (1995). *Social literacies: Critical approaches to literacy development, ethnography, and education.* New York: Addison Wesley.

INDEX

Note. Page numbers followed by *f* or *t* indicate figures or tables, respectively.

A

ACADEMIC LANGUAGE, 25–28
ALLEN, J., 128, 130–133, 135–136
ALVERMANN, D., 142
AMANTI, C., 63, 133
AMERICAN EDUCATOR, 25
ANGELOU, M., 136
APPLEMAN, D., 52–53
ARTIFACTS: cultural, 129
ATWELL, N., 19
AUTOBIOGRAPHY: Critical Race Theory on, 37–39

B

BAKHTIN, M.M., xii, 2
BALDWIN, L., 25
BARTON, D., xii, 14–15
BASIC INTERPERSONAL COMMUNICATION SKILLS (BICS), 82
BAUDRILLARD, J., 109
BEHAR, R., 51
BELL, L., 55
BILINGUAL STUDENTS: cultural-historical approach for, 60–77; sociocritical literacies and, 68–73
BIRCH, M., 55
BISHOP, R.S., 39–40
BOAL, A., 106
BOMER, R., 110
BRAGG, R., 128
BRANDT, D., 24, 50
BRONFENBRENNER, U., 127
BURNS, M.S., 25

C

CARBONE, P., 69
CHALL, J.S., 25
CHRISTIAN, J., 106
CLASSROOM: cultural-historical approach and, 64; diverse, culturally relevant pedagogy and, 109–124; research, sociocultural theories and, 49–59; sociocultural principles in, 88–89

CLASSROOM APPLICATIONS: of critical literacy and multimodality, 107; of Critical Race Theory, 46–47; of cultural-historical approach, 75–76; of culturally relevant pedagogy, 121–122; of decontextualized language, 31–32; of family–school partnerships, 138–139; of New Literacy Studies, 21–22; of popular culture, 149–150; of research, 57–58; of science fairs, 90–91
CLINTON, K., 50
COACHES: definition of, 120
COCHRAN-SMITH, M., 49
CODE SWITCHING, 4, 82
COGNITIVE ACADEMIC LEARNING PROFICIENCY (CALP), 82
COLE, M., 14, 61–62, 64–65
COLORBLIND DISCOURSE, 34, 113
COMBER, B., 92, 94
CONDUCTORS: definition of, 120
CONFIANZA, 135
CONSENT: informed, 55
CONTEXT: Critical Race Theory on, 37–39; cultural-historical approach and, 60–61; factors in, 21; investigation of, 128–130; and literacy development, xii; of students, building on, 84–85. *See also* funds of knowledge
CONTEXTUALIZED LANGUAGE, 24–25; all language as, 28–31
COPE, B., 15
CORREA-CHAVEZ, M., 61
COUNTERNARRATIVE, 41, 44
COUSIN, T., 146
COWLEY, J., 145–146
CRENSHAW, K.W., 35
CRITICAL LITERACY, 92–108; definition of, 94; and dramatic play, 96–105; mediated discourse analysis in, 105–106; and popular culture, 148; recommendations on, 107
CRITICAL RACE THEORY (CRT), 34–48; applying, 42–45; literature review on, 34–36; recommendations on, 46–47

CRITICAL THEORY: and teacher research, 53
CULTURAL COMMUNITY: definition of, 60
CULTURAL FACTORS: and literacy development, xi–xvii, 151–153
CULTURAL-HISTORICAL APPROACH: to literacy development, 60–77; recommendations on, 75–76
CULTURAL INSIDERS, 39
CULTURALLY RELEVANT PEDAGOGY (CRP), 109–124; characteristics of, 118–119; components of, 120; definition of, 119–120; engaged approach to, 116–118, 121–122; evaluation of, 124; pitfalls in, 112–116, 118–119; profiles in, 110–119, 124; recommendations on, 121–122
CULTURALLY SPECIFIC/CONSCIOUS LITERATURE: applying diversity wheel to, 42–45, 43t; examples of, 40; selection of, 39–41, 145–146
CULTURAL MEMOIRS, 128–130; resources on, 128
CULTURE: definition of, 61; role in learning, 61–63, 62f. See also sociocultural theories
CUMMINS, J., 24, 82
CURRICULUM: cultural-historical approach and, 63–65

D
DECONTEXTUALIZED LANGUAGE, 24–33; Critical Race Theory on, 39; definition of, 24–26; recommendations on, 31–32
DEFICIT MODEL, 84
DELGADO, R., 35, 41
DELGADO BERNAL, D., 35
DELGADO-GAITAN, C., 53, 128, 137
DICKINSON, D.K., 25
DISCUSSION: cultural-historical approach and, 65–68, 71–73; of cultural influences, 129–130; in family–school partnerships, 136–138; of popular culture, 144–145
DIVERSITY: Critical Race Theory on, 35; culturally relevant pedagogy and, 109–124; and family–school partnerships, 125–140; and literacy development, xi–xiii
DIVERSITY WHEEL, 42f; application of, 42–45, 43t; and text selection, 41
DORNER, L., 69
DOWDY, J.K., 38
DRAMATIC PLAY, 99f–100f, 104f; critical literacy and, 92–108; mediated discourse analysis of, 102–105; problem and solution in, 98–101, 103–104; structuring and creating, 97–98
DUNCOMBE, J., 54
DWORIN, J.E., 110
DYSON, A.H., 142–143, 148

E
EDELSKY, C., 20
EDUCATIONAL DEBT, 110
EKSNER, H.J., 69
ENCISO, P., 49
ENGLISH LANGUAGE ARTS INSTRUCTION: Critical Race Theory and, 34–48
ENGLISH-LANGUAGE LEARNERS (ELLs): cultural-historical approach and, 61, 65–68; recommendations on, 90–91; and science fairs, 81–91
ETHNOGRAPHIC RESEARCH: dilemmas of, 51–52; role of researcher in, 53–54; solutions for, 56–57; value of, 50. See also research; teacher research
EVANS, J., 141, 148

F
FAMILY: and decontextualized language, 4, 25; funds of knowledge, 133–136; and literacy development, 3–4, 3t; and popular culture, 146; and schooling, 85–87; stories of, 132–133
FAMILY–SCHOOL PARTNERSHIPS, 125–140; cultivating, 130–133; importance of, 126–127; recommendations on, 138–139
FERDMAN, B., xii
FISHER, M.T., 142
FLINT, A.S., 94
FLOOD, J., 128
FOSTER, M., 110–111, 120
FREIRE, P., 125, 136–137
FUNDS OF KNOWLEDGE, 63, 75–76; family, 133–136

G
GALLEGO, M.A., 64
GAL'PERIN, P., 95
GATTO, L., 16
GEE, J.P., xii, 8, 14–15, 24, 26, 29, 31
GENDER: and material selection, 145, 148
GONZALES, R., 135
GONZÁLEZ, N., 63, 133–134
GOODY, J., 24
GORSKI, P.C., 110
GOTANDA, N., 35
GRAFF, H., 14
GREEN, D., 52
GREER, S., 135
GRIFFIN, P., 25, 65
GUTIÉRREZ, K., 60–61, 69, 76

H
HAGOOD, M., 142
HALLIDAY, M.A.K., 27, 29–30

HAMILTON, M., xii, 14–15
HAND-OFF CHAT, 134
HARRIS, V.J., 36
HAVELOCK, E.A., 24
HEATH, S.B., 14, 25, 147
HELMS, J.E., 38
HENDERSON, A., 126
HENSLEY, M., 134
HIP-HOP, 142, 144, 146
HISTORY: in cultural-historical approach, 60–77; family–school partnerships and, 128–130, 133–136; and literacy development, xii, 1–2
HOME READING JOURNALS, 131–132
HOOKS, B., 138
HULL, G., xii, 15
HURSH, D., xi

I

IDENTITIES: and literacy development, xii; and social languages, 31
IDEOLOGY: family and, 4–5; and literacy development, xii
IMMIGRATION POLICIES, 70; bilingual students and, 70–73, 71f. See also English-language learners
INFORMED CONSENT, 55
INITIATION-RESPONSE-EVALUATION (I-R-E), 64–68, 72–73
ITO, M., 14
IVANIČ, R., xii

J

JACOBS, V., 25
JANKS, H., 106–107
JESSOP, J., 54–55
JOHNSON, A.G., 39, 41
JONES, R., 93, 105
JONES, S., 105
JOURNALS: of home reading, 131–132

K

KALANTZIS, M., 15
KAYZAR, B., 126
KNOBEL, C., 14–15
KNOWLEDGE. See funds of knowledge
KRESS, G.R, 15, 94
KYLE, D., 135

L

LABBO, L., 125
LABORATORY OF COMPARATIVE HUMAN COGNITION, 64
LABOV, W., 26, 95
LADSON-BILLINGS, G.J., 35, 110, 119–120, 146–147

LANGUAGE: decontextualized, 24–33, 39; forms of, 82–83; and schooling, 82–84; social interaction and, 83–84; sociocultural strategies and, 152t
LANGUAGE ARTS INSTRUCTION: Critical Race Theory and, 34–48
LANKSHEAR, C., 14–15
LAPP, D., 128
LARSON, J., 14–15, 17, 19–21
LAWRENCE, C.R. III, 35
LAWRENCE-LIGHTFOOT, S., 137
LEARNING: cultural-historical approach and, 63–65; family–school partnerships and, 134–135; social interaction and, 83–84
LEISTNYA, P., 37
LeMOINE, N., 147
LEWIS, C., 49–50, 57–58
LEWIS, J., 110
LEWISON, M., 94
LISTENING: in family–school partnerships, 137; and use of popular culture, 141, 144–145
LITERACY DEVELOPMENT: cultural factors and, xi-xvii, 151–153; popular culture and, 141–150
LITERACY EVENTS: term, 14
LITERACY PRACTICES: definition of, 3; family and, 3–4, 3t; New Literacy Studies and, 15, 15t
LOCAL PROBLEMS: critical literacy and multimodality and, 92–108
LODEN, M., 41–42
LUKE, A., 15
LYTLE, S., 49

M

MAHIRI, J., 94, 142
MAIER, M., 20
MAPP, K., 126
MARSH, J., 14–15, 19–20
MARTIN, J.R., 27, 29–30
MARTÍNEZ, R., 69
MATSUDA, M., 14
MATSUDA, M.J., 35
MATTINGLY, D.J., 126
MAUTHNER, M., 55
MAY, L., 110
McBRIDE, J., 128
McINTYRE, A., 38
McINTYRE, E., 135
McKENZIE, T.L., 126
MEDIATED DISCOURSE ANALYSIS (MDA), 93–95; in critical literacy, 105–108; of dramatic play, 102–105; resources on, 96
MEHAN, H., 64
MELSER, J., 146

MEMOIRS: Critical Race Theory on, 37–39; cultural, 128–130
MEZA, M., 69
MICHALOVE, B., 130
MILLER, L.S., 24
MILLER, T., 55
MILLER, W., 106
MITCHELL, C., 146
MODES, 94
MOJE, E., 49
MOLL, L.C. 61, 133
MOORE, G., 135
MORRELL, E., 142–143, 148
MOSLEY, M., 96
MOUTOUSSAMY-ASHE, J., 136
MULTICULTURALISM: Black woman teacher on, 117–118
MULTICULTURAL/MULTIETHNIC LITERATURE: selection of, 39–41
MULTIMODALITY, 92–108; definition of, 94–95; and dramatic play, 96–105; popular culture and, 142; recommendations on, 107
MUSIC, 142, 144, 146
MYERS, W.D., 42, 44

N

NARROW/SUPERFICIAL FOCUS ON READING, 21, 152; effects of, xi
NATIONAL COMMISSION ON EXCELLENCE IN EDUCATION, xi
NATIONAL INSTITUTE OF CHILD HEALTH AND HUMAN DEVELOPMENT, xi
NEFF, D., 63
NEUMAN, S.B., 25
NEW LITERACY STUDIES (NLS), 13–23; in classroom, 16–20, 18f–19f; definition of, 14–15; principles of, 15t; recommendations on, 21–22; tips on, 16
NICHOLS, S., 150
NIETO, S., 37
NIXON, A.S., 76
NO CHILD LEFT BEHIND ACT, xi
NONVERNACULAR LANGUAGE, 26–28
NORRIS, S., 93, 105
NYSTRAND, M., 20

O

OBSERVATION: in ethnographic research, 50–52; sociocultural strategies and, 152t; students and, 17, 18f
OKABE, D., 14
OLSON, D.R., 24
ONAFOWORA, L., 110
ORELLANA, M.F., 69

OUELLETTE, G., 25

P

PACHECO, M., 69
PAINTER, J., 141
PARENTS. See family
PARTICIPATION: patterns of, 83
PATTERSON, L., 135
PEDAGOGY: critical, 94–95, 105–106; culturally relevant, 109–124; popular culture and, 142; terminology in, 2. See also sociocultural theories
PELLER, G., 35
PENDERGAST, C., 36
PESHKIN, A., 50, 53, 56
PHOTOGRAPHS: cultural, 129; of local knowledge sources, 135–136
PICKERING, C., 141
PLAY. See dramatic play
POETRY: spoken word, 142; by student, 4f
POKÉMON, 142–143
POPULAR CULTURE: and literacy development, 141–150; recommendations on, 149–150; student resources on, 143
PORTER, G., 146
POVERTY: workshop approach to, 109–110
POWER: Critical Race Theory on, 36; family–school partnerships and, 136–138; and literacy development, xii; research and, 54
PRATT, S., 31
PROFESSIONAL DEVELOPMENT: culturally relevant, 109–124
PUBLICATION: precautions on, 55–56

R

RACE: in Critical Race Theory, 34–48
RADMILA, P., 126
READING JOURNALS: home, 131–132
READING RECOVERY: popular culture and, 141, 143–147
REFUGEES. See English-language learners
REMEDIAL INSTRUCTION: cultural-historical approach and, 65; popular culture and, 141, 143–147
REPERTOIRES OF PRACTICE, 60
RESEARCH: effects on subjects, 51–52, 53f; questions on, 52; recommendations on, 57–58; sociocultural theories and, 49–59. See also ethnographic research; teacher research
RESEARCHER: relation with subjects, 54–55; role of, 53–54
REYNOLDS, J.F., 69
RHYTHMIC TEXTS, 146–147

RODNEY, D., 25
RODRIGUEZ, ALICIA (PSEUDONYM), 1–10, 151–153
RODRIGUEZ, J.L., 126
RODRIGUEZ, R., 128
ROGERS, R., 96, 106
ROGOFF, B., 18, 60–61
ROSE, M., 20
ROSENER, J., 41

S

SCHLEPPEGRELL, M., 27
SCHOOL CONTEXT: attitudes to, sample, 7t; and decontextualized language, 24; language and, 82–84; and literacy development, 7–8
SCHULTZ, K., xii
SCIENCE FAIRS: recommendations on, 90–91; sociocultural approaches to, 81–91
SCOLLON, R., 25, 94–95
SCOLLON, S.W., 25
SCRIBNER, S., 14
SECOND GRADE: critical literacy and multimodality in, 92–108
SELF-REFLECTION: sociocultural strategies and, 152t
SEMINGSON, P., 110
SEMIOTIC SIGNS, 70, 71f, 94
SÉNÉCHAL, M., 25
SHERBLOM, S.A., 37
SHOCKLEY, B., 130–133
SIEGEL, M., 94
SIGNS, 70–71, 71f, 94
SMITH, K., 142
SNOW, C.E., 24–25
SOCIAL LANGUAGES, 26–28; characteristics of, 28
SOCIAL PROCESS: in classroom, 18–19; culture and, 61–63, 62f; examples of, 5–7; and language, 83–84; literacy development as, xii
SOCIOCRITICAL LITERACIES, 68–73, 71f
SOCIOCULTURAL THEORIES, xi–xvii, 151–153; applications of, 152t; beginning with, 153; New Literacy Studies, 13–23; and research, 49–59; rethinking of, 57; and science fairs, 81–91; and students/classrooms, 1–10
SOCIOECONOMIC DIVERSITY: workshop approach to, 109–110
SOCIOHISTORIC LENS: definition of, 37
SOLÓRZANO, D.G., 36
SOUNDING OUT: term, 2
SPINA, S., 34
SPOKEN WORD POETRY, 142
STEFANCIC, J., 35, 41
STEREOTYPES, 125–126, 138
STREET, B., xii, 3, 14–15, 20–21, 24, 151
STUDENTS: interests of, and instruction, 141–150; as subjects of research, 51–52, 53f, 54–55

SUBJECTS, RESEARCH: effects of research on, 51–52, 53f; informed consent by, 55; relationship with, 54–55; voice of, 56
SWEAZY, R.A., 135

T

TAI, R., 34
TATE, W.F., 35
TATUM, B.D., 38
TAYLOR, D., 25
TEACHER: and cultural memoirs, 128–130
TEACHER RESEARCH: dilemmas of, 51–52; presentation of, 55–56; questions on, 52; sociocultural theories and, 49–59; solutions for, 56–57. See also ethnographic research; research
TEACHING: cultural-historical approach and, 63–65; practices, sociocultural strategies and, 152t; sociocultural principles and, 88–89
TELL ME ABOUT YOUR CHILD, 130–131
TEXT SELECTION: Critical Race Theory on, 39–41; for remedial instruction, 145–146
THOMAS, K., 35
THOMSON, P., 92
THORNE, B., 55–56
TRANSLATION: bilingual students and, 68–73; challenges of, 69–70

U–V

UNITED STATES DEPARTMENT OF JUSTICE, 44
VAN LEEUWEN, T., 94
VAN SLUYS, K., 94
VASQUEZ, V.M., 94, 142
VERNACULAR LANGUAGE, 26

W

WALETZKY, J., 95
WATERS, M.C., 38
WATT, I.P., 24
WELLS, M., 92
WERTSCH, J.V., 50, 94–95
WHITE PRIVILEGE, 34–35, 38, 45, 118, 129
WIEDER, D.L., 31
WILHELM, H., 145
WILLIAMS, G.L., 44
WILLIAMS, K., 131
WILLIS, A.I., 35
WINTER, J., 96
WOODRUM, A., 37
WORKSHOP APPROACH, 109–110
WRITING: remedial instruction and, 146–147

Y

YOSSO, T.J., 35–36